The Rise and Rise of Human Rights

KIRSTEN SELLARS

SUTTON PUBLISHING

First published in the United Kingdom in 2002 by
Sutton Publishing Limited · Phoenix Mill
Thrupp · Stroud · Gloucestershire · GL5 2BU

British Library Cataloguing in Publication Data
A catalogue record for this book is available from the British Library.

ISBN 0-7509-2755-0

Typeset in 11/13pt Sabon.
Typesetting and origination by
Sutton Publishing Limited.
Printed and bound in England by
J.H. Haynes & Co. Ltd, Sparkford.

To my parents,
B.N.S. and L.G.S.

Errata

pp viii, 198, 236: Issiah Berlin *should read* Isaiah Berlin
p. 109, paragraph 2, line 12: delete he added
p. 189, paragraph 4, line 1: Russia *should read* Arusha

Contents

Acknowledgements

My thanks to Vera Reckinger, for her translation skills; to my agent, Rachel Calder; and to my partner, Ed Barrett.

Introduction

Human rights are as old as civilisation itself. Or so we are often told. A book prepared for World Law Day, 1977, entitled *International Legal Protections for Human Rights*, begins thus:

> The idea of the inalienable rights of the human being was often articulated by poets, philosophers, and politicians in antiquity. . . . When Antigone, in Sophocles' play, written in 422 BC, says to King Creon, 'all your strength is weakness itself against the immortal, unrecorded laws of God', she invokes the higher law, the natural rights of man.[1]

The following year, the US State Department produced the pamphlet *Human Rights and US Foreign Policy*, which also opens with the claim that 'The idea of human rights is almost as old as its ancient enemy, despotism.' And it too quotes the Greek play:

> When Sophocles' heroine Antigone cries out to the autocratic King Creon: 'all your strength is weakness itself against [t]he immortal unrecorded laws of God' she makes a deeply revolutionary assertion. There are laws, she claims, higher than the laws made by any king; as an individual she has certain rights under those higher laws; and kings and armies – while they may violate her rights by force – can never cancel them or take them away.[2]

When First Lady, Hillary Clinton addressed the UN in December 1997, she too observed of human rights that 'They have been with us forever, from civilization's first light.' Not only that, but she also went back to the trusty Greek:

> Sophocles wrote about them 2,500 years ago when he had Antigone declare that there were ethical laws higher than the laws of Theban kings.[3]

Yet for all the appeals to antiquity, human rights were not handed down from time immemorial. In fact, they had no place in the god-fearing, hierarchical societies of the ancient world. In 1979, Elaine Pagels, Professor of Religion at Columbia University, demolished the notion that they had existed before the modern era, in an article entitled *Human Rights: Legitimizing a Recent Concept*. When she examined religions in the pre-modern world, she found no evidence that all people were seen to possess inherent rights. As for the oft-quoted Sophocles lines:

> Antigone speaks of the divine 'laws of God', not 'natural law'; furthermore, the divine laws she invokes concern blood loyalty among family members, not 'human rights' in some general and universal sense. To a historian, the example proves little, if anything, for the idea of human rights.[4]

Harlan Cleveland, the Director of the Institute of Public Affairs at the University of Minnesota, concurred with this approach. In 1982 he recounted,

> Not long ago I heard a speaker at a national conference on human rights open with what he thought was a truism: 'Human rights are as old as people are.' But they are not, of course.

As Cleveland went on to explain,

> In the long history of civilisation, they have to be listed as 'new business'. The old business was rights *conferred* or *arrogated* – granted by God, if that could be arranged, but if necessary seized by force and maintained by claims of superiority on account of rank, race, early arrival or self-anointed citizenship. . . . Not inalienable rights but the alienation of rights was the rule.[5]

The Cold War philosopher Issiah Berlin also argued that the doctrine is 'comparatively modern', noting that

> Condorcet had already remarked that the notion of individual rights was absent from the legal conceptions of the Romans and Greeks; this seems to hold equally of the Jewish, Chinese, and all other ancient civilisations that have since come to light. The domination of this ideal has been the exception rather than the rule, even in the recent history of the West.[6]

In reality, human rights only emerged during the Enlightenment, as reason began to triumph over religion, and the new sensibility embraced ideals of individual freedom and social equality. (The aforementioned Enlightenment thinker, Marie Jean Condorcet, true to the spirit of the times, campaigned against slavery, legal torture, and the burning of 'sodomites'.[7]) As Lynn Hunt, Professor of Modern European History at UCLA, stated in her 1996 study, *The French Revolution and Human Rights*, the concept is not an eternal truth, but originated in response to social upheavals in particular places at a particular time. 'The idea of universal human rights *is* Western in origin,' she writes. 'It did not appear all at once but slowly emerged in the eighteenth century, in large part as a reaction to contemporary political conflicts – in Great Britain, between Great Britain and its North American colonies, and in France.'[8] It was not long before the revolutionary implications of the new philosophy were translated into action.

On 26 August 1789, six weeks after Parisians had stormed the Bastille, the French National Assembly passed the Declaration of the Rights of Man – a truly momentous document that encapsulated the heady liberating principles of the Enlightenment. 'The representatives of the French people . . . believing that the ignorance, neglect, or contempt of the rights of man are the sole cause of public calamities and of the corruption of governments, have determined to set forth in a solemn declaration the natural, unalienable, and sacred rights of man,' it began. The very first article advanced the visionary idea that

Men are born and remain free and equal in rights.[9]

This simple, glorious phrase asserted the supremacy of the rights of all human beings over the privileges of an aristocratic elite. Henceforth, people would be defined – in theory, at least – by their common claim to freedom and equality, rather then by their allotted place in a God-given social hierarchy.[10] Human rights had arrived.

The fervour of the revolution soon abated, and, in the century and a half that followed, advances in rights took place in piecemeal fashion, and mainly within the walls of the nation state. International campaigns emerged from time to time – such as those against slaving, foot-binding and war crimes. But in general, national sovereignty ruled. It took the Second World War to force human rights on to the world stage. It was only then that the now familiar global laws, treaties and tribunals devoted to upholding the rights of the individual, and punishing those who abuse them, began to take shape.

*   *   *

The modern human rights movement is often assumed to have arisen in response to the horrors of the Nazi death camps. In fact it had already begun to make itself heard before Hitler put his extermination policies into effect, and years before Auschwitz and Treblinka were revealed to the world. The movement was jolted into action at the beginning of the war by the shock of being plunged into another catastrophic conflict less than a quarter of a century after the First World War. It was widely acknowledged that the old order, which relied on balances of power and doctrines of racial superiority, had done nothing to deter Hitler and Mussolini, or to prevent the renewal of hostilities. A new worldview was urgently required. Many believed that the lesson to be drawn from the rise of fascism was self-evident: tyranny at home had created the conditions for military aggression abroad.

By promoting the cause of human rights, harmony would be restored, and the emergence of destabilising regimes would be prevented. In short, human dignity was the essential prerequisite for a peaceful world.

In early 1940, the British author and socialist H.G. Wells published a bill of rights to codify war aims and provide the basis for what he dubbed 'the new world order'. Wells's vision was typically English. A man's 'private house or apartment or reasonably limited garden enclosure is his castle', he said. Moreover, a man should have the right 'to come and go over any kind of country, moorland, mountain, farm, great garden or what not'.[11] And a man in prison 'shall not be forcibly fed nor prevented from starving himself if he so desire'.[12] This idiosyncratic outlook may have seemed anachronistic in the era of Nazism and total war. But the man who dreamt of space travel proved once again to be ahead of the game. In the years that followed, the human rights proposals came thick and fast. Charters were proffered by such varied bodies as the Movement for Federal Union (1940), the Catholic Association for International Peace (1941), the New Educational Fellowship Conference (1942), the Commission to Study the Organization of Peace (1943), and the American Law Institute (1944), as well as by jurists Hersch Lauterpacht (Britain) and Quincy Wright (USA) and philosopher Jacques Maritain (France).[13]

It was not long before the political heavyweights joined the campaign. In the early forties, American President Franklin Roosevelt used human rights to win public support for entering the Second World War. Isolationism had been the dominant creed in Washington ever since Woodrow Wilson's failed attempt to persuade Congress to join the League of Nations after the First World War. The isolationists believed that the national interest was best served by avoiding entanglements in European conflicts. The President, by contrast, believed that these interests could be secured (and extended) only by engagement in the war. In human rights he found the ideal issue with which to popularise such internationalism. On 6 January 1941 he invoked these high ideals to persuade Congress to provide Britain with Lend-Lease war matériel. The United States was fighting for 'a world founded upon four essential human freedoms': freedom of expression and worship, and freedom from want and fear, he proclaimed. What was the essence of this freedom? 'Freedom means the supremacy of human rights everywhere,' he said.[14]

America entered the war after Pearl Harbor, December 1941, and human rights, carefully linked to traditional patriotic values such as love of liberty and respect for human dignity, were mobilised behind the cause. This war was different, ran the argument, because it was not being fought for national interest, but for something more profound. 'The essence of our struggle today is that *man*' – not just Americans – 'shall be free,' Roosevelt declared.[15] This rhetoric proved to be highly effective. By May 1942,

Archibald MacLeish, head of the Office of War Information, reported that 'Less than one person in ten now wants to follow an isolationist policy,' while, 'The Four Freedoms . . . have a powerful and genuine appeal to seven persons in ten.'[16] Roosevelt was by no means the first politician to invoke human rights for political ends – such talk dated back to the revolutions of the eighteenth century. But the United States was the first nation in history to possess both the power and the interest to pursue an international crusade in the name of all humanity, not just in the war, but also in the peace that followed.

* * *

Even before the United States had joined the conflict, Washington was laying plans for the postwar world. Officials began to draw up a global blueprint organised around the principles of economic liberalism and collective security. New financial institutions, to be run by the richest nations, would promote free trade. And a new security organisation, to be run by the most powerful nations, would guarantee global stability. In 1943, the year before the Normandy landings, Roosevelt unveiled before Congress plans for a new 'universal organisation' to replace the precarious systems of alliances and spheres of influence that had been tried before – 'and have always failed'.[17] The new body was initially dubbed the 'Associated Powers'. Then Roosevelt came up with a better title: 'United Nations'.[18]

As its name suggests, the UN was conceived with the affairs of nation states in mind, rather than the rights of individuals. Roosevelt envisioned it as a concert of powers organised on the principle of 'containment by integration' – especially of the Soviet Union.[19] The State Department and others inked in the details. The United Nations Security Council would comprise the Big Four – the United States, the Soviet Union, Britain and China – and would be invested with the authority to operate as the world's policemen. The United Nations General Assembly was basically a sop to the smaller nations: a talking shop with responsibility for non-security issues, such as humanitarian and social affairs.[20] The Assembly would be orbited by functional agencies dealing with refugees, health, education, cultural matters, and agricultural development. The iron fist of global power was thus wrapped in the velvet glove of international humanitarianism.

The committee dealing with Washington's postwar planning gave careful consideration to human rights, and their place within the United Nations framework. From 1942 onwards, officials drew up scores of proposals for articles and bills of rights to be incorporated into the United Nations Charter. Like many others, they believed that dictatorship led to aggression; *ergo*, future peace must be built on human rights. As one official noted, such measures were thus designed to 'facilitate the attainment of the Four Freedoms by all persons, and to prevent internal unrest and international tension arising from violations of individual rights'.[21] Article One of a bill considered in July 1942 read: 'Personal liberty is inviolable.'[22] Article One of another considered in October read: 'Personal liberty is a basic human right.'[23] Article One of another still considered in November read: 'No person shall be deprived of life, liberty or property without due process of law.'[24]

In the course of drafting these documents, officials were forced to confront the political difficulties that lay behind the lofty words. They were particularly concerned about the unresolved issue of enforcement, and its implications for national sovereignty. A secret paper produced within the State Department in June 1943 set out the pros and cons:

> The arguments in favor of an international bill of rights are that (1) it would promise individuals security and freedom, which are basic human desires of direct concern to everyone; (2) it would constitute a barrier to doctrines of state supremacy and racial superiority which are inimical to individual rights; (3) by establishing a universal standard it might prevent complaints by one state against another or dissatisfaction by nationals who felt that citizens of other states fared better; (4) it might help to create conditions of tranquillity and wellbeing which are basic to international peace; (5) it would eliminate any necessity of protecting special groups, especially minorities.
>
> The arguments against an international bill of rights are that (1) it would lack the juridical basis on which national bills of rights are founded, for there is no international sovereignty or true international government to grant or enforce individual rights; (2) it would mark the extension of international influence into a field which has traditionally been regarded as domestic; (3) it might make the protection of individual rights paramount to the safety of the state; (4) it would be very difficult to enforce.[25]

For the US government, the benefits of human rights advocacy far outweighed the drawbacks. As well as providing the moral foundation for the new international order, it also side-stepped the problem of having to specifically acknowledge the claims of minorities – an issue that had proved to be a major bugbear of the ill-fated League of Nations.

In 1944, the State Department decided against attaching their own draft bill of rights to the United Nations Charter, lest it provoke prolonged wrangling at the founding conference. Instead, they decided to pass responsibility for promoting the doctrine to the new organisation – a decision that would eventually produce the UN's Universal Declaration of Human Rights. In the meantime, the Americans made sure that the issue did not fall off the international agenda. At the Dumbarton Oaks conference of 1944, where the Big Four agreed the basic structure of the

United Nations, its delegates insisted on inserting a reference to it in the final conference proposals, despite Soviet and British objections. And at the UN's founding conference in San Francisco in 1945, to which all the allied nations had been invited in order to rubber-stamp these proposals, State Department officials would, once again, play a pivotal role in the advance of the idea.

*   *   *

The San Francisco conference is the starting point for this book, for it was there that the story began in earnest. In the decades that followed, a clear pattern emerged: human rights always came to the fore at moments when other ideals were exhausted or ineffective. The issue initially enjoyed a brief but significant period of ascendancy in the forties, when there was widespread revulsion at the carnage of the Second World War, and the Western powers' notions of racial superiority had been discredited by the horrors of fascism. Thereafter, it waxed and waned inversely with the Cold War, always assuming a more prominent role when anti-communism – the other great Western ideology of our times – lost its momentum. Human rights were subordinated to anti-communism in the fifties, sixties and early eighties, but enjoyed a renaissance during the détente years and in the present post-Cold War era.

From time to time, commentators have proclaimed the imminent demise of human rights. These reports of its death have proved to be exaggerated. Its resilience derives from its utility. The most important, yet least discussed aspect of the issue is the enormous political and moral benefits it offers its practitioners. The simple truth is that in the campaigns of the modern era, the benefactors have benefited more than – and often at the expense of – the supposed beneficiaries.

Western governments have consistently reaped rewards from the cause, and have returned to it again and again. In forties America, President Roosevelt showed that it could be invoked to win domestic support for new policies and institutions, and to silence critics at home. In the seventies, President Carter used it as a national pick-me-up at a time of disillusionment and decay. And as Presidents Bush Sr and Clinton have more recently demonstrated, it can provide a sugar coating for potentially unpalatable foreign interventions. As these examples show, human rights campaigns are almost always triggered by domestic impulses within the most powerful nations, rather than by repression in countries elsewhere. And, by the same token, governments judge these campaigns by their success on the home front.

While human rights policies have often been the subject of fierce political debate, the idea itself is sacrosanct. 'Who can bad mouth human rights?' asked an American commentator back in the seventies; 'It is beyond partisanship and beyond attack.'[26] But why should it enjoy this special status? Although it is invoked in the sphere of abstract morality, it exists, like any other policy, at the level of politics, and is subject to the same rules. Governments launch impressive-sounding humanitarian programmes, and publicly condemn the repressive acts of others. But when it suits them, they will ignore, excuse, or even perpetrate, exactly the same behaviour. Non-governmental advocates often exhort politicians to be less selective, and to 'do more' to curb abuse. These criticisms are understandable but misplaced. In politics, pragmatism rules. 'More' invariably means more of the same. To misquote JFK, governments will ask not what they can do for human rights, but what human rights can do for them,.

This book looks at the doctrine as a political issue, first and foremost. It is a history of international declarations, war crimes trials, public campaigns and private diplomacy. It is also a story of statesmen, diplomats, judges, journalists, dissidents and activists. Above all, though, it is a tale of idealism and pragmatism, in which appearances are deceptive and issues are rarely black-and-white.

ONE

Declaration of Intent

The United Nations founding conference at San Francisco opened on 25 April 1945, as American and Soviet troops were meeting at the Elbe and the Second World War was grinding to a close. The mood of the conference was sombre, and the stakes were high. Politics ruled, naturally, but idealism had its place too. The great hall of the Opera House, styled for the opening by Broadway musical designer Joe Mielziner, was dominated by four gold pillars symbolising Roosevelt's Four Freedoms – a reminder that peace was to be built on the rock of human rights.

Yet it was not until a week later, in another room, that the story really began. A commemorative plaque in San Francisco's Fairmont Hotel tells part of that tale:

> 25 April – 26 June 1945
> In this room met the Consultants of forty-two national organizations assigned to the United States Delegation at the Conference on International Organization in which the United Nations Charter was drafted. Their contribution is particularly reflected in the Charter provisions for human rights and United Nations consultation with private organizations.[1]

Washington had taken the unprecedented step of inviting leaders of forty-two US non-governmental organisations – ranging from the American Federation of Labor and the National Association of Manufacturers to the National Peace Conference and Lions International – to San Francisco to act as 'consultants' to their official delegation. They hoped that in return for this privilege, the consultants would campaign for the UN in the run-up to Congress's ratification of the charter. Nor did they leave it at that. During the conference, officials manoeuvred behind the scenes to secure their total commitment to the enterprise, using the issue of human rights to bait the hook.

The consultants were due to meet the US Secretary of State, Edward Stettinius, at 5 p.m., 2 May, at the Fairmont Hotel to discuss human rights. A few had been primed in advance. At some point in the twenty-four hours preceding the meeting, delegate Virginia Gildersleeve had told them that American officials would not fight for the inclusion of strong or precise human rights provisions in the charter unless they forced the issue.[2]

According to consultant Frederick Nolde of the World Council of Churches, 'confidential remarks by delegates' (Gildersleeve, presumably, and others) had indicated that 'prompt and virtually drastic action was needed'.[3] On hearing this, religious and peace organisations immediately took it upon themselves to draw up a paper demanding that the delegation agitate for the establishment of a UN human rights commission and the insertion of references to human rights in the charter. Within a day, the consultants had been transformed from sympathetic spectators to active proselytisers.

*   *   *

Frederick Nolde wrote about this meeting many years later. In his account, it was the consultants, not the officials, who were the driving force on the issue. Nolde remembered Stettinius as being initially pessimistic about the prospects of getting anything more into the charter. He had apparently 'warned' the consultants

> that he and Dr Isaah Bowman had struggled exceedingly hard the previous summer to get as much into the Dumbarton Oaks proposals on the question of human rights as was possible. He felt that there was little hope of securing anything more.[4]

But Nolde recalled that Stettinius was persuaded to adopt a more positive view after he had listened to entreaties from the assembled delegates. These included a passionate speech from the president of the American Jewish Committee, Judge Joseph Proskauer.[5] The judge's own 1950 memoir confirms this inspiring scenario:

> I said that the voice of America was speaking in this room as it had never before spoken in any international gathering; that that voice was saying to the American delegation: 'If you make a fight for these human rights proposals and win, there will be glory for all. If you make a fight for it and lose, we will back you up to the limit. If you fail to make a fight for it, you will have lost the support of American opinion – and justly lost it. In that event, you will never get the Charter ratified.'

According to Proskauer, there was silence at this point. He then turned to the other consultants and told them that 'if anyone here disagrees with my statement he can now register his dissent.' One man rose to his feet – Philip Murray, the head of the Congress of Industrial Organizations, who pointed to Stettinius.

> 'Mr Secretary,' he said, 'I didn't sign that paper.' He paused for a moment and my heart pounded harder. 'The only reason I didn't sign it,' he went on, 'was that they didn't get it to me. I am here to tell you that I believe that I am

speaking not only for the CIO, but for all labor when I say that we are 100 percent behind the argument which has just been made.'

Proskauer recalled that Edward Stettinius then 'rose to his feet impulsively and exclaimed that he had had no idea of the intensity of the feeling on this subject', and promised to raise the issue with the US delegation immediately.[6] This he did. Then after discussions with the other major powers, commitments to promote human rights and to establish a commission were duly written into the UN Charter. A State Department official, Walter Kotschnig, later told the consultants that

I have never seen democracy in action demonstrated so forcefully. . . . It is the participation meeting we had in this room when Mr Nolde first introduced the matter, which really changed history at this point.[7]

Edward Stettinius topped this commendation by saluting the consultants' action in his end-of-conference report.[8] Meanwhile, they proudly proclaimed what they believed to be their decisive role in this achievement – a view that has been reiterated by historians and activists ever since.[9] According to this received wisdom, the movement for international human rights was born of the American citizens' passion for freedom and justice, and of their powers of moral persuasion.

This uplifting portrayal of events is not borne out by the documentary evidence, however. The verbatim record of the meeting, held in the US National Archives at College Park, Maryland, shows that things did not unfold in the way that was later recounted. The record indicates that Stettinius was far from downbeat about the proposals, and that he did not declare that he had 'no idea of the intensity of the feeling' on the subject. It also shows that the speech by Proskauer was considerably less florid than the version in his memoirs, and that he did not challenge the other consultants to register their dissent. Murray's speech was also a good deal less dramatic than it was later portrayed.[10] These were relatively minor distortions – possibly the result of faulty memory. But the general thrust of these recollections was that the consultants had single-handedly persuaded Stettinius to back the human rights provisions. This interpretation is plainly wrong. Had the Secretary of State been genuinely reluctant to agree to the consultants' demands, it is highly unlikely that he would have been swayed by a few speeches in a hotel room. And even if he had been convinced by their rhetoric, it is almost inconceivable that American human rights policy, which had been painstakingly worked out over several years, would be suddenly wrapped up in a consultative meeting that lasted less than half an hour.

In fact, as State Department documents show, Washington was already firmly committed to a UN human rights commission and other additions to the charter before the conference began. A month prior to the Fairmont Hotel meeting, a department official, Alice McDiarmid, had drafted a secret paper on this issue (reviewed, incidentally, by Walter Kotschnig, who later praised the consultants for changing history). McDiarmid noted the clamour from 'various governments and private organizations' for a greater stress on human rights than had appeared in the Dumbarton Oaks proposals the previous year. She wrote,

> [T]here have been expressions of dissatisfaction with the Proposals on the grounds that they lack ideological content and do not establish a standard of justice and human well-being. Religious groups have been particularly emphatic in demanding that the Charter be strengthened in the field of human rights; newsmen have demonstrated keen interest in freedom of information; and groups of lawyers and others interested in international relations have put forward proposals for an international bill of rights.[11]

The White House and the State Department had every intention of capitalising on a groundswell of opinion that they themselves had created. The issue was not whether or not they would advocate human rights, but when they would do so, and how far they could go without endangering their own sovereignty. The McDiarmid paper proposed several 'limited steps' towards human rights – the same steps later demanded by the consultants.[12] The UN Charter

> (a) should contain fuller provisions than those contained in the Dumbarton Oaks Proposals recognizing the promotion of respect for human rights and fundamental freedoms as a responsibility of the Organization, and (b) should ensure that a Commission on Human Rights and Fundamental Freedoms should be one of the commissions established under the authority of the [UN's] Economic and Social Council.

This would entail new references to human rights in the 'purposes' and 'principles' of the United Nations, and a new clause proposing the establishment of the commission. As McDiarmid pointed out, these were not radical proposals that might encroach on national sovereignty. The Human Rights Commission, for example,

> should not become a court of appeal from national courts or a means of super-national government. It might, however, exert a beneficial influence and make a substantial contribution to the stability and well-being upon which peaceful and friendly relations of states depend.[13]

Washington was clearly determined to press ahead with its human rights proposals at some point, and expected to get its way at San Francisco.

At the same time, it recognised the advantages of allowing the consultants to claim the idea as their own. To this end, the delegation nudged them into action. As well as encouraging them to take 'drastic' steps, they made sure that the issue was raised at the Fairmont Hotel meeting itself. Frederick Nolde recalled that while Stettinius was speaking, Archibald MacLeish, the Assistant Secretary for Public Affairs, 'came down to my chair and urged me to get to my feet immediately upon the completion of the remarks by the Secretary of State' to present the case for the commission.[14] Nolde did so. Government officials thus found themselves in the agreeable position of being exhorted by their guests to do the very thing that they wanted to do anyway. At the same time, the consultants were flattered into feeling personally responsible for the initiative. With both parties benefiting from this conceit, there was no reason to challenge it, and it duly became accepted as the truth, commemorated on a plaque, and immortalised in human rights histories.

*   *   *

The United States, as first among equals, acted, in the words of one historian, as 'both good and bad fairy at the christening' of the United Nations.[15] It hosted, funded and organised the San Francisco conference. It also controlled the agenda, monopolised the chair, stacked the votes, and orchestrated the discussions. The State Department had been laying plans for the new organisation since the beginning of the war, and was not leaving anything to chance. Even the smallest details were attended to by American officials: as well as crafting the UN logo, a team seconded from the Office of Strategic Services (forerunner of the CIA) also designed security passes and other conference paraphernalia.[16] And if the American delegation occasionally displayed an uncanny prescience about the direction of debates, it was because the War Department had been secretly intercepting the embassy cable traffic of all the allies (with the possible exception of the United Kingdom and the Soviet Union).[17] This advance knowledge of other delegations' bargaining positions enabled it to railroad the converence along Washington-approved lines.

Although the Pacific War was still raging, the conference laid the foundation of the postwar world. And although peace and human rights were invoked at every opportunity, hard-nosed pragmatism reigned supreme. For the Big Five nations – the United States, Soviet Union, Britain, China, and the latest addition, France – security was the top priority. Even as the conference convened, rifts were opening up between these major powers, most obviously between the United States and the Soviet Union. As they had long recognised, security could only be achieved by abandoning the precarious pre-war system of balances-of-power, and replacing it with a single conglomerate that would safeguard the new global arrangement.

To this end, they urged the other nations attending the conference to approve the establishment of the UN Security Council. Its controlling mechanism would be a veto, which established co-dependency and guaranteed security by allowing each member of the Big Five to halt any council action that it considered to be a threat to its own national interests. They were all thus protected from each other, while being locked together in a mutually beneficial embrace. Not for nothing did the senior US delegate, Senator Thomas Connally, describe the veto as 'the heart and the stomach and the liver' of the United Nations.[18] The major powers were ruthless in their determination to establish this arrangement, and swept aside objections from smaller countries that resented their monopoly of power. The Security Council, complete with veto, was duly enshrined in the UN Charter.

But whatever their differences on this particular issue, the delegates could all agree on one thing. The 'civilisation' upheld by the old order had died with Kristallnacht, and a new one could only be built on the foundation of human dignity. At a press conference held midway through the conference, Edward Stettinius explicitly contrasted the failed ideas of the past with the humane aspirations of the present:

> The people of the world will not be satisfied simply to return to an order which offers them only worn-out answers to their hopes. They rightly demand the active defense and promotion of basic human rights and fundamental freedoms. It is a matter of elementary justice that this demand be answered affirmatively.[19]

British diplomats also spoke the new language of human rights. At San Francisco in June 1945, Guildhaume Myrddin Evans gave a striking speech in which he made extravagant claims on behalf of the United Kingdom. 'In matters affecting the liberty of the individuals *[sic]*, in matters of social progress, in humanitarian and other fields . . . we can claim that our country has been a pioneer – and we intend to remain in that position,' he proclaimed (turning a blind eye to the colonies). Myrddin Evans also claimed that Britain had fought the war for the sake of human rights – a classic case of rewriting history:

> If there is one thing which the free democracies prize above all else, even above life itself, it is the freedom of the individual, because it is that which symbolises the dignity of the human soul. During the last six years we have, in common with other freedom-loving nations, not only sacrificed the treasure of the best amongst our youth, we have voluntarily surrendered many liberties which our fathers fought for. We did this in the sure and certain knowledge that, if we kept the faith those liberties would not only return to us in due course, but their temporary surrender would prove to have assisted in the

restoration of freedom to other people. That hope has not been disappointed. The time for its realization has not completely come but it is near. Will anyone dare to say that the sacrifice was not worth while?[20]

Everyone, even delegates from notoriously repressive regimes, indulged in the new rhetoric. The Big Five – all of which violated the rights of their citizens, or colonial subjects, or both – proposed that the United Nations's purposes include the promotion of 'respect for human rights and for fundamental freedoms for all without distinction as to race, sex, language, or religion'. The preamble – which reaffirmed faith in 'the dignity and worth of the human person' – was first drafted by Jan Smuts of South Africa, a nation soon to become a global pariah.[21] The charter must express 'what is in the hearts of the men and women', Smuts argued, by upholding 'social progress' and the 'ultimate value of human personality'.[22]

Yet while these powerful states regarded human rights as a splendid unifying ideal, they were also anxious to pre-empt any intervention in their own affairs. At one of the meetings between the consultants and officials, Walter White, the head of the National Association for the Advancement of Colored People, pointed out that a blanket ban on domestic interference would, had the United Nations existed earlier, have prevented it from protesting against Hitler's racial policies. Delegate Harold Stassen gave a reply that summed up Washington's approach:

> If you give [the UN] power to go into domestic affairs they can come in and change, for instance, your immigration policies. They can come in and change your tariff set-ups. Now maybe you want them to . . . but we are not ready for anything like that.[23]

Other countries shared the United States' fears about potential breaches of sovereignty in the name of human rights. A briefing paper drafted by Egyptian officials for their delegation to San Francisco (and secretly passed on to the American Legation in Cairo by a 'confidential source') argued that although they could not avoid supporting the doctrine,

> it should be borne in mind that the application of this principle may lead to dangerous evils as a result of the unjustified interference of foreign powers in the internal affairs of other powers. It has happened in the past that the question of minorities has been taken advantage of on numerous occasions to justify such interference; a late example of this sort was one of the causes of the outbreak of the war – the interference of Germany in the Sudeten question.[24]

It is thus not surprising that the lofty ideals incorporated into the charter were tempered by legal caution. While human rights were sweepingly affirmed as the essential foundation of peace, they were simultaneously blotted out by the almighty 'sovereignty article' (Article 2, Paragraph 7) which banned the UN from intervening in matters 'essentially within the domestic jurisdiction' of member states.[25]

*   *   *

A fortnight after the Fairmont Hotel meeting, Edward Stettinius gave a press conference to announce that his government expected the UN to establish a Human Rights Commission to 'promptly undertake to prepare an International Bill of Rights'.[26] What did the British make of this? 'It is said that he was under pressure both from various currents among the consultative organisations attached to his delegation,' British diplomats reported back to London, 'and also from the Latin American states following on Resolution 40 of the Mexico City Conference calling for modification of the rights of man.'[27] R.H. Hadow expanded on this theme:

> The reason for Mr Stettinius's sudden statement to the Press with regard to an International Bill of Rights will – according to information given me confidentially in the US Delegation – I fancy, be found to be a desire to compensate, to certain Latin American governments, for countervailing concessions on the part of the latter with regard to regional autonomy in the Act of Chapultepec.

Hadow added,

> The Latin American jurists are, I understand, raring to 'get a move on' with a typical string of pious [human rights] platitudes which seem to place them in the vanguard of progress and yet involve no enforcement of inconvenient standards in their home towns! . . . Hence Stettinius's sop; and also, I am led to believe, a far less easy side-tracking of the issue than Alger Hiss (who is evidently not in the know) seems to have indicated.[28]

The operative words here are 'Stettinius's sop'. A controversy had blown up over the Security Council's power to over-ride regional security pacts, codified, in Latin America's case, by the Act of Chapultepec. The US delegation had smoothed over this row by offering their Southern neighbours various sweeteners, including the promise of a future bill of rights (although they were not prepared to discuss its content at the conference). If the British were right about this, it shows that State Department officials, who already intended to push for a commission and a bill of rights, had cunningly killed two birds – consultants and Latin Americans – with one human rights stone.

The United States had every reason to be satisfied with the way the conference had played out. The question was, would the public buy it? The obvious people to ask were the consultants, who had been given the responsibility for selling the UN project. Did they believe in the product? The answer was a resounding 'yes'. They not only believed in it; they identified closely with it, regarding it as their own.

Some of the consultants reported on their San Francisco experience to a conference of non-governmental organisations (NGOs) held in New York in June 1945. A British diplomat, vice-consul Leonard Holliday, was present at the meeting, and he was unimpressed by what he heard. He described how Judge Joseph Proskauer, one of the chief protagonists in the encounter with Stettinius,

> introduced into the proceedings a note of emotion which won him several rounds of applause. The Board of Consultants, he claimed, had made it possible for the first time for the voice of the people to be hear[d] directly in the formulation of an international charter and as a result this document was the first of its kind to guarantee certain rights not to states, not to groups but to individuals. The credit for this he claimed principally for Dean Gildersleeve, Philip Murray and himself who had told Secretary Stettenius that the consultants could not support the Charter without the Human Rights provisions.

Holliday added: 'It was noticeable that Judge Proskauer glossed over the fact that most of the Human Rights provisions of the Charter are, in fact, permissive, not mandatory and he was several times taken up on this during the question period which followed.'[29]

Other consultants spoke too. William Carr of the National Education Association 'showed even less of a sense of proportion', Holliday said, when he had argued that 'trade and treaties, armament and disarmament, security and sanctions' were outmoded concerns, but the 'explicit inclusion of education' was the charter's 'greatest single achievement'.[30] Meanwhile, Jane Evans of the National Peace Conference gave an address purporting to take the audience behind the scenes at San Francisco. Holliday described it as being 'of little general interest', except for her clear antipathy towards 'government as such and for diplomatists whom she compared to Dickens's oyster – "solitary, secret and self-contained".' He was equally disparaging about the audience made up of people from non-governmental organisations, claiming that they 'held views inspired by unbridled idealism rather than shrewd common sense', and were more interested in 'justice in the abstract rather than in pragmatical solutions'.[31]

This report was passed to the British Ambassador in Washington, and then to the Foreign Office – past masters in the manipulation of non-governmental groups. Holliday's superiors had to admit that Washington's unusual decision to invite the consultants to San Francisco had been a masterstroke. Lord Halifax, in Washington, noted that the State

Department's decision to do so, 'which at the time appeared alarming', had turned out far better than expected, as they 'were proud of the results of the Conference and claimed them as their own work'.[32] Back in London, Gladwyn Jebb disdainfully noted that

> We had quite underestimated the apparent power of the American administration to delude these simple folk and to make them think that their objectives had been achieved in the present Charter. I very much doubt whether 42 British groups of the same character would have come to the same conclusion. However, despite the fact that they all agree that the Charter is admirable and that they themselves had the principal responsibility for writing it, nearly all of these 'consultants' talked the most fearful nonsense, the gem being in my view the speech of Mr William G. Carr.[33]

Were the consultants really as credulous as the British implied? Walter White of the National Association for the Advancement of Colored People complained that their presence at San Francisco was nothing more than 'window dressing', and he was right to be sceptical.[34] Washington was not seeking their expertise or advice, it was merely exploiting them as cheerleaders for the United Nations. The consultants, for their part, were not cynical or corrupt, but they were guilty of two other political sins: vanity and wishful thinking. They allowed themselves to be flattered by government, and acquired an exaggerated sense of their own importance. More seriously, because they wanted to believe that San Francisco heralded a brave new world of human rights, they shut their eyes to the realities of power politics. Instead of seeing the United Nations for what it was – a security organisation run for and by the world's most powerful states – they saw it for what they wanted it to be: a vehicle for the advancement of the rights of the disenfranchised and dispossessed. In this respect, they were just the first of a long line of non-governmental organisations to suffer such delusions.

*   *   *

After the portentous San Francisco conference, the first meetings of the preparatory UN Nuclear Commission on Human Rights were something of an anti-climax. Joseph Lash, the biographer of his friend, the former First Lady, Eleanor Roosevelt, set the scene:

> On a Monday morning late in April, 1946, a tall woman in black, black stockings, a black gauzy scarf around her neck, emerged from the last stop of the Bronx subway and with swift stride began to cross the Hunter College campus. . . . Behind her, an impeccably dressed gentleman in a dark suit tried to catch up with her without breaking into a run. This was James P. Hendrick, Wall Street lawyer during the Thirties, War Department aide during the war,

and now assistant to the chief of the International Affairs Division of the State Department.[35]

When Hendrick finally drew level with Eleanor Roosevelt, he introduced himself as her advisor. They were both about to embark on a tumultuous political journey.

These earliest meetings of the fledgling human rights body took place in a college reading room smelling of old books and wood polish. Observers and advisors were placed on creaking wooden benches brought in for the occasion. There were no microphones. The half dozen international delegates elected Roosevelt as chairwoman, a move that would have pleased Washington. But a third of the commission's members did not show up, and those that did, Hendrick thought, were not (other than Roosevelt and the French delegate René Cassin) 'sufficiently distinguished'.

> Mr Hsia, China, and Mr Neogy, India, were useful members but neither of them is a figure of world-wide importance. Mr Brkish, Yugoslavia, with halting French and no English, was able to make no contribution of any real value but he was on the whole co-operative. Mr Borisov, USSR, arriving at the last moment was a completely inflexible exponent of the messages he had received from Moscow.[36]

The nuclear commission proposed drafting an international bill of rights. It also advocated the establishment of an International Agency of Implementation. This suggestion refocused attention on the central question posed by human rights – intervention or non-intervention; human rights or sovereignty? James Hendrick commented that:

> The [implementation] proposal goes beyond what had been outlined in the United States agenda for the Commission and is bound to be highly controversial. Its strongest proponent on the Commission was Professor Cassin who . . . feels that had the world been able to stop the monstrous acts of Germany towards the Jews after Hitler's accession to power, war might have been avoided. There is no question but that the Commission's work will be of little use without implementation. The difficulty is that effective implementation cannot be achieved unless the Commission interferes with the internal problems of nations.[37]

So could governments accept the idea that governments should intervene in the affairs of other governments in the name of human rights? Hendrick left the question dangling.

The full UN Commission on Human Rights, comprising eighteen members, first met in January 1947 at the United Nations's first home – the wartime Sperry Gyroscope factory at Lake Success, New York. The Americans again proposed Roosevelt as their delegate, and predicted that it was 'quite likely' that she would be voted chairwoman – which she was.[38] They decided that, on balance, this would be a good thing, because she would be able to direct the discussion 'by recognizing or not recognizing particular speakers at critical moments'.[39] Nationalist China's Chang Peng-chun and Lebanon's Charles Malik were appointed deputy chair and rapporteur respectively. The State Department was satisfied with this outcome: Chang and Malik were both seen as being broadly sympathetic to America's views – as indeed, were almost all delegates, save those from the three Soviet republics and Yugoslavia.

Like the Americans, the British Foreign Office saw the new commission as being potentially 'of considerable importance'.[40] One official correctly predicted that it would become an arena for the 'big battles in the United Nations on the fundamental ideological issue of Western democracy as opposed to Soviet totalitarianism'.[41] Another suggested that the bill of rights might rank 'second in importance to the Charter itself'.[42] They agonised over their choice of delegate, scouring the ranks of the great and the good for an 'eminent non-official person' who was 'high-powered, not too old and well-known in public life'.[43] The name of author and broadcaster J.B. Priestley was discarded ('a great name but . . . would he get on with his colleagues?')[44] Also jettisoned was the Liberal politician Sir Geoffrey Mander, after the Lord Chancellor described him as 'a bit of a windbag'.[45] The economic historian Professor R.H. Tawney was deemed to be too old.[46]

Whitehall also considered for the job Britain's foremost international law specialist, Professor Hersch Lauterpacht – an eminently qualified candidate who had already written *An International Bill of the Rights of Man*, the first book urging the global protection of human rights by legal means. The Americans obviously recognised his credentials because they had added him to their wish list of commission members.[47] But the Foreign Office declined to appoint him. Expressing a prejudice that the commission was established to eradicate, its legal advisor, Eric Beckett, insisted that it would be 'quite disastrous' to make him His Majesty's Government's delegate, for

> Professor Lauterpacht, although a distinguished and industrious international lawyer, is, when all said and done, a Jew fairly recently come from Vienna. Emphatically, I think that the representative of HMG on human rights must be a very English Englishman imbued throughout his life and hereditary to the real meaning of human rights as we understand them in this country.[48]

Having discarded Lauterpacht, they appointed the Foreign Secretary's nominee, the former trade union leader and very English Englishman Charles Dukes (born Stourbridge, Worcestershire). He was far from being the ideal choice, being old, sick and reluctant to take the job. He made little mark on the proceedings and died shortly after.

The Human Rights Commission set itself the initial task of drawing up a bill of rights, which was to include a non-binding declaration, a binding covenant, and measures of enforcement. The declaration was intended to be an inspiring statement of principles, that would play a moral and educational role. The covenant, meanwhile, would be drawn up as a formal treaty, which would impose legal restraints on the signatories. Having decided on the form, the commission then began to discuss its content, and immediately discovered that human rights were much easier to invoke than to define. Would these rights be pre-existing or aspiring; individual or collective; secular or God-given; government-proof or government-endowed?

The inordinately long debates about the declaration's first article signalled the magnitude of the task ahead. First, the French delegate René Cassin, proposed,

> All men are brothers. Being endowed with reason, members of one family, they are free and possess equal dignity and rights.

Delegates immediately expressed their disquiet about the first two words: 'all men'. The Soviet delegate, Vladimir Koretsky, challenged the view that all men meant all people. That was just an 'historical reflection on the mastery of men over women', he said.[49] The Indian delegate, Hansa Mehta, and members of the Commission on the Status of Women also objected to 'all men', and proposed instead 'all people' or 'all human beings'. Roosevelt was not in sympathy with these sentiments: American women, she argued, did not feel excluded by the Declaration of Independence's reference to 'all men'.[50]

Various alternatives were proposed. The French suggested 'all members of the human family', while the British and Indians jointly offered 'all people, men and women'. Yet as the Russian delegate, Alexei Pavlov, pointed out, the phrase 'all people, men and women' suffered in translation to Russian, because in that language 'women were automatically included in the notion of "people"'. The Belgian delegate, Ronald Lebeau, indicated that the phrase looked just as bad in French: 'tous les hommes, hommes et femmes'.[51] So Article One was redrafted as:

> All human beings are born free and equal in dignity and rights. They are endowed by nature with reason and conscience and should act towards one another like brothers.

The final phrase too was eventually changed to 'in a spirit of brotherhood' at the behest of the Women's Commission.

More discussion ensued over whether human 'reason and conscience' was bestowed by God or by nature. In the commission, Charles Malik had proposed a reference to 'The Creator' in the discussion of another article, but had been successfully rebuffed by Alexander Bogomolov of the USSR who argued that 'the Declaration was meant for mankind as a whole, whether believers or unbelievers'. But when the draft declaration wended its way from the commission to the UN's Third (Social and Humanitarian) Committee prior to the final debate in the General Assembly, the debate about God was resurrected with regard to Article One. There, the Brazilian delegation suggested that the second sentence should be changed to,

> Created in the image and likeness of God, they are endowed with reason and conscience.

Other delegates opposed this suggestion. Ernest Davies of the United Kingdom, for example, thought that it would alienate communist delegations 'representing more than half the world's populations'. In the end, Henri Carton de Wiart of Belgium proposed a trade-off: no reference to God, but no reference to nature either.[52] The 'by nature' phrase was deleted, and the Universal Declaration acquired its secular form, beginning with Article One:

> All human beings are born free and equal in dignity and rights. They are endowed with reason and conscience and should act towards one another in a spirit of brotherhood.[53]

*   *   *

The Americans quickly forged a close working relationship with the British on the commission. Durward Sandifer, deputy director of the Office of UN Affairs, was impressed by the smooth machinations of British diplomacy and wrote to James Hendrick and James Simsarian that

> The longer I have worked in the human rights field the more convinced I have been that in order to achieve anything really worth while it is essential that the British and the United States work together as a team. This does not mean that we have to knuckle under and yield to them on all their pet projects; by the same token it does mean that we have to give up some of our pet projects. In dealing with the British it is essential to note that they are far more skilled in negotiation on an international level than we are; that they give the impressions of being very fine and straight-forward but in fact they are extremely slick customers. There are a few points on which we can 'twist their arm' quite effectively if need be. . . . They are . . . sensitive to a degree which I have thought was true only of the USSR, to any attempt to inquire into colonial affairs. To propose, for example, that the Covenant contain a

provision on the rights to vote is to send cold chills up and down the British spine and make them extremely amenable to accepting our suggestions on other points if only we will not push the right to vote.[54]

Cold chills on democracy notwithstanding, they together pressed for a 'clear and concise declaration . . . and the elimination of provisions . . . which were objectionable'.[55] One provision that they found particularly unacceptable was the 'rebellion' article. Originally proposed by Latin American nations, it was intended to uphold the right to oppose Nazi-style tyranny. The State Department, working on the premise that citizens should not be encouraged to overthrow governments, opposed it from the start. As a briefing paper argued,

> Presumably all states would admit that they exist for the purpose of assuring order and justice through law. . . . However, to admit the right of forcible resistance, or rebellion, is another matter entirely, for this involves the negation of law, and in this sense of the state itself.

It suggested that the declaration should promote stability, not revolt. It also suggested that oppression could and should be fought by legal means – the important and generally unquestioned assumption that underpins all discussion of human rights.

> The purpose of the proposed bill of rights is to facilitate the task of the United Nations in promoting immunity from oppression and tyranny by peaceful means. Forcible resistance should be the last resort after it has become clear that no other means can be effective to achieve a just result. A man is arrested by a policeman for insufficient reason. This may well be a case of tyranny or oppression. Yet the proper course for the man is not to resist; it is to accept the arrest and get his remedy at law.

So the United States braced itself for a fight over the rebellion article, alone if necessary:

> It must be recognized that solitary opposition to this article would be unpopular but it is hard to explain in a headline failure to support a statement which has the ring of a battle cry. But it is not expected that there will be much difficulty in securing agreement by others to its deletion. Should this prove impossible, it is believed that substantial drafting changes would be necessary to render the article satisfactory.[56]

As it turned out, Britain and the United States worked in tandem to squeeze the right of rebellion out of the declaration. They abstained on a crucial vote, watered it down, and rendered it harmless by burying it in the preamble.

These two nations would not have been able to exercise the power they did without allies on the various human rights committees. Both kept a beady eye on comings and goings at the UN and fought hard to place preferred candidates in the right positions. Among Britain's favourites on the Human Rights Commission was Charles Malik (a 'fervent individualist' who challenged the 'dialectical materialists'), and Hansa Mehta of India (who gave British positions 'powerful & constant support').[57] The Americans, meanwhile, maintained close and cordial relations with Malik, Chang Peng-chun and Carlos Romulo of the Philippines. But they were unenthusiastic about the French delegate, René Cassin, whose preparedness to hew an independent line earned him the reputation of being awkward, and worse. In September 1948, for example, the US Ambassador in Paris, Jefferson Caffery, reported that he was 'manifesting fellow traveller tendencies . . . [which] consist of the usual crypto-communist habit of directing criticism against United States while maintaining silence on worst features of Soviet regime'.[58] (This assessment might have startled Cassin's wartime comrade-in-arms, the deeply conservative Charles de Gaulle.)

The British were more inclined to view Cassin as vain and verbose, and wrote that,

> Professor Cassin is a difficult Commission member to work with as he can rarely be persuaded to compromise on his favourite principles and is apt to press for the inclusion of unnecessary details. His fondness for indefinable phrases like 'judicial personality' & 'social security' caused endless discussion, & in regard to the economic and social rights he gave the Commission a great deal of trouble, & the Slav members much satisfaction, by insisting on the duty of the State to guarantee these rights.[59]

Claws were unsheathed in discussions of other nations' delegates, too. In 1947, Foreign Office officials suggested that the Belgian, Joseph Nisot would be 'a very suitable rapporteur' for the Discrimination and Minorities Sub-commission, adding: 'he is a lawyer without many original ideas'.[60] In the run-up to elections for the Freedom of Information Sub-commission in early 1948, the Americans expressed their preference for Mr Lomakin of the USSR ('heavy-footed' and 'predictable') to Mr Sychrava of Czechoslovakia ('ineffective and inarticulate').[61] And in 1947, neither wanted Bodil Begtrup of Denmark to chair the Women's Commission – indeed, a British diplomat read a telegram out to an American colleague which 'equalled any virulence that has been expressed around here about Mrs Begtrup's qualifications'.[62] They were dismayed when she was elected nevertheless.

*　　*　　*

Eleanor Roosevelt was the jewel in the crown of the commission. She already enjoyed immense fame. Millions of Americans read her 'My Day' column, and thousands of Europeans turned out to see her wherever she travelled.[63] Many American commentators regarded her as a national treasure, and penned sycophantic profiles, which provided the raw material for a subsequent slew of hagiographies. But although she enjoyed a left-of-centre reputation, she was neither a political maverick nor a humanitarian paragon. Her human rights advocacy was almost always conducted through the prism of official foreign policy. She accepted, and respected, the constraints imposed on her by the State Department and the Truman Administration. There is little evidence that these restrictions troubled her unduly; in any case, as one advisor James Green noted, her views 'did not differ much from those of the State Department on human rights questions'.[64] Throughout her tenure on the commission, she sometimes made decisions at odds with her reputation, but never at odds with America's foreign interests.

She was briefed and guided by two official bodies in Washington. The Subcommittee on Human Rights and the Status of Women, set up under the auspices of the Interdepartmental Committee on International Social Policy in 1946, scrutinised and advised on every aspect of the negotiations. This subcommittee was first chaired by Walter Kotschnig, and was attended by representatives from the departments of State, Commerce, Labor, Interior and the Federal Security Agency. Meanwhile, responsibility for preparatory work fell to the newly formed human rights branch of the State Department's Division of International Organisation Affairs under its first appointed head, James Hendrick, and later, John Halderman. These two bodies – the earliest human rights components in the modern American bureaucracy – produced a veritable avalanche of briefing papers, position papers, memoranda and proposals to guide the development of every aspect of the declaration and covenant.

Roosevelt thus received a constant drip-feed of written instructions from Washington, as well as minute-to-minute counselling from State and Justice Department lawyers and aides, who always sat within whispering distance while she chaired the commission in Geneva or Lake Success. She noted,

> Mr [Durward] Sandifer was always seated just behind me, to give me guidance. As time went on I got so I could tell merely by his reactions whether the discussion was going well or badly. If I could feel him breathing down my neck, I knew there was trouble coming, usually from the Russians.[65]

Occasionally these over-the-shoulder communications were hindered by her deafness. James Hendrick at first tried to murmur instructions into her good ear, but eventually resorted to scribbling notes. A typical example read, 'On Philippine resolution, assume you will vote yes.' Or, 'If there is a subcommittee of three, suggest – Malik, Dukes, Mora.'[66] Or, less helpfully,

> You will just have to play this one as well as you can. Our position paper finds 'serious difficulties' with the right to work. On the other hand, you can't very well argue against the President's speech.[67]

Roosevelt soon grew into her role of commission chairwoman. 'Two and a half years ago, she was an indifferent parliamentarian . . . but nowadays she can chairman a meeting as expertly as if she had been born with an "Out of Order" on her lips', commented the author of a flattering profile in the *New Yorker*.[68] A British delegate concurred, remarking after a particularly gruelling series of debates that 'Mrs Roosevelt has performed an unusually exacting task of chairmanship with her usual distinction.'[69] Her colleagues greatly admired her parliamentary guile: after witnessing a clash between her and a Soviet delegate, one official purred: 'Never have I seen naïveté and cunning so gracefully blended.'[70]

But although other nation's envoys respected her ability as chair, they resented her occasional use of the position to push through US-inspired initiatives. The British representative, Geoffrey Wilson, was among those aggravated by her partisanship – even though he was still prepared to give her the benefit of the doubt. 'Mrs Roosevelt, in ignorance, I think, more than anything else, uses her position as chairman to try to force through American ideas with the result that we have to be constantly on guard to prevent American clauses drafted in the most general terms from being substituted for the Clauses appearing in [the existing draft].' Wilson was so incensed by their habit of trying to put one over on the commission that on one occasion he 'had this out' with Hendrick and Herzel Plaine of the Justice Department.[71] (On other occasions, Wilson happily collaborated with the Americans, and informed Hendrick that he 'deplored the fact that [Roosevelt] was unable to do more speaking as an advocate and had to rely very largely on unofficially persuading other members to take the initiative in introducing US views'.[72])

In fact, unofficial persuasion was Roosevelt's great forte. Her skill as behind-the-scenes vote-catcher was highlighted by Durward Sandifer in a memo he wrote in July 1948, bringing Hendrick and Simsarian up to speed on the declaration's progress from the commission to the Third Committee (where she also represented the United States). 'Always remember that there are some votes which can be secured only if Mrs Roosevelt speaks to the delegates herself,' he counselled. There seemed to be little risk of that not happening. In fact, just about everybody – those who supported America's views, those who opposed them, and especially the waverers – was grist to her mill. Sandifer wrote:

As you know, Mrs Roosevelt makes it a practice of entertaining all the delegates on the Third Committee during the course of the session. This is done by small luncheons and by evening sessions. You and Otis Mulliken should make sure people are lined up for luncheon every day and you should also make plans for evening sessions. In each case the group invited must be carefully picked out so as to secure maximum efficiency in lining up votes.[73]

The State Department's prime aim was to maintain America's moral leadership of the human rights initiative without becoming entangled in any concrete obligations. The non-binding declaration did not require Senate approval, but all the same, officials had no intention of setting precedents that would upset politicians in Washington. In July 1948, during the final stages of the negotiations over the declaration, Sandifer briefed his colleagues on the thorny question of implementation:

If changes must be made in the Declaration I believe the one tendency which should be fought more strongly than any other is the tendency to put measures of implementation in the Declaration. This is a matter which you will have to watch like a hawk because once any member has succeeded in putting in only one sentence indicating implementation the precedent will have been established and you will be lost. You remember the fight we had to take out of the Declaration the statement that 'The Government shall conform to the will of the people.' This statement was one with which we very fully sympathized and we hated to argue for its deletion; yet had it not been deleted we would have been completely lost when it came to the social and economic rights.[74]

The United States was not the only nation wary of commitment: the Soviet Union and others were also against creating machinery that might be turned against them. The commission is consequently famous more for its fine words than for its bold deeds.

*   *   *

In 1947, thousands of desperate people petitioned the United Nations Secretariat, calling for support against injustice. The Human Rights commission's tepid response to this deluge was a model for future inaction. Its members dutifully debated whether to campaign on behalf of wronged individuals over the heads of national governments, and, prodded along by the major powers, regretfully opted for a self-imposed doctrine of impotence. The commission declared that it had 'no power to take any action in regard to any complaints concerning human rights' and kicked the matter upstairs to the Economic and Social Council (ECOSOC). In turn, the council confirmed the commission's decision, and (wrote a human rights advocate) 'salted the self-inflicted wound by deciding that

Commission members should not even review the original text of specific complaints by individuals lest, one supposes, the horrors recounted therein inspire second thoughts about the virtues of self-restraint'.[75] John Humphrey, the Canadian head of the UN Secretariat's Human Rights Division, described the process in his diary as 'probably the most elaborate wastepaper basket ever invented'.[76]

Among the petitions consigned to the wastepaper basket in 1947 was one entitled 'An Appeal to the World' by the National Association for the Advancement of Colored People (NAACP). This report, which documented lynching, Jim Crow and other forms of racial discrimination in the United States, caused quite a stir.[77] Executive secretary, Walter White, initially believed that they had an ally in Eleanor Roosevelt, a member of the NAACP board and a declared opponent of segregation. But recent research reveals that both she and John Humphrey played their part in freezing this embarrassing document off the United Nations agenda.

When the report's author, W.E.B. Du Bois, approached the Human Rights Division about putting the petition before the General Assembly, Humphrey coolly informed him that Washington had decided that 'no good would come' of it.[78] Roosevelt's response to the proposal was even less encouraging. In fact, Du Bois reported, she threatened to resign from the American delegation if it was raised in that forum.[79] A State Department briefing paper records one icy encounter between the two of them over this matter:

> Mrs Roosevelt informed Dr DuBois [sic] it seemed to her that the best interests of the colored people in the United States and elsewhere would be better served in the long run if the NAACP Appeal were not placed on the Agenda of the Third Session. Dr DuBois, on the other hand, felt that it would help if the world at large were informed of their status and treatment in this country. He did not anticipate that any particular action would result from discussion of the Appeal in the General Assembly, but he had the feeling that the discussion itself would be a good thing. He had not expected the United States to agree to place the Appeal on the Agenda, but he said he knew of several other delegations willing to do so. He gave no clue as to which delegation he had in mind. Mrs Roosevelt pressed the view that it would be better to look for and work for results within this country without exposing the United States to distorted accusations by other countries.[80]

The unwanted petition was finally shunted into the Discrimination and Minorities Sub-commission, where it found an opportunistic champion in the Soviet delegate, Alexander Borisov. After days of accusation and counter-accusation about the 'Negro problem', the American, Jonathan Daniels, managed to suppress it on procedural grounds, thus sparing the United States the embarrassment of having the finer points of Southern lynch-law discussed on the floor of the General Assembly. Roosevelt expressed her satisfaction with this result, telling Walter White that she agreed with Daniels' stance because American delegates could not just 'stand by and let the Soviet Union attack the United States'.[81] This argument would not have cut much ice with Du Bois, who, referring to a racist Mississippi governor, had once written that the main threat to America was 'not Stalin . . . but Rankin.'[82]

While the NAACP petition was being cold-shouldered in 1947, Edward Lawson, an American section head of Humphrey's Human Right's Division who regularly liaised with Roosevelt's Human Rights Commission, was seeking accommodation in New York. When he applied for a lease in a Manhattan apartment complex, the landlords turned him down. Housing there was for whites only, he was told.[83]

*   *   *

In September 1948, after discussion spread over two years, the commission passed the draft declaration to the Third Committee, where it was picked over once again in eighty-five grinding sessions. Some articles sparked off weeks of debate. The first two articles took seventeen days. The seemingly uncontroversial article that states that 'everyone has the right to life, liberty and security of person' took a week.

The declaration that began to take shape was pointedly non-ideological – the words, 'democracy', 'fascism' and 'communism' do not appear anywhere in the document. But the universal desire to prevent a resurgence of oppression and conflict left indelible birth-marks on every draft. The preamble's first stanza, which proclaims that 'freedom, justice and peace' are founded on 'the equal and inalienable rights of all members of the human family', looks forward to an era of peace. The preamble's second stanza, which asserts that 'disregard and contempt for human rights have resulted in barbarous acts which have outraged the conscience of mankind', looks back at the outrages of the Nazi regime.

The document upholds economic and social as well as political rights, reflecting the welfarist orthodoxy of the time. During the drafting, everyone from Soviet Stalinists and Latin American Socialists to British Keynesians and American Democrats, agreed that such rights were appropriate additions to the document. But they parted company over definition. The draft article beginning 'Everyone, as a member of society, has the right to social security' was one of those that caused problems in the Third Committee. As the discussion progressed it became clear that while some delegates, such as the British, interpreted 'social security' narrowly as social insurance, others interpreted it broadly as the right to a secure place within society. A British participant wryly reported that the debate then entered a different realm altogether:

Panama pressed for social security 'from the cradle to the grave', which was amended by Venezuela to read 'from conception till death', and subsequently by Syria to 'from conception to disintegration'. This so amused the Russians that they accepted the loss of their own amendment without the usual protest.[84]

Meanwhile, some proposed changes were rejected out of hand. Among these was the Soviet Union's propagandistic bid to abolish the death penalty in peacetime. The Western powers had no intention of giving up capital punishment: the Belgians wanted the right to shoot people in peacetime, the British wanted the right to hang them, and the Americans wanted the right to electrocute them. In response to this initiative, the French representative enquired whether the Russian practice of sending people to prison camps was not also a death sentence. The Soviet delegate retorted that such punishment 'did not lead to death, but rather to the reform of persons'.[85] The Russians returned to the subject of capital punishment in the pages of the *Literaturnaya Gazeta*, translated here by the US Embassy in Moscow:

> The impeccable Mrs Roosevelt voted against the Soviet proposal together with the Greek delegate. Otherwise it might have been necessary to send for scrap such a masterpiece of American technology as the electric chair and the gallows which have been erected in Greece for the destruction of patriots.[86]

After a long debate – 'for some extraordinary reason every delegation considers it necessary to explain its position', a Secretariat member complained – the Soviet amendment fell.[87] No reference to the death penalty survived.

The declaration was not a radical document. Rather, it accurately reflected the conservative social mores and liberal economic values of the immediate postwar era. It proclaimed trade union rights and the right to enter into and dissolve marriage freely, but also reaffirmed the family as the 'natural and fundamental group unit in society' and carefully re-asserted 'the right to own property'. Even so, the drafters feared that they had not been circumspect enough. So although it was intended to be a simple statement of general principles, they slipped in a qualifying article – Article 29 – at the end. This reminded the world that the individual bearer of rights also has 'duties to the community', and that the exercise of rights and freedoms must meet 'the just requirements of morality, public order and the general welfare in a democratic society'. This ultra-cautious, belt-and-braces approach set the pattern for human rights treaties in the future.

*   *   *

The General Assembly finally voted on the Universal Declaration of Human Rights at the Palais de Chaillot, just across the river from the

Eiffel Tower, on 10 December 1948. The French government was
delighted: henceforth, the world would see Paris as 'the cradle of the . . .
Declaration'.[88] The document was passed with a resounding forty-eight
votes. Eight nations abstained. The Soviet Bloc (USSR, Ukraine,
Byelorussia, Poland, Czechoslovakia and Yugoslavia) was dissatisfied with
it because it did not sufficiently uphold economic and social rights and
failed to denounce fascism. Saudi Arabia opposed the right to change
religion. And South Africa rejected the rights of movement and
participation in government. Yemen and Honduras were absent from the
chamber that night.

Ideas always transcend national barriers, human rights among them. But
the declaration is nevertheless cast in distinctly American idiom. Every stage
of the process was indelibly stained with their effort, from the creation of
the institutional framework, to the appointment of Eleanor Roosevelt, to
the labour of State Department officials. It was a heavy investment and it
paid off handsomely. At the end of the first commission session in early
1947, an American report noted that 'the United States position was
accepted on all important points'.[89] Half way through the drafting process,
another report indicated that 'the provisions conform as well as could be
expected to United States laws'.[90] At the end of the last commission session
in mid-1948, another report showed that of thirty-three articles, twenty-
four passed exactly or almost exactly to their specifications, seven passed in
part, and only two did not conform to their wishes.[91]

Many American officials embraced the declaration as the nation's own.
Louis Hyde, an ECOSOC delegate, proudly asserted that

> The United States had blazed the trail for internationalizing human rights
> through the United Nations . . . and had watched the rest of the world flock
> to this common standard in such unity that even the arch-antagonist had
> found it the better part of valor merely to abstain . . .

As Hyde and many others saw it, 'traditional American rights and
freedoms' had been transported to the rest of the world.[92] They believed
that the American Dream had finally grown wings.

The euphoria did not last long though. At the high water mark of the
nation's engagement with human rights, the Republican John Foster Dulles,
who supported the declaration, sensed trouble ahead. At a meeting of the
American delegation to the General Assembly in September 1948, he read
out the clause stating that 'everyone has the right of access to public
employment', and raised an eyebrow. Had he not signed an oath stating
that he was not a communist, upon his appointment to the delegation?[93] At
another meeting, he warned that Republicans might pick up on isolated
phrases such as the one on public employment, which could be interpreted

as 'agreeing to employment of Communists in such agencies as the Atomic Energy Commission'.[94]

Dulles's instincts were accurate. The declaration did indeed provoke the first rumblings of dissent in the United States. Who were these foreigners – Soviets among them! – to lecture Americans about rights? Who were they to declare that people should have the right to marry regardless of race; or that children should have protection 'whether born in or out of wedlock'? Just a few months later, a discomfited James Simsarian, reported that members of the influential American Bar Association were claiming the declaration was 'totalitarian'.[95] The issue of human rights was set to become a force for national division rather than unity.

*   *   *

The declaration was an important accomplishment, but it was not the only development that was taking place in the human rights field. San Francisco promised a new dawn, but before then there were still some dark hours to endure. The other side of the project involved the prosecution of wartime enemies at major war crimes tribunals at Nuremberg and Tokyo. It is to those that we now turn.

TWO

Nuremberg Revisited

In October 1945, the British Attorney-General, Hartley Shawcross, and other senior silks issued a resolution that effectively prohibited English barristers from defending Nazi leaders at Nuremberg, on the grounds that it was 'contrary to the public interest'.[1] This action raised important questions about the tribunal, such as – would justice be served if the defendants were presumed guilty before the trial had even begun?

The decision immediately stirred up controversy. Barrister Harvey Moore dispatched a letter to *The Times* from his chambers in Fountain Court, complaining that this was a scandalous breach of ethics. 'If a doctor or a lifeboatman were warned by his professional or national superiors not to succour a fellow man in peril because of his vile character or political past, such a ukase, in British lands, would receive universal condemnation.' So too for lawyers, he argued: 'Can those whose profession is justice any less refuse their duty wherever their services are sought, and are permitted to be exercised?'

Moore highlighted the inconsistency of allowing prosecutors (led, as it turned out, by none other than Hartley Shawcross), but not defenders, to play a role at the tribunal:

> [T]he Nuremberg trial is either a proceeding of high political policy – which some will think reminiscent of Thomas Cromwell's 'the Abbot of Glaston to be tried at Glaston, and also hanged there'! – or it is, in embryo, an international court of criminal justice. If it is to be the latter, the services of impartial judges as of competent prosecutors and freely chosen defenders are necessary. If it is the former, it may be expedient; but if it is no place for skilled defenders it is also no place for distinguished British judges sworn to the difficult task of 'doing right to all manner of persons without fear of favour, affection or ill-will'.[2]

The Times letters page was soon abuzz. Some lawyers favoured the Shawcross ban, but most objected to it, including Serjeant-at-law Alexander Sullivan KC, one-time defender of the Irish nationalist, Roger Casement. Sullivan contended that the ban 'repudiates the two great characteristics of a true member of the Bar – his independence and his impersonality', and that every English judge and lawyer should refuse to attend the tribunal if it was to be 'deprived of all chance of true judicial determination'.[3] In another letter, six Lincoln's Inn briefs argued that the resolution contradicted an 'elementary principle of justice'. They stated that:

> if there is to be a trial, then surely it should not be merely a more prolonged and solemn method of execution, but a true judicial trial in which either of the two verdicts is admissible, and in which the accused are presumed innocent until they are proved guilty, and afforded every assistance in presenting such case as they can.[4]

The Bar resolution was not lifted however, and no British or other Allied defence counsel ever appeared in the Nuremberg courtroom. Nor was this the only peculiarity of the assize.

*   *   *

The International Military Tribunal was born out of a bitter bureaucratic struggle in Washington in autumn 1944. Up until that point, the Roosevelt administration had not given much thought to how it would deal with the defeated Nazi leaders. The previous year, it had, along with Britain and the Soviet Union, issued the Moscow Declaration pledging to punish war criminals, but it was not until victory in Europe was within grasp that it began to work out the practicalities.

A trial was by no means a foregone conclusion. At the Moscow conference, Secretary of State Cordell Hull had declared himself in favour of summary execution:

> If I had my way, I would take Hitler and Mussolini and Tojo and their arch accomplices and bring them before a drumhead court-martial. And at sunrise on the following day there would occur an historic incident.[5]

Treasury Secretary Henry Morgenthau, meanwhile, advanced a comprehensive plan for imposing a Carthaginian peace on Germany, which involved executing the Nazi leaders without trial and putting the SS to work in massive penal labour battalions, as well as flattening its industrial areas. His plan initially attracted the nominal support of President Franklin Roosevelt, but the Secretary of War, Henry Stimson, thought it too harsh and impracticable. He did not want his department, which would have to deal with the defeated nation, committed to a long-term, arduous and expensive occupation.

Stimson's bureaucratic counter-offensive against Morgenthau's punitive peace plan began in early September 1944, when he suggested that the Americans set up an international tribunal to try the top Nazis. This would enable them to highlight the bestiality of Hitler's regime, while heralding the virtues of the Allies who had put a stop to it. Why execute the Nazis – such a *fascist* solution to the problem – and pass up a perfect opportunity to showcase justice in action?[6] In a letter to Roosevelt, Stimson argued that the United States should observe 'at least rudimentary aspects of the Bill of Rights' in their handling of enemy leaders – a calculated swipe at Morgenthau.[7] Meanwhile, a War Department lawyer, Lieutenant Colonel Murray Bernays, began to work out the details of a trial plan. Like Stimson, Bernays believed that shooting Hitler would 'do violence to the very principles for which the United States have taken up arms, and furnish apparent justification for what the Nazis themselves have taught and done'.[8] A trial, by contrast, would provide a dignified solution to the problem of the disposal of the Nazi leaders, and underline the 'menace of racism and totalitarianism'.[9] 'Not to try these beasts,' he argued, 'would be to miss the educational and therapeutic opportunity of our generation.'[10]

To this end, Bernays and other departmental lawyers drew up a plan to try the top Nazis (and 'criminal organisations' such as the Gestapo and SS) for conspiring to launch illegal wars of aggression; and, while doing so, committing outrages against their own people and people of other countries. Of all these, the United States was most concerned about prosecuting the Nazis for aggression. This focus reflected *America's* experience of the war. Despite genuine disgust at Nazi atrocities, Washington believed that the regime's most heinous crime had been to draw the Allies into a ruinous global conflict.[11] A hierarchy of iniquity was thus later established at Nuremberg, with the Americans and British prosecuting the central case, 'crimes against peace', and the Soviets and the French conducting the cases on war crimes and 'crimes against humanity'.

Bernays and his collaborators paid scant attention to existing international law. Nazi crimes demanded new laws, they reasoned, or old laws bent to fit. When the War Department privately submitted their plan to acting Harvard Law School dean, Edmund Morgan, he identified some proposals as retroactive, and others as 'not only unwise but unjustifiable'.[12] The criminalisation of aggressive war was especially contentious, and later sparked off fierce debates in legal circles. Some jurists pointed out that waging a war had never previously been a supreme crime. Washington retorted that the League of Nations (which the USA had refused to join) and the 1928 Kellogg–Briand Pact (which it had shot full of holes[13]) outlawed aggression. Jurists counter-claimed that even if true, responsibility for war-making and treaty-breaking then rested with states, not individuals – *ergo*, Nazi leaders were being charged for actions, which, although morally reprehensible, were not illegal when they were committed.

A well-received report written in June 1945 by American prosecutor Colonel Telford Taylor suggests that he was dubious at best about the legal provenance of the concept of aggression. Taylor wrote that the phase of the case dealing with the 'illegal launching' of war is based on the assumption that it is, or will be declared, a punishable offense to plan and launch (and lose?) an aggressive war, particularly if treaties are thereby violated. Although the phrase 'illegal launching' is a 'law idea', and although much legal paraphernalia will be and must be invoked to validate the assumption, the thing we want to accomplish is not a legal thing but a political thing. Its accomplishment depends on persuading the several participating nations to take the political step of committing themselves to this doctrine. Whether the doctrine is presently a juridically valid doctrine is an interesting question.[14]

Despite the liberties taken with international law, Stimson's argument for a trial prevailed over Morgenthau's argument for a punitive peace. This was not because it was uniquely appropriate to the German situation, but because it satisfied American concerns[15] – appealing to policy-makers who were wary of long-term commitments in Europe, or who envisaged Germany as a future shield against the Soviet Union.

Once Stimson has won his battle in Washington, the United States set to wooing its allies to the idea of a tribunal. The Soviets, despite some claims to the contrary, supported the idea from late 1944.[16] So did Charles de Gaulle. But the British were opposed to a trial. Prime Minister Winston Churchill favoured shooting international 'outlaws' within hours of their capture and identification.[17] A 1942 Foreign Office paper, which summarised Britain's position, advised that 'there should be no question of such leaders being tried either by national or international tribunals'. Instead, the 'fate of outstanding enemy leaders should be decided as a political question by the United Nations as in the case of Napoleon'.[18] Their stance was coloured by their experience of the Leipzig trials after the First World War: they wanted to avoid another situation in which 'far-reaching threats of punishment only result in a handful of trials and in inadequate sentences, as happened after 1918'. Whitehall thus recommended that the punishment of war criminals be 'disposed of as soon as possible' in order to pre-empt lynchings, and to encourage the rapid return of peace to Europe.[19]

The Americans eventually persuaded the British to drop their opposition to the tribunal at the San Francisco conference. After all, the prime candidates for Churchill's firing squads – Hitler, Mussolini, Goebbels and Himmler – were all dead by then. The four Allies involved: the United States, the Soviet Union, Britain and France, formalised their commitment to prosecute war crimes by signing the London Agreement on 8 August 1945; two days after the bombing of Hiroshima, a day before the bombing of Nagasaki. Henceforth, the Allies' Temple of Peace was built on two pillars: the human rights programme (which symbolically created the benign values of the future) and the war crimes trials (which symbolically destroyed the malign forces of the past).[20] Lofty claims were made on behalf of the forthcoming assize. As well as punishing the Nazis, it would educate the world at large about the criminality of Germany's war; establish international law as the guardian of peace; and leave a historical record of Nazi horrors.

*   *   *

The International Military Tribunal was held in the Bavarian Central Courts of Justice, one of the few buildings in Nuremberg that had survived the war more or less intact. In spring 1945, the besieging Americans had bombed the city to its foundations in their attempts to dislodge two SS divisions holed up in the centre. Then they had fought their way in, street by street. The old part of town, which had once provided a picturesque backdrop to some of Hitler's earliest newsreels, was now just a wreck, pocked by vast bombshell craters and scarred by blackened walls. Tens of thousands of corpses, and tens of thousands of unexploded munitions, lay entombed in the rotten debris. (Judge Francis Biddle recalled the whiff of rotting flesh in warm weather.[21]) Ninety per cent of the city had been destroyed, and 250,000 people were living in holes.[22]

When the Americans gave the judges a tour of the Courts of Justice a few months before the trial, the corridors were choked with rubbish and the main courtroom, used as a GIs' recreation hall, had a beer keg propped jauntily on the judges' bench. When the builders moved in to restore the room, the floor collapsed.

The trial opened on 20 November 1945 in a blaze of klieg lights and flash-bulbs. The notoriety of the accused and the gravity of the charges had turned it into a full-blown media spectacular. All eyes naturally fixed on the former Nazi leaders, who sat in the dock, blinking slightly in the glare. Sir Ivor Pink, deputy political advisor to the British Military Governor, sent home a long report about the appearance and demeanour of the accused.

> Goering, who sits in the front row . . . is clearly the leading personality in the gang. His dove-grey uniform with its brass buttons hangs in folds around him, but it is obvious that prison diet and the resultant loss of several stone have done him good. He looks surprisingly young, takes a lively interest in the proceedings and clearly enjoys being the centre of attention. . . . He will give the prosecution some trouble before they are through with him. Hess, next along the line, looks shrunken, sallow and mad. After spending the first few hours looking around the court as if searching for a familiar face, he has settled down to read a novel and appears to take no more interest in the proceedings. Ribbentrop, his neighbour, looks a broken man, grey, drawn and haggard. Keitel, in a plain uniform without decorations, is stiff and sour, fuming behind his moustache. Rosenberg looks ill and worried; his eyes are as pouchy as Ribbentrop's. Frank is a noticeably evil man, even in such a gathering, though there seems little to choose between him and his

neighbours, Frick and Streicher. At the end of the row are Funk and Schacht. The latter started off with an air of jaunty unconcern which is already wearing thin. . . .

In the second row the two Admirals, Dönitz and Raed[e]r, sit impassive and silent. Von Schirach looks relatively civilised in comparison with his neighbour Sauckel, a repulsive specimen of the worst kind of petty Nazi tyrant and clearly the ideal man for his job of exploiting slave labour. Jodl seems more the military historian than the soldier, while the diplomatists, Papen and Neurath, sit calm and unmoved, observing the proceedings with professional detachment. Seyss-Inquart has the air of an unsuccessful schoolmaster, while Speer, like Schirach, is an improvement on his neighbours. Last of all is Hans Frit[z]sche, the relatively unknown Editor of the DNB, who only appears as understudy for his dead master Goebbels and is obviously alarmed at finding himself in such company.[23]

The prosecution – comprising enough high officials to form a small government – was responsible for breathing life into the charges hatched in Washington the previous year.[24] The Nazis were accused of three capital crimes: conspiracy to commit 'crimes against peace' (the 'planning, preparation, initiation or waging of a war of aggression'); 'crimes against humanity' (murder, extermination, enslavement, deportation, and 'persecutions on political, racial and religious grounds'); and traditional war crimes (violation of the laws of war).[25] For the first time, a group of political leaders – ministers, generals, financiers, diplomats – were brought before the international bar to answer for the actions of their state. They were not allowed to hide behind sovereign immunity, or to pass responsibility on to higher authorities. The buck stopped with them. With the exception of war crimes, these were new legal principles, which had to be applied with delicacy. As the author of a Quay D'Orsay circular pointed out, not only did the court 'operate retroactively', but the Allied judges also had to preside over a war that their nations had just won. They were, in other words, 'enemies sitting in judgement over enemies'.[26]

On the second day of the trial, the American Robert Jackson stood up to deliver the opening address for the prosecution. He tried to dispel this notion that Nuremberg was victors' justice.

Unfortunately, the nature of these crimes is such that both prosecution and judgment must be by victor nations over vanquished foes. The worldwide scope of the aggressions carried out by these men has left but few real neutrals. . . . We must never forget that the record on which we judge these defendants today is the record on which history will judge us tomorrow. To pass these defendants a poisoned chalice is to put it to our own lips as well. We must summon such detachment and intellectual integrity to our task that this Trial will commend itself to posterity as fulfilling humanity's aspirations to do justice.[27]

These were arresting and uplifting words, but the main issue was not the composition of the court – whether it was made up of victors or of neutrals – but the *constitution* of the court. The Nuremberg Charter, the court's founding document, was notable for the amnesty that the Allies had granted themselves. As it plainly indicated, the tribunal was set up to punish only the crimes of the defeated enemy, not aggression or war crimes in general. Article One restricted its remit to the 'the trial and punishment of the major war criminals of the European Axis'. Article Six reiterated that the only crimes on trial were those committed 'in the interests of the European Axis countries'. And Article Three expressly forbade legal challenges to this mandate.[28] Thus, the Allies criminalised Germany's war, while ennobling their own. Yet their reluctance to relinquish victors' immunity and openly acknowledge their own actions laid the tribunal open to the very accusation that Jackson sought to deny – that Nuremberg represented selective justice, or, as some argued, no justice at all.

This charge of victors' justice was made as soon as the court was set up, and it is still made today – even by those who have inherited Nuremberg's mantle (David Scheffer, President Clinton's war crimes ambassador, stated that 'Victors' justice prevailed'[29]). It has been made for the best of motives, such as those objecting to the arrogance of Allied power, and it has been made for the worst, such as those seeking to deny the Holocaust. Even at the time, some key participants recognised that the Allies' self-declared immunity would undermine the court's credibility. Among them was the British judge, Norman Birkett, who stated during an address at Chatham House in 1947 that,

> One could not, for example, bring before the court, say, the Soviet Union because of what they did in Finland, or because of what they did in Poland. You could not bring the United States of America, or indeed Britain to judgement for dropping the atomic bomb on Japan. It does not apply. If it continues to apply only to the enemy, then I think the verdict of history may be against Nuremberg.[30]

Prosecutor Robert Jackson was sensitive to charges of hypocrisy before the trial had even begun, and complained to President Harry Truman, in October 1945, about the behaviour of the Allies who 'have done or are doing some of the very things we are prosecuting Germans for'. He elaborated: 'We are accusing Germans of mistreatment of prisoners of war',[31] but

> The French are so violating the Geneva Convention in the treatment of prisoners of war that our command is taking back prisoners sent to them.[32]

France's mistreatment of the Germans was just too reminiscent of Nazi practices. Jackson continued:

We are prosecuting plunder and our Allies are practising it.[33]

This may have been a reference to the British, who, under the direction of Sir Percy 'Robber' Mills, were busy plundering German industrial plant and patents. He continued:

We say aggressive war is a crime and one of our allies asserts sovereignty over the Baltic States based on no title except conquest.[34]

This was, of course, a reference to the Soviet occupation of Estonia, Lithuania and Latvia. He continued,

We are charging spoilation, looting, enslaving of labour and interference with religion. Suppose a counter charge as to eastern areas is made?[35]

This was another reference to the actions of the Soviet Union.

How would Nuremberg deal with this awkward problem of selective justice? Before the trial began, the Americans anticipated the arguments that might be raised against them in court. For example, a secret memo, probably drafted by the State Department in summer 1945, predicted defence strategies against the charge of aggression:

English support of German 'equality' in arms.
English sanction of German acquisition of areas occupied by 'racial' Germans (Runciman Report, in particular).
French and possibly English consent to German 'free hand' in the East (Bonnet–Ribbentrop Accord of December, 1938).
Colonel Beck's refusal to negotiate the Danzig issue.
Beck's declaration that 'anschluss' of Danzig with Germany would be cause of war.
Polish atrocities against Germans in Poland, 1938–39.
Mobilization of Poland in August 1939.
Alleged British–French plans to invade Norway.
Alleged 'encirclement' of Germany.
Defence against bolshevism.
War is no crime.
Imperialism of British.
Dollar diplomacy of Americans.
Russian aggression against Finland.[36]

In different circumstances, some of these arguments might have been used at Nuremberg to justify the launching of the war ('Alleged "encirclement" of Germany', 'Defence against Bolshevism'). Others might have been used to highlight the Allies' pre-war complicity with Germany (the little-discussed matter of 'French and possibly English consent to German "free hand" in the East'). Others still may have been used to highlight Allied occupation and exploitation of nations abroad ('Imperialism of British'). But we will never know, because the Americans banished from Nuremberg all evidence – *mitigating* evidence – arising from events that had taken place before 1 September 1939, the start of the war. As Telford Taylor had earlier advised,

> It is important that the trial *not* become an inquiry into the *causes* of the war. It can not be established that Hitlerism was the sole cause of the war, and there should be no effort to do this. . . . The question of causation is important and will be discussed for many years, but it has no place in this trial, which must rather stick rigorously to the doctrine that the planning and launching of aggressive war is illegal. . . . Contributing causes may be pleaded by the defendants before the bar of history, but not before the tribunal.[37]

Although the deck had been stacked in favour of the prosecution, it was less easy to suppress evidence of Allied culpability once the trial had begun. The case of Admiral Karl Doenitz – charged with violating the laws of marine warfare because he had ordered U-boats to sink merchant ships and abandon survivors – was one such example. The defence contended that the Allies had been as ruthless as the Germans on the high seas. Had not the Americans established sink-on-sight zones in the North Atlantic; had not their submarines abandoned Japanese survivors in the Pacific War? The British prosecutor, David Maxwell-Fyfe, protested vigorously: 'the question whether the United States broke the laws and usages of war is quite irrelevant; as the question before the Tribunal is whether the German High Command broke the laws and usages of war'. He added that the accusation 'raises the old problem of evidence directed to *tu quoque*' – you also – 'an argument which this Prosecution has always submitted throughout this Trial is irrelevant'.[38]

There the matter might have rested, but for a deposition from Admiral Chester Nimitz, commander-in-chief of the US Pacific Fleet. In it, he made clear that the Americans had fought just as mercilessly as the Germans. He said that it was customary for his submarines to attack merchantmen without warning 'with the exception of hospital ships and other vessels under "safe conduct" voyages';[39] and that they did not rescue enemy survivors 'if undue additional hazard to the submarine resulted or the submarine would thereby be prevented from accomplishing its further mission'.[40] Confronted with this evidence, the judges ruled that Doenitz had indeed broken laws of maritime warfare, but that he would not be so heavily penalised for it because the Allies had indulged in similar practices (he was sentenced to ten years). Rebecca West, who reported the trial for the *Daily Telegraph*, was impressed with this decision, which she called 'a step further on the road to civilisation'.[41] She later wrote:

This *nostra culpa* of the conquerors might well be considered the most important thing that happened at Nuremberg. But it evoked no response at the time, and it has been forgotten.[42]

It was forgotten because it was the exception to the rule. Although the judges had no intention of operating as mere political pawns, and from time to time made decisions that discomfited the prosecuting powers, they were compelled to act within the constraints of the court's charter. The defence of *tu quoque* was not completely prohibited from the courtroom, as the Doenitz case showed, but it was rarely allowed to progress quite so far.

Nonetheless, the German defence lawyers persisted in their attacks on the Allies' behaviour, for want of a better strategy. Had not Britain planned to invade Norway in April 1940, at the same time as Germany had done? (The British had indeed been engaged in what one official called 'funny business' over Norway.[43] But after a scramble to find exonerating evidence, they refused to present documents to the court on the instruction of the Prime Minister, Clement Attlee, who decreed: 'We are not on trial and should not put ourselves on the defensive.'[44]) And what of the Soviet invasions of Finland and Poland, the American occupation of Iceland and Greenland, the French plans to blow up oil-fields? The judges were having none of this. In May 1946, the Foreign Office official, Patrick Dean reported to London, 'all documents on alleged Allied plans to invade Greece and Yugoslavia to block [the] Danube and to bomb Caucasian oil wells were struck out'.[45]

As for war crimes, the defence complained that Allied pilots had machine-gunned farmers, bombed open cities, and sunk rescue craft. In March 1946, the bench decided that they would henceforth reject evidence of Allied atrocities. Patrick Dean, was relieved: 'This is an important decision and may save much time and embarrassment', he cabled London.[46]

One of the embarrassments to which Dean may have been referring was the British commando's handbook, *Close Combat Regulations*, which the defence was pressing to have entered into evidence. In this instance, Alfred Jodl's lawyer, Franz Exner, ingeniously got around the *tu quoque* problem by arguing that if the Allies also engaged in certain activities, then those actions must have been legal. He thus maintained that if the commando's regulations 'should happen to include illustrations . . . of the shackling of prisoners and orders for doing so, one would be obliged to say that the British Government does not consider this kind of treatment illegal and . . . we cannot be censured for it'.[47] This was a sensitive point. The British military historian, Basil Liddel Hart, later warned against prosecuting the Germans for anti-commando measures. '[Y]ou might perhaps find it worthwhile to enquire, for your own guidance, about the methods that our Commando troops were taught, and encouraged, to practise,' he advised the Lord Chancellor, William Jowitt, because he had met French resistance members who 'had themselves seen the dead bodies of German soldiers, with their hands bound, who had been killed by our Commandos'.[48]

The Soviets, who led the Nuremberg charge against Nazi war crimes, harboured their own black secrets. There was, for example, the pressing question of who had murdered 15,000 Poles in the Katyn Forest during the war. The Soviets claimed that the Germans had murdered the Poles in 1941, when the Wermacht controlled the Smolensk region. The Germans claimed that the Soviets had murdered the Poles in 1940, when the Red Army controlled it. Although the finger of suspicion had already begun to drift towards the Soviet Union, Prosecutor General Roman Rudenko still added the massacre to the tribunal charge-sheet.[49] Such was the prerogative of the victor. (Few Western court officials were happy about the Soviet presence at Nuremberg. Sir Ivor Pink complained that 'an NKVD man, Nikitchenko' sat on the bench, and that it was 'a little hard to understand why the representative of a regime which maintains concentration camps in Siberia or the Urals should sit in judgement on those who maintained similar establishments in Germany'.[50])

In fact, none of the Allies could point to a war record that was beyond reproach. They were well aware that their own actions had at times mirrored those of their enemies, and there was thus considerable scope for embarrassment. That tribunal was thus notably circumspect about aerial bombing. The Luftwaffe had laid waste to European cities, but the RAF and US Air Force arguably had a greater case to answer. The War Department supremo, Henry Stimson – creator of Nuremberg, destroyer of Hiroshima – once confided to Harry Truman that he was worried about dropping the bomb because 'I did not want to have the United States get the reputation of outdoing Hitler in atrocities.'[51] Telford Taylor said that it was 'difficult to contest the judgement that Dresden and Nagasaki were war crimes'.[52] In 1948, military historian Basil Liddell Hart wrote to the Lord Chancellor setting out the dangers of prosecuting German military leaders:

> [A] weakness in our case . . . would seem to lie in the directive which the Government gave to Bomber Command early in 1942, for a policy specifically designed to strike at 'the German civil population' – this substituting the method of terrorisation for legitimate military aims. Because of its early date, this directive is in some ways more significant than the more discussed use of the atom-bomb to bring about the collapse of the Japanese people's will to resist.[53]

Interestingly, the Nuremberg judges declined to penalise former Luftwaffe chief Hermann Goering for the destruction of Warsaw, Rotterdam and Coventry, perhaps sensing that it was a double standard too far.

In May 1946, the British court president, Geoffrey Lawrence, declared from the bench: 'We are not trying whether any other powers have committed breaches of international law, or crimes against humanity, or war crimes; we are trying whether these defendants have.'[54] But by rejecting evidence of Allied crimes, the tribunal distorted the truth about the Second World War – namely, that all sides fought a savage war, unbound by either morality or the Geneva Convention. As Churchill had once said, 'In the struggle for life and death there is in the end no legality,' and so it had proved.[55] Of course, it was within the Allies' power to portray the war as a German crime, and they succeeded in large measure. However, by attempting to sanitise and justify the conduct, Nuremberg effectively relinquished its declared aim of providing an impartial historical record. It bequeathed to posterity a flattering portrait of a black-and-white war.

*   *   *

The trial had its moments of horrible revelation. On one occasion, the prosecution showed the court a film of Dachau and Buchenwald, taken just after the opening of those camps. Some of the Nazi defendants, spot-lit in a darkened courtroom, recoiled in disgust and turned their heads away. Goering, the architect of the concentration camp system, complained afterwards that 'they showed that awful film, and it just spoiled everything.'[56]

On another occasion, Rudolf Hoess, the commandant of Auschwitz (called, remarkably, as a defence witness), nodded as his affidavit was read out loud: 'I . . . estimate that at least 2,500,000 victims were executed and exterminated there by gassing and burning, and at least another half million succumbed to starvation and disease.'[57] His dreadful testimony mocked the top Nazis' pleas of 'not guilty' to extermination:

> *Dr Kauffmann:* And after the arrival of the transports were the victims stripped of everything they had? Did they have to undress completely; did they have to surrender their valuables? Is that true?
> *Hoess:* Yes.
> *Dr Kauffmann:* And then they immediately went to their death?
> *Hoess:* Yes.[58]

At those moments, one of the defence attorneys said, it 'rained blood' and 'the smell of burned corpses poisoned the atmosphere.'[59]

Yet the predominant mood of the trial was not horror, but boredom. Most of the evidence on aggression and conspiracy, as opposed to extermination, was mind-numbingly dull. Lawyers with no jury to persuade spent hours reading aloud from official documents. The journalist Rebecca West reported that the courtroom was 'a citadel of boredom', and every person within it was 'in the grip of extreme tedium'.[60] The British judge Norman Birkett railed against wasted time in his diary (some of which seems to have been written on the bench):

> *23 May [1946]:* The trial has now got to a stage when nobody makes any effort to consider time. . . . I used to protest vigorously and suggest matters to save time, but I have now got completely dispirited and can only chafe in impotent despair.[61]
>
> *21 June:* The emotions are too deeply stirred. Irritation, I suppose, is the chief feeling, for not only is the whole proceeding a grave and wicked waste of time, but the illiterate translation is really a torture of the spirit. Time simply stands still, and at the moment at which I write, there is almost half an hour to go, thirty minutes of sheer, unadulterated misery.[62]

Outside the courtroom, Western officials were impatient too. They wanted the rapid disposal of the Nazis, and the quick satisfaction of public opinion. Besides, the vaunted unity between the Allies involved was starting to crumble. Every month that passed brought them closer to disaster. The tribunal had already made its point, had it not? In January 1946, just two months after the trial began, the Foreign Office legal advisor, Eric Beckett, fretted:

> I think that already from the point of view of public opinion the Nuremberg trials are too long and too complicated. As Mr Feller of the United States delegation said to me last night, 'By the time the Nuremberg trials really finish the American public will have long ago supposed that all the accused were dead.'[63]

When the judgement was handed down on 1 October 1946, twelve top Nazis were condemned to death, including Martin Bormann, controversially tried *in absentia*, and Hermann Goering, who cheated the hangman by poisoning himself. Of the rest, seven were sentenced to jail terms ranging between ten years and life. Three defendants – von Papen, Schacht and Fritzsche – were acquitted, setting off storms of protest in Germany and France.

When Winston Churchill was told of the verdict, he seems to have suffered the sensation of someone walking across his grave, for he confided to Lord Hastings Ismay, his wartime chief-of-staff, that,

> It shows . . . that if you get into a war, it is supremely important to win it. You and I would be in a pretty pickle if we had lost.[64]

Not all leaders favoured the judgement. The President of Cuba, Ramon Grau San Martin, wrote to each of the Allies' embassies in Havana, to indicate his desire to see the death sentences commuted to life imprisonment.[65] The Republic of Ireland's Prime Minster, Eamon de Valera, sought out the British representative, Sir John Maffey, to say that the executions would be 'a tragic mistake'.[66] And the Colombian Senate passed a motion saying that 'their guilt is evident . . . but executions could prove to be counter-productive'.[67] Yet these criticisms came from nations that had not fought against Germany. In the countries that had, most people thought that the Nazis got what they deserved. Nuremberg may have been poor justice, but it was richly satisfying nonetheless.

*   *   *

Politics led the advance to Nuremberg, and politics sounded the retreat, with the Cold War killing off Western enthusiasm for the punishment of their war time enemies. The imbroglio over the trial of four Nazi generals by the British in the late forties – set out in documents held at the Public Record Office at Kew, Surrey – illustrate this process. General Gerd von Rundstedt had directed the Ardennes offensive and *blitzkrieg* against Poland and France; General Erich von Manstein had been von Rundstedt's chief-of-staff and the scourge of the Crimea; Field Marshal Walther von Brauchitsch had been commander-in-chief of the Wermacht; and Colonel-General Adolf Strauss had led the Ninth Army. All four were being held as prisoners-of-war in Britain. Yet in August 1947, when the Americans lodged evidence with London that they were implicated in war crimes on the Eastern Front, Clement Attlee's Labour government was reluctant to start new trials. They tried to pass this hot potato back to Washington, without success. It was only then that the British legal machinery creaked into action, accompanied by loud squeals of protest from Parliament.

By now, many, including members of Attlee's Cabinet, took the view that Germany should be built up against the Soviet Union rather than crushed for its former sins. Those who shared former Prime Minister Winston Churchill's view that the Allies had 'slaughtered the wrong pig' turned their fire on the Allies' military trials of the 'lesser' Nazis.[68] The case of the four generals acted as the lightning rod for such sentiment. Tory grandees made much of the Attlee administration's discomfort, arguing that it was unfair to put the generals on trail so long after their initial incarceration as prisoners-of-war. The former Conservative Foreign Secretary, Anthony Eden, argued that it was 'wholly repugnant to British traditions that after so long a period of imprisonment charges should so belatedly have been brought'.[69] Winston Churchill also joined the fray, declaring to the House of Commons that:

> Revenge is, of all satisfactions, the most costly and long drawn out; retributive
> persecution is, of all policies, the most pernicious. Our policy . . . should

henceforward be to draw the sponge across the crimes and horrors of the past – hard as that may be – and look, for the sake of all our salvation, towards the future. There can be no revival of Europe without the active and loyal aid 'of all the German tribes'. . . . Nothing should stand in the way of enabling them to render to Europe the great services which are in their power.[70]

These arguments were driven in the main by unvarnished anti-communism. But there was also empathy with class brethren fallen on hard times. English Church, Parliament and civil service leaders spoke out on behalf of well-connected German kinsmen. The military top brass, sobered by the fate of Keitel and Jodl at Nuremberg, was especially solicitous about the treatment of defeated generals and admirals, as they hoped fellow generals and admirals might one day be towards them. The military governor of the British Zone, Air Marshal Sholto Douglas, counselled leniency, as did his deputy, General Brian Robertson, who urged government ministers to drop the case against the generals because they were 'old men'.[71] (The oldest of them, Rundstedt, was seventy-three; all had commanded armies a few years earlier.)

This sense of common cause with German compatriots was evident in a letter written by the Admiral of the British Fleet, the Earl of Cork and Orrery, to the *Daily Telegraph* in 1948. 'Eminent generals and admirals whose only fault appears to have been that they carried out their military duties with loyalty and success have been treated with, to say the least of it, indignity and want of consideration,' he wrote:

It is difficult to forget Field-Marshal von Rundstedt's treatment when his son lay dying or that when certain prisoners of war of high rank were moved from one place to another many of our papers reported that these officers were carrying their own baggage. At the time there were thousands of their fellow-countrymen available to do it for them.[72]

R.M. Tyrrell of London SW7 replied:

Sir – The thought of German officers having to carry their own baggage had haunted me ever since I read of it. This is scarcely playing the game. Even the victims of the gas-ovens in the concentration camps were spared the indignity of carrying their own belongings on the last journey. Their possessions had thoughtfully been confiscated before then.

Yours faithfully –[73]

In May 1949, three of the generals were pronounced medically unfit to stand trial, to the evident relief of Whitehall's law officers. That left one general to face the music. Erich von Manstein was one of Hitler's most effective and ruthless generals: his Eleventh Army had rolled over the

Crimea and rolled up Sevastopol during Operation Barbarossa. Yet his case became a British *cause célèbre*. The Lord de L'Isle and Dudley and General Lord Bridgeman got up a collection for £2,000 to pay for the defence; Winston Churchill donated £25. Although Conservative politicians led the assault on Attlee's squirming government, the issue was not divided on purely party-political lines. Sections of the Labour backbench were also opposed to such trials on the patriotic grounds that it violated the norms of British justice and represented a punitive peace. The Labour MP Michael Foot argued in the Commons that the issue should be dropped because speedy justice had not been done, and that it was 'the duty and privilege of this country to set an example to the whole world'.[74] The leftwing publisher Victor Gollancz wrote to Prime Minister Clement Attlee in similar vein, saying that the trial might be unfair, and that 'justification for even a suspicion of such unfairness is deplorable, in view of our traditions'.[75]

Erich von Manstein stood trial in Curio House in Hamburg in late 1949. To the horror of Labour Party leaders, the English barrister and Labour MP, Reginald Paget, represented him. The general was eventually indicted for nine of seventeen counts, and sentenced to eighteen years imprisonment for various crimes, including the maltreatment of Soviet prisoners-of-war and civilians. While Manstein was sitting out his sentence in Werl Prison, Westphalia, penning his autobiography, Paget was writing his biography, *Manstein: His Campaigns and His Trial*, published in 1951. The foreword, written by Sir Maurice Hankey, a former cabinet secretary and leading campaigner against the trials, compared Manstein's tribulations with other 'shabby episodes' in English justice, including the beheading of Charles I, the execution of Admiral Byng, the impeachment of Warren Hastings, and the burning of Joan of Arc.[76]

In the United States, meanwhile, disillusion with the war crimes programme fixed on the case against seventy-three SS-men, who, in December 1944, had murdered seventy American prisoners of war in a Belgian field near Malmédy during the Battle of the Bulge – the biggest single atrocity committed by the Germans against Americans. But during the trial in 1946, which had convicted all and condemned forty-three to death, the prisoners claimed that they had been tortured to extract confessions. Cold Warriors and conservatives, as well as civil libertarians and pacifists, took up their cause in the USA, and in 1949 Senator Joseph McCarthy of Wisconsin, a publicity-hungry Republican politician from a state with a large German population, excoriated the US Army for using 'Gestapo and OGPU tactics'.[77] (Washington's rightwingers were in no mood to recall Nazi atrocities, and while they were campaigning for SS men, they were successfully campaigning against support for the UN Genocide Convention.[78]) After numerous reviews, the Malmédy death sentences were rescinded and the prisoners released. Although awkward at the time, this controversy smoothed the path for the general clemency programme for German war criminals introduced in 1951.

After the creation of the Federal Republic of Germany in 1949, Washington was keen to put its relationship with its new ally on a more equal footing. It was well aware that West German public opinion was hostile to the continued incarceration of the war criminals. In January 1951, the US High Commissioner, John McCloy, announced sentence reductions for seventy-eight of the eighty-seven war criminals held at Landsberg Prison in Bavaria. Some were set free, including top executives from IG Farben and Krupp who had been responsible for working tens of thousands of slave labourers to death. (On release, McCloy's officials reunited Alfried Krupp with the vast fortune that they had earlier confiscated from him – an act so generous that even the pro-industrialist British found it hard to swallow.[79] Another freed prisoner, the IG Farben scientist Fritz Ter Meer, commented that the Americans were friendlier '[n]ow that they have Korea on their hands'.[80]) A poll conduced after the releases showed that the German public regarded the clemency programme as an 'American retreat from Nuremberg to outright political expediency'.[81]

Nine condemned prisoners in Landsberg were denied reduced sentences because of the enormity of their crimes. They included Oswald Pohl, head of Himmler's Economic-Administrative Main Office which had controlled concentration-camp labour; Otto Ohlendorf, commander of Einsatzgruppe D which had massacred 90,000 people on the Eastern Front; and Paul Blobel, commander of Einsatzgruppe C which had murdered Kiev's Jews at Babi Yar. Yet when the Americans carried out executions of some on 8 June 1951, the outcry that ensued emphatically underscored Nuremberg's failure to shape public opinion in West Germany. Instead of being shamed by the actions of the condemned men, Germans aggressively demanded the end of American-imposed punishments. Nor did this sentiment abate: a poll conducted in 1952 indicated that only one in ten Germans supported the war crimes trials.[82]

By December 1952, the State Department's Office of Political Affairs sought a 'political solution' to the war criminals problem. Yet John Auchincloss of its Legal Advisors' Office was loath to totally abandon the Nuremberg legacy:

> The solution proposed would remove all legal basis for the trials by showing what little respect for them we have. It would discredit everything the Allies have done in this field. There is so much background to the question, the Moscow declaration, the trials themselves, the expectations they would serve justice and create new principles of law, the international acceptance of these

principles by the General Assembly, that an American yielding to a German demand for the release of war criminals would be a concession of uncommon significance.[83]

But the tide of politics was now running against such views. By 1953, the Cold War had effectively called a halt on punishment for past crimes. American and West European politicians had moved on, and were bent on clearing out their remaining German prisoners and preparing for the debate about the Federal Republic's participation in Western European defence arrangements. The French cut back sentences and passed responsibility for the remaining prisoners to the German authorities, despite ongoing trials at home and flak from the Left. (During the 1953 trial in France of the SS-men who had massacred 642 inhabitants of Oradour-sur-Glane, a communist deputy, Marcel Rosenblatt, said of the proposed European Army: 'You know full well that the Americans have called the SS the best European soldiers. That's why you need them.'[84]) The British were also trying to reduce the numbers of inmates. General Erich von Manstein, for example, spent early spring 1953 on sick leave in the small spa resort of Allmendingen under the vague supervision of the British authorities, and was set free in May, less than four years after his trial.

In the summer of that year, American officials accelerated the clemency programme in order to assist the election prospects of their chosen candidate for West German Chancellor, Christian Democrat Konrad Adenauer. In the week before the election in September, they eased parole conditions and set up a US-German 'Interim Mixed Parole and Clemency Board' to regularly review cases. They also encouraged their allies to make similar concessions. ('As the German elections draw closer you are likely to be under increasing pressure from the Americans to take measures calculated to bring electoral advantage to Dr Adenauer,' the British High Commissioner, Sir Ivone Kirkpatrick warned the Foreign Office.[85]) Adenauer did not squander these electoral gifts. During his campaign he paid a surprise visit to the inmates of the British-run Werl Prison in Westphalia, and declared that all held on war crimes charges should be released. He won the election by a landslide.

Britain's conciliatory attitude towards Germany was brought into sharp focus by the 1954 controversy over the best-selling book, *The Scourge of the Swastika*. Its author, Lord Russell of Liverpool, was an archetypal establishment man. His grandfather had earned his peerage as editor of the *Liverpool Daily Post*; Russell himself had made his mark in the military. He won a chestful of decorations for his exploits during the First World War (MC and two bars), and another chestful for his exploits during the Second (despatches, OBE, CBE). He then rose steadily through the ranks of the Army's legal services, serving as the senior legal advisor to the British Rhine

Army during the trials of German war criminals, and then as Assistant Judge Advocate General. (A few years earlier, he had contributed to the shrinkage of Manstein's sentence by reducing it from eighteen to twelve years.) By 1954, a newspaper photograph showed a conventional well-upholstered man in a formal suit, with slicked-back hair, heavy-framed spectacles, and a dog on his lap.[86] A quiet retirement was not on the cards, though.

Russell was inspired to write *The Scourge of the Swastika* by his experiences prosecuting German war criminals. Using evidence produced at these trials, he described Nazi atrocities in concentration camps, slave labour factories, and the occupied territories, and, unusually for those less Holocaust-aware times, devoted a chapter to the extermination of the Jews.[87] Along with *The Diary of Anne Frank* (which had first appeared in the UK in 1952), *The Scourge of the Swastika* was one of the first popular books about Nazi crimes published in Britain after the war. Yet if officialdom had had its way, it would never have seen the light of day. Nuremberg had once been promoted as a 'lesson of history', but the government now wanted to forgive and forget. The last thing it needed during delicate discussions about German participation in West European defence was a book reminding everyone that a mob in Huchenfeld had lynched British airmen during the war.[88] Whitehall tried to suppress it. Russell himself was threatened with the sack, and defiantly resigned amidst a furious debate about government censorship.

A week before the dispute went public on 11 August 1953, Sir Edward Bridges, the Permanent Secretary of the Treasury, met Sir George Coldstream, the Permanent Secretary of the Lord Chancellor's Office, at their club, the Athenæum. Bridges asked Coldstream how the Lord Russell 'story' was developing. It was not good news. Apparently Lord Simonds, the Lord Chancellor, had read *The Scourge of the Swastika* manuscript and was up in arms about 'certain objectionable passages' as well as 'the effect of the whole'. But if the Lord Chancellor was thinking about suppressing the book, his task would be made more difficult by an unanticipated problem. Coldstream confided that Lord Russell's superior, Judge Advocate General Sir Henry MacGeagh, had carelessly given him permission to publish it. There was thus the risk that Russell would say he had incurred loss because of MacGeagh's negligence. 'On this I made a very nasty face,' Bridges wrote to a colleague. He added that the whole situation was 'very frightful and very awkward'.[89]

While top civil servants were chewing over the problem in their clubs, Lord Simonds wrote a letter to Russell making his case against the book's publication. There were conflicting stories about the contents of this correspondence. The Lord Chancellor publicly claimed that the objections he had raised were 'not based upon the nature of the views set out in it, but upon the undesirability of the holder of a judicial office expressing views which are intended to affect, or which may affect, a matter of present public controversy'.[90] Then Russell publicly brandished a private letter from Simonds that showed that, in fact, he had been very concerned about the content of the book:

> The whole treatment of the subject, including the publisher's wrapper and most particularly the photographs, are such as to stir up hatred of the German people as a whole, and therefore give support to the opinions of those who are most strongly critical of the policy of giving Germany an opportunity, by rearmament or otherwise, of exerting an interest in world affairs.[91]

Russell explained that Simonds had also objected to specific passages, despite his claims to the contrary:

> [He] took exception to descriptions of German brutalities in Russia which were accepted as true evidence in the Nuremberg trials. He objected to a statement that on many occasions unarmed British airmen who had been shot down over Germany were beaten and killed by German crowds. He did not like the evidence that a large section of the German public knew about the crimes being committed in their name in concentration camps.[92]

Lord Simonds left Russell in no doubt about what would happen if he went ahead with publication: he would 'be obliged to consider' his position – in other words, sack him.[93] Russell refused to withdraw the book and resigned his job. Soon afterwards, he called a press conference to explain why he would not be muzzled. Civil servants were appalled by such treachery. 'I think that anyone really soaked in the Service unwritten code would have abstained from this course,' one Treasury official wrote to another.[94] The newspapers quickly reached their own conclusions: 'A Monstrous Act of Censorship,' said the *Daily Express*; 'They Cannot Gag Him,' said the *Daily Worker*; 'This Impudent Censorship,' said the *News Chronicle*.[95] The *Manchester Guardian* took a more measured view:

> an enlightening thing about the whole incident is that it gives the public an unusual insight into the fact that a concealed censorship of publications works all the time. Service departments in particular are often able to 'persuade' publishers of the unwisdom of carrying out certain enterprises, and in the name of 'security' more than one work had been suppressed or mutilated, sometimes quite rightly.[96]

The press did not pass up the opportunity to chide the government for its expedient attitude to West Germany, either. A month before the controversy broke, Dr Otto John, the head of the Federal Republic's counter-spy service, had apparently defected to East Germany. John had been an opponent of Hitler, a translator at Nuremberg, and an assistant to the prosecution on the Manstein case. He disappeared from West Berlin on 20 July 1954, and reappeared in East Berlin three days later, when he made a public statement saying that he had gone to the GDR as a protest against the West's rearmament politics and the re-emergence of Nazis in the Federal Republic.[97] This was strong stuff, and in Britain, it seemed to affirm the view that the government was 'rearming Nazis'. Russell's book gave more grist to this mill.

Critics of Churchill's Conservative Party (now returned to power) complained the loudest. 'So now we know how low the Government will sink in order to revive the German military machine,' said *Tribune*, the journal of the Labour Party's left. It added that the Lord Chancellor was not alone in thinking it 'inopportune to revive' memories of the concentration camps, for there were also in Germany 'the host of leading ex-Nazis who have crawled from underneath their stones and are now riding arrogantly back to supremacy'.[98] Russell probably shared this view, although perhaps not *Tribune*'s avowed radicalism. He told the *Daily Express* that he had written *The Scourge of the Swastika* because 'my own friends were forgetting the lessons of Belsen and Buchenwald'. He added, 'Its emergence at a time when it happened to be politically inexpedient to recall what the Germans did when they were armed was purely coincidental.'[99]

* * *

Proving the adage, 'who controls the present controls the past', the Allies invoked, and then revoked, the lessons of Nuremberg in the decade after the war. The Soviets made sure that most of the surviving Nazi leaders served out their terms in Spandau Prison, but every other war criminal convicted by the Western Allies had been released by 1958. When the Americans turned loose the last four prisoners from Landsberg prison on 9 May, they were clearly relieved that the Nuremberg episode had finally drawn to a close. '[I]t is pleasant to feel that this diplomatic pebble has been removed from the State Department's shoes,' wrote Spencer Phoenix, the US representative on the mixed parole board. Doubtless the released prisoners – three of whom were Einsatzgruppen members whom Phoenix described as the 'ultra hardcore' – shared this sentiment.[100] The experiment was over, repudiated by the very powers that had created it in the name of political expediency.

Judged by its own declared aims, Nuremberg was a failure. In place of its lofty vision of international justice, a compromised 'victors' justice' prevailed. Instead of a definitive document for posterity, it provided a diminished, selective account. And rather than educating German opinion, it invited accusations of Allied arrogance. Nor did it create peace: indeed, the war criminals controversy impeded rapprochement between the Allies and its former foe. Yet the tribunal also served undeclared political aims. By donning winged collars and gowns, it recast politics as justice. And by denying that it takes two to tango, it pinned war guilt to Germany. In a secret paper drafted before the beginning of the trial, Telford Taylor argued that the prosecution's main objective at Nuremberg was

> To give meaning to the war against Germany. To validate the casualties we have suffered and the destruction and casualties we have caused. To show why those things had to be done.[101]

Nuremberg retrospectively validated the Allied cause. While its publicly proclaimed aims were abandoned one by one, its creation of the legend of the 'Good War' was its enduring legacy.

THREE

Trouble at Tokyo

In early 1947, a Chinese military tribunal found Yonemura Haruchi – the 'Wolf of Changshou' – guilty of burying Chinese victims alive; and Shimoto Jiro – the 'Tiger of Kiangyin' – guilty of torture, rape and plunder. Both Japanese were sentenced to death. Six months later, they were driven along the Bund and the Nanking Road in Shanghai, where dense crowds had gathered to watch. They were then shot at the Kiangwan Execution Ground before a huge throng: the first public execution of Japanese war criminals to have taken place in the city. The British Consul-General in Shanghai, A.G.N. Ogden, reported all this to the British Ambassador in Nanking:

> It had been announced that the two Japanese were to be paraded in Chinese carts, but possibly owing to a delay in the start, the procession actually consisted of military motor vehicles, with the Japanese in an open truck under a heavy armed-guard. Crowds estimated at about 150,000 in all shouted and cheered as the parade passed and it is said that at some points stones were thrown at the condemned men, who preserved a stolid and unmoved attitude throughout, although they had refused a narcotic injection offered to them before the procession set out.

Ogden reported that Shanghai's foreign language newspapers condemned the public parade and execution, 'deploring the fact that such proceedings should still be regarded as natural and unobjectionable by the Chinese authorities'. He was also moved to comment on a perceived double standard in the treatment of former enemies. 'It is interesting to compare the relentless attitude of the Chinese authorities towards Japanese accused of war crimes and Chinese "traitors",' he opined, 'with their complacency regarding the continued presence in this country of certain Germans who, although objectionable on political grounds, were granted exemption from deportation presumably because they were regarded as being useful in post-war trade activity.'[1]

Ogden's report was forwarded to London, where it elicited a sharp retort from Frederick Garner in the Foreign Office's War Crimes Section. Perhaps detecting a racist undercurrent to criticisms of Chinese behaviour, he minuted:

As a matter of fact the Chinese have been quite moderate about Japanese war criminals. Considering the immense number of crimes committed they have executed very few. They have preferred to make a public example of notorious cases rather than execute large numbers privately. I do not consider that the Chinese have behaved any worse than many European countries – in fact they have I think behaved better. The Pacific Sub-Commission of the United Nations War Crimes Commission was able to wind up in March last but the parent body still drags on. As regards letting useful Germans stay on in China, what about von Paulus in Russia and the German 'rocket' scientists in the USA and in this country?[2]

While the Chinese were disposing of the 'Wolf of Changshou' and the 'Tiger of Kiangyin' in Shanghai, the Allies was disposing of their political and military superiors in Tokyo, at the second great postwar assize. And the whiff of double standards was just as strong.

*   *   *

The International Military Tribunal for the Far East was established in 1946 to punish Japan's war leaders for aggression, as well as war crimes and crimes against humanity. The court derived its charter, appointments and indictments from the United States, and operated under the aegis of General Douglas MacArthur's occupation administration in Japan. Eleven Allied nations were represented on the judge's bench, led by the Australian court president, Sir William Webb, and on the prosecution team, led by American chief of counsel, Joseph Keenan.[3] Like Nuremberg, the Tokyo court aspired to promote peace and international law as well as punish the guilty. Beyond that, it aimed to offer a lesson to the future, and to educate the Japanese about the sins committed in their name. MacArthur was especially keen publicise Japanese atrocities, and reminded local newspaper proprietors that it was in their interest to give the trial full coverage[4] – no mean feat, given that papers then consisted of a single tabloid page.

Court officials needed little reminder of the barbarities of the war just concluded – evidence of it was all around them. The US Air Force had set out to 'bomb the hell out of Tokyo'; and on 9/10 March 1945, it had saturated the city with napalm, setting off vast firestorms that burned alive 80,000 people.[5] So great was the devastation that when the American strategists convened in April to decide which Japanese cities were suitable targets for the A-Bomb, they noted that that there was almost nothing left of Tokyo to hit. The city was 'all bombed and burned out and . . . practically rubble with only the palace grounds left standing'.[6] Some of the judges at the tribunal were struck by the awful message of the devastation: 'It was horrible that we went there for the purpose of vindicating the laws of war,' said the Dutch judge, Bernard Röling, 'and yet saw every day how the Allies had violated them dreadfully'.[7]

The trial opened on 3 May 1946 in the auditorium of the former Imperial Army Officers' School. 'The klieg lights suggested a Hollywood premiere,' wrote the *Time* correspondent. The courtroom had been fitted out with 'dark walnut-toned paneling, imposing daises, convenient perches for the press and motion picture cameramen', but the Tokyo proceedings lacked the 'majesty' of Nuremberg, *Time* claimed, because:

> The German production had a touch of Wagner – elaborate vaunting of guilt, protestations of heroic innocence. Tokyo's had the flavour of Gilbert & Sullivan. . . . In the shadow of reckoning and doom, [the defendants] giggled and gossiped. . . . Prosecutor Keenan (who looks like W.C. Fields) had to deal with the *opéra bouffe* element which the West so often finds in the Japanese character. The chief Jap defendant, Hideki Tojo, picked his nose unconcernedly and flirted with an American stenographer. Hiroshi Oshima, wartime ambassador to Germany, affected the dandy, with white pocket handkerchief, smart bow tie and black-ribboned pince-nez. Shumei Okawa, onetime Manchurian railway official, carried comic indifference into broad buffoonery.[8]

The judges were stationed atop a vast mahogany bench, which, one observer commented, 'on first appearance seemed to be excessively high'.[9] All had been transported to this elevated spot on the ship of low politics. Some had been appointed because Washington – which wanted to give the Tokyo Tribunal an international flavour – had insisted upon it. The Canadian judge, for example, was appointed as a result of a trade-off between Washington and Ottawa over war-crimes trials elsewhere.[10] Other judges were appointed in response to pressures from within the colonies or elsewhere. The Indian judge was appointed because the British – presumably as a sop to Indian opinion – had insisted that her colony 'has suffered . . . certainly more than French or Dutch'.[11] The Filipino judge was appointed because the Philippines had an equal claim to suffering as India.

The defence soon contested the judges' credibility. American counsel, George Furness, argued that because they were 'representatives of the nations which defeated Japan and which are the accusers in this action, a legal, fair and impartial trial is denied to these accused by arraignment before this Tribunal'.[12] Prosecutor Joseph Keenan retorted that 'it would be necessary perhaps to wait until our scientists could perfect a safe rocket ship to go up to Mars . . . and there find some neutral nations or peoples to come and sit upon judgement of those responsible for aggressive war.'[13] (He then contradicted himself by sarcastically adding that 'we might turn this whole business over to a tribunal composed of the representatives, perhaps of the Argentine Republic, Spain, perhaps Sweden, and we might add Erin.'[14])

More damagingly, some judges had a history that should have automatically disqualified them from the job. The Australian William Webb had in 1943–4 conducted three major investigations for the Canberra government into Japanese atrocities against Australian troops. (When queried, Webb said that he had already considered his own suitability for the role, and had deemed himself eligible 'without difficulty'.[15]) The Soviet, Major General I.M. Zaryanov, spoke neither Japanese nor English, the court's working languages.[16] The Filipino, Delfin Jaranilla, had not only been held as a prisoner-of-war by the Japanese for the duration of the conflict, he was also a survivor of the Bataan Death March – experiences likely to have prejudiced him against the defendants.[17]

As at Nuremberg, the Allies at Tokyo were far more concerned about punishing aggression than they were with war crimes. This preoccupation was understandable, even if it was not entirely conscious. By putting conflict into a courtroom, one could transform a war over colonies and spheres of influence into a campaign against Japanese criminality. Even hugely controversial events such as the bombing of Hiroshima and Nagasaki could be recast as a legitimate response to an international crime. As Keenan asserted at the beginning of the trial,

> We admit that great force and violence, including the Hiroshima bomb, have been employed by the Allies, and we make no more apology for that than does a decent, innocent citizen walking home from his office, his factory or shop . . . and his family employ the use of force to prevent his life being taken by an outlaw.[18]

The prosecution thus unveiled thirty-six charges out of a total of fifty-five against the defendants for various 'crimes against peace' dating back to 1928. In his opening speech, Joseph Keenan accused the Japanese of nothing short of launching a 'war upon civilisation':

> Together they planned, prepared and initiated aggressive wars against the great democracies enumerated in the indictment. They willingly dealt with human beings as chattels and pawns. That it meant murder and the subjugation and enslavement of millions was of no moment to them.[19]

The prosecution's focus on aggression served another purpose too – namely, to buttress the Nuremberg judgement. Allied governments were well aware that 'crimes against peace' had shallow roots in international law, and that the charge was regarded with scepticism in some legal circles. In London, Eric Beckett, the Foreign Office legal advisor, stressed the importance of the Tokyo prosecution winning its battles over 'crimes against peace'. '[T]he greatest effort should be made in defeating the defence on *this* point because to fail . . . would *inter alia* mean that the Tokyo tribunal was saying that the Judgement of the Nuremberg tribunal was based at any rate in part upon bad law,' he wrote. That would mean, 'the Allies had been guilty of infringing the principle *nulla poena sine lege'* – no punishment without law – 'which is supposed to be one of the fundamental principles of justice'.[20]

The prosecution had eighteen years' worth of Japanese foreign policy with which to establish their case, but their attempts to strong-arm the defendants into admitting the criminality of their wartime policies were often clumsy. The former Prime Minister Tojo Hideki, for one, easily parried Keenan's loaded questions about aggression:

> Q: [Keenan] Mr Tojo, wouldn't you agree with me that wars are crimes of the highest nature? Let me simplify the question. Wouldn't you agree with me that wars are crimes against the people?
> A: [Tojo] I don't agree with your statement that war is a crime, but I do agree with you so far as to say that wars have an unfortunate effect upon the people, and that unfortunate effect is the same for the victor as for the vanquished.[21]

William Webb, who had little time for Joseph Keenan, was unimpressed by the standard of cross-examination. On one occasion, he was heard saying *sotto voce* into an open microphone: 'This is dreadful.'[22]

The defence, meanwhile, tried to defend the accused against charges of aggression by arguing that Japan's foreign policy was a defensive reaction against the spread of Soviet and Chinese communism. It was no coincidence that they began to pursue this strategy just after President Truman first outlined his doctrine of communist containment on 12 March 1947, when he famously called on Congress to aid the Greeks and Turks in their fight against the spread of Soviet influence. Yet despite the outbreak of Cold War outside the courthouse, Webb tried to stop the defence from following Cold War logic inside it.

One incident highlighted this anomaly. In April 1947, defence counsel George Lazarus tried to argue that Japan's actions in China were motivated by their 'reasonable fear' of the spread of communism.[23] Lazarus continued,

> President Truman we feel has said exactly what these people have been saying all along, and we want to introduce President Truman's address as justification, even at this late date, for what they themselves foresaw beginning in 1937 when the China Incident broke out.[24]

This was too much for Webb, who announced that he would not put up with slurs against one of the Allied nations, the Soviet Union, in his court:

> As American counsel, do not take advantage of the great tolerance displayed by this Allied Court to indulge in what might be termed enemy propaganda.[25]

Lazarus, unbowed by Webb's admonitions, shot back:

> we must state that we never expected that evidence of the remarks by the President of the United States to the Congress of the United States would be called enemy propaganda.[26]

Webb retorted, 'That is utter nonsense you are putting to us now,' and reiterated that he would 'not stand for gratuitous insults' against members of the court.[27] According to a report in *The Times*, 'The exchanges between Sir William Webb and the counsel for the defense were conducted with the greatest acrimony, the latter taking the line that it was their duty as United States citizens to defend the Japanese at all costs.'[28]

That was not the end of the matter, either. Debates were 'particularly animated' during this phase of the trial, reported the French prosecutor, Robert Oneto.[29] Shortly after his clash with Lazarus, Webb convened a meeting of defence lawyers, in which he rebuked them for 'repeatedly tendering "statements in the nature of [Japanese] propaganda".'[30] When, in midsummer, the defence tried to argue that incidents on the Manchurian border had been prompted by Japan's fear of the Soviet Union, the bench rejected scores of documents intended to show grounds for this alarm.[31] In this respect, the Tokyo Tribunal must have been the only institution in the world to set its face against Truman's anti-communist crusade with the full endorsement of Washington.

The 'crimes of peace' charge had implications that extended far beyond the walls of the courtroom in Tokyo. The outlawry of 'aggressive' war attempted to freeze the global *status quo* at a point somewhere in the late forties. 'Whatever grievance a nation may have . . . aggressive warfare is an illegal means for settling the grievances or for altering those conditions,' Robert Jackson had stated at Nuremberg.[32] In other words, the struggle against colonialism – the central question in Asia at that time – was prohibited under Nuremberg and Tokyo law. The Indian judge, Radhabinod Pal, was aghast. War, or what he called 'self help by force', was now banned, and the colonies would simply have to accept their lot. 'At any rate in the present state of international relations such a static idea of peace is absolutely untenable', he wrote, because 'dominated nations of the present day *status quo* cannot be made to submit to eternal domination only in the name of peace'.[33]

The colonial question cast a long shadow across the tribunal. Asia and the Pacific were still mottled with the territorial possessions of the white colonial powers, and would remain so until after the trial (India and the Philippines gained their independence while the court was sitting). So when the Allies accused Japan of pursuing an aggressive foreign policy, they were really accusing it of rudely elbowing its way into other powers' colonies, and presumptuously overturning the pre-existing colonial arrangements. This imperial perspective was reflected in the composition of the bench and the prosecution. Japan's accusers at Tokyo were not its former colonies (Korea, Formosa and Manchuria), nor, aside from China and the Philippines, were they countries occupied or fought over by Japan during the war (Malaya, Dutch East Indies, Burma, New Guinea and many more). In fact, none of these nations had been invited to participate. By contrast, all the colonial powers in Asia and the Pacific (Britain, France, the Netherlands, USA, Australia) whose rule had been so inconveniently interrupted by Japan, were present and correct at Tokyo.

While condemning Japanese colonial practices, prosecutors could not avoid parallels with those of their own nations. The American prosecutor, Solis Horowitz, for example, later recapped his denunciation of Japan's spoliation of parts of China under the puppet leadership of Wang Ching-wei:

> Japanese officials were placed in key posts and 'national policy' companies were created under the protection and supervision of Japan to ensure control of the economic system. Banking privileges were available only to the Japanese although all persons were compulsorily required to deposit a portion of their earnings in the banks. Land was confiscated and turned over to Japanese immigrants, while the Chinese farmers were moved into undeveloped lands. All Chinese from 18 to 45 were required to render labour service to the Japanese Army. Chinese property was confiscated. China's resources and wealth were stolen, depleted and despoiled. Plants were denuded and mines worked out. Equipment was sold, destroyed or removed. Industries were taken over at a fraction of real value. . . .[34]

Other members of the court, especially those from Britain, France, the United States and the Netherlands must have listened to such evidence with unease. Could not the same accusations have been levelled at their own nations' China policy at some time or another? Four decades after the event, Professor Yu Xinchun of Nankai University, touched on this point during a symposium in Tokyo about the tribunal:

> From the Chinese standpoint, the first people who stole from China were the English. At the Tokyo trial, however, England was on the side doing the judging. Then came the Dutch, and then the French, and finally the Americans. In the Chinese view, they were all thieves. So those who had stolen judge one who had stolen – thieves judging a thief.[35]

What was especially ironic was that the 'aggression' indictment was being framed at the very time that the prosecuting powers themselves were aggressively fighting their way back into their old colonial possessions.

Indeed, in a few places, the Europeans re-established their rule with the help of the departing Japanese – a baton change from one occupying power to another. This happened in the Dutch East Indies. It also happened in Vietnam. Here the French rulers were deeply unpopular because they had plundered rice stocks throughout a famine that killed a million Vietnamese during the war. The Japanese had ejected the French in 1944. When envoys from Paris reappeared in Hanoi in August 1945, they were greeted by violent demonstrators bearing banners proclaiming 'Death to French Imperialism', held in check by Japanese troops.[36] The following month, American war crimes investigators arrived in Saigon with the intention of arresting members of the Kempei Tai, the notoriously brutal Japanese gendarmerie. They postponed their plans when they discovered that the French, British and Indian forces occupying the country had given the Kempei Tai their guns back in order to help them fight a common enemy – the Viet Minh.[37]

*   *   *

The Tokyo trial was as notable for what it omitted as for what it included. The most conspicuous absentee was the Emperor Hirohito, who was never called to account for his actions, even though seven of his subordinates were hanged. At first, the Americans were not sure about how to deal with him. George Atcheson, the acting political advisor in Japan, thought that Hirohito should be tried. 'I believe (and some of our allies may insist) that the Emperor is a war criminal', he argued in a January 1946 report to Truman.[38] But the supreme commander of the American occupation forces, General Douglas MacArthur, had different ideas. Destroy the Emperor, he said, 'and the nation will disintegrate'.[39] Perhaps he really believed that Hirohito was the last bastion against chaos (although there was little evidence to support this view), or perhaps he saw the throne as a foil for his own mighty power. For whatever reason, the Emperor was transformed into the figurehead of MacArthur's ship of state, a 'reserved occupation' which exempted him from appearing in the dock.

   While the trial was in progress, the Americans made every effort to cast Hirohito as a cardboard king. They tried to claim that he had spent the war cocooned in the Imperial Palace with his butterfly collection, only dimly aware of the plans being hatched by the military. MacArthur, for example, described him as 'a complete Charlie McCarthy' – a ventriloquist's dummy.[40] Inside the courtroom, prosecutor Joseph Keenan did his best to lead defendants away from incriminating testimony about Hirohito. Outside it, the defendants were discreetly encouraged to abet the Allies in this exculpatory enterprise. On one occasion, an American official instructed defence counsel George Lazarus to visit the military defendants at Sugamo prison. Here he was to put it to them delicately that they 'go out of their way during their testimony to include that fact that Hirohito was only a benign presence when military actions or programmes were discussed at meetings that, by protocol, he had to attend'.[41]

In fact, the Emperor had been anything but disengaged with wartime politics. He had the final say on the conduct of foreign policy and had ruthlessly disposed of high officials who had questioned his judgement. As the French prosecutor, Robert Oneto, privately noted, he 'could not be refused anything'. Oneto added that his absence from the court created problems for the prosecution because it 'made it easier for the defendants to implicitly blame the Emperor' for the acts of which they were accused.[42] Several allusions to his enormous power slipped out during testimony. When Tojo Hideki was asked whether Kido Koichi had ever acted against the Emperor's will, Tojo said that no Japanese subject, particularly a high government official, would contradict him. From the bench, William Webb, who barely disguised his disgust at Hirohito's absence from the dock, observed pointedly, 'Well, you know the implications from that reply.'[43] In January 1948, the British prosecutor, Arthur Comyns Carr, referred to this matter in a letter to Hartley Shawcross:

> Incidentally, the defendants if they have done nothing else, have proved the guilt of the Emperor pretty conclusively, which, in view of the decision not to prosecute him, we had been trying to keep in the background, and K [Keenan] has been going out of his way, quite unsuccessfully to disprove. Of course, they have all been parading their loyalty to him, but that is the practical effect of their evidence.[44]

Most Allied governments echoed the American line that Hirohito bore no responsibility for Japan's actions. But as soon as it transpired that he had endorsed the attacks on Pearl Harbor and elsewhere, the Western press adopted a more critical tone. The *New York Times* called for Hirohito's abdication, and the *Manchester Guardian* said that his non-appearance had a 'lamentable effect' on the trial. 'It is no good laying down a principle that crimes against peace mean – for the conquered – death, if one starts to discriminate.'[45] Western governments could do nothing more than dig in under fire. '[T]he Emperor cannot escape a measure of guilt', a Foreign Office official wrote, but 'anything we might do would only draw undesirable attention to it'.[46] A few years later, in 1950, even the chief prosecutor, Joseph Keenan, admitted that 'strictly legally' Hirohito should have been tried and punished as a war criminal.[47] If the tribunal proved only one thing, it was that men could be hanged for obeying the will of a monarch rendered untouchable by political expediency.

There were other striking omissions too. Some of the atrocities that are now seen as the defining features of a barbaric war were not fully examined during the proceedings. Discussion of the bombing of Hiroshima and Nagasaki was limited, with many statements and papers being rejected by the court. Discussion of Unit 731's grotesque germ war medical experiments was suppressed after the Americans struck an amnesty-for-data deal with the Japanese officers involved. Discussion of the terrible suffering of the Chinese was not pressed because Chiang Kai-shek, leader of the Kuomintang government, had no interest in highlighting war crimes committed against the Communist Chinese.

*   *   *

The court was riven by internal conflicts. The eleven judges were deeply divided over the question of war guilt, and acutely sensitive to negative comparisons with the Nuremberg Tribunal, which ended when the Tokyo assize began. In March 1947, Justice Harvey Northcroft wrote a despairing letter to his superiors in New Zealand:

> I fear the result of this long trial will be futile and valueless or worse. This court will not speak with a clear voice upon any topic whether of law or fact. If a court of this standing is seriously divided, and I feel sure it will be, then the modern advances in international law towards the outlawry of war may suffer a serious set-back. . . . Varying opinions from this Court including sharp dissent from Nuremberg must be disastrous. This I feel sure will happen.[48]

Such complaints caused concern among officials back in Western capitals. In London, for example, the future Ambassador in Tokyo, Esler Dening, went straight to the heart of the matter. 'Here we have a predominantly Western tribunal sitting in the Far East to try Japanese war criminals', he wrote. 'If the tribunal fails to fulfil its task, Western justice will become the laughing-stock not only of Japan but of the Far East in general.'[49] After the war-era military debacles of Singapore and Pearl Harbor, the last thing the colonial powers in Asia needed was more damage to white prestige.

In Tokyo, the judges took out their frustrations over the progress of the trial on the court president, Sir William Webb – a man who apparently made little attempt to endear himself to his highly-strung colleagues. The British judge, Lord William Patrick, described Webb as 'a quick-tempered turbulent bully'[50] whose behaviour was 'offensive', and occasionally 'grossly offensive'.[51] Justice Harvey Northcroft of New Zealand, meanwhile, vented his spleen in a six-page letter to the Chief Justice in Wellington. The Australian, he wrote, lacked gravitas in court, displaying 'an unfortunate manner of expression, generally querulous, invariably argumentative and frequently injudicious'. Worse still, he did not accord the other judges the respect that they deserved, behaving 'as a presiding Judge sitting with a jury, never as *primus inter pares*' – first among equals.

It was a situation that they just had to endure, Northcroft said, despite the social indignities.

> The other day McDougall and I had lunch at the dining room at the Court building and were joined by Zaryanov, so that we were three Judges together. At another table was a Lieutenant Colonel, an Officer of the Secretariat, with another officer as his guest. Webb came in with his Associate, looked around and without even a friendly gesture or comment to us went to the table of the two American Officers. . . . It looked like, and I think it was in fact, a wilful avoidance of us. The mischief in this occasion was the inference the American Officers would almost certainly draw of division among the Judges.[52]

This crescendo of complaint eventually grew so loud that the New Zealand Prime Minister, Peter Fraser, made personal representations to the Australian Premier, Ben Chifley, requesting Webb's recall.[53] Whitehall, meanwhile, seriously contemplated sending Lord Wright, former chairman of the United Nations War Crimes Commission, out to Tokyo to smooth things over. In November 1947, Webb was briefly summoned back to Australia on a flimsy pretext, while the American judge, Myron Cramer, stood in as court president. More drama was to follow on Webb's return.

*   *   *

The prosecution had its own problems. The main recipient of opprobrium was its chief prosecutor Joseph Keenan, or 'Joe the Key', as he was known in Democrat circles back in Washington. He was a fixer, a New Dealer, and President Truman's placeman at the Tokyo Tribunal. He was also a drunk, and, some claimed, incapable. Reports of his misdemeanours were legion, and even General MacArthur felt compelled to set his security 'watchdogs' on the wayward brief to keep him off the drink and out of trouble.[54]

One of Keenan's harshest critics was the British prosecutor Arthur Comyns Carr, who wrote frequently to London, cruelly chronicling Keenan's losing battle with the bottle. He reported in December 1946 that Keenan has been 'drinking heavily again for the last six weeks, with recent renewed semi-public exhibitions'.[55] He recounted in October 1947 that 'Keenan, although, or perhaps because he's apparently still on wagon, has been playing merry hell with the case . . . and seems finally to have disgusted most of the Americans, though none of them has the guts to tell him so.'[56] These criticisms were not entirely disinterested, of course. The ambitious Comyns Carr (backed by Whitehall) made a play for Keenan's job when the latter returned home for an operation during the trial, only to be angrily rebuffed by General MacArthur, who denounced this 'dastardly act to stab a man in the back'.[57]

Back in London, Comyns Carr's waspish letters created *frissons* in the law and foreign departments as the circle of gossip widened. 'Dear Lord

Chancellor,' Hartley Shawcross, the former Nuremberg prosecutor, wrote
to William Jowitt in January 1948,

> I don't know whether you have been hearing from time to time of the progress
> of the War Crimes Trial at Tokyo. The whole thing has really been most
> disastrous and, but for Comyns Carr, I think the proceedings might well have
> collapsed in complete fiasco. Not only is the tribunal too large; not only has
> the President (an Australian judge) been absent for some time . . . not only
> have there been other changes in the course of the trial on the Bench; but the
> American lawyer, one Keenan, who is in charge of the prosecution, is at all
> times hopelessly incompetent, and at most times also completely intoxicated.
> It is, I believe, literally true, as [Maurice] Reed of my Department, who went
> out there, assures me, that Keenan often has to be put to bed before dinner,
> which seems to indicate that he is even unable to organise his drinking
> activities to his best advantage.[58]

Joseph Keenan eventually met his nemesis in the shape of wartime premier
Tojo Hideki. There was no doubt in anybody's mind that Tojo's appearance
in the dock would be the climax of the trial. Even the British diplomatic
representative, Alvary Gascoigne, lapsed into movie metaphors when he
described this very blackest of courtroom dramas. He reported that

> Tojo provided one of the biggest 'box-office attractions' of the Occupation,
> and certainly the biggest of the trial, so that the spectators overflowed from
> their usually half-empty galleries into that reserved for the press. But those
> who went with a morbid interest in seeing the chief prisoner metaphorically at
> bay – and they must have been many on the Allied side – were rewarded with
> the spectacle of a star turn, a role which it was apparent that Tojo himself
> realized he filled. It was easy to understand from the quickness of his
> perception, the clarity of his answers, his air of command, and the way in
> which he handled his interlocutor (Mr Keenan . . . whose measure he has had
> ample time to take since the trial started) why Tojo had been Japan's wartime
> leader.[59]

Tojo's defence, set out in a 250-page affidavit presented by his defence
lawyer, Kiyose Ichiro, addressed accusations of aggression and conspiracy.
The core of his argument was that Japan had not waged an aggressive war,
but that it had been forced into conflict with the West in order to defend its
legitimate national interests. His subsequent court performance did much to
restore his personal credibility among those Japanese who had earlier been
unimpressed by his botched attempt to commit suicide. Gascoigne noted
that 'his defence of the Emperor . . . and his offer of himself as a scapegoat
for defeat has probably given comfort', and that the 'private comment we
have heard from Japanese has been to the effect that he has stood up to his
accusers "like a true Japanese".'[60]

The prosecution case against Tojo got off to a bad start and never really recovered. Comyns Carr described how John Fihelly, the former chief of the US Attorney General's Office criminal division, had spent a year preparing the case against Tojo and had naturally assumed that he would question him in court. Joseph Keenan had other ideas, however.

> Until the actual morning when the XXN [cross-examination] started he had been repeatedly assured by Keenan that he was to do it. Then K applied to the court for permission to do half of it himself and leave the other half to Fipelly [*sic*], which is against the rules here, as he well knew. He then complained of the ruling that he couldn't do this, and announced that he would do it all himself. Fipelly walked out of court and left him to it. The whole thing is a farce. The results are best summarised by a girl from the British Embassy who was in court this morning and said, 'Tojo had a good morning hanging Keenan.'[61]

At this point, Alvary Gascoigne took up the story about Keenan's botched interrogation:

> Mr Keenan had to conduct the whole cross-examination himself, which it is to be supposed he was not very fully prepared to do. His first question, which started with the sneer – 'Accused Tojo, I shall not address you as General because, of course, you know there is no longer any Japanese army', was disallowed. Tojo's first reply to him was a trenchant 'That is not a direct question.' This will perhaps suffice to convey the atmosphere in which the four-days' cross-examination was conducted. Tojo's contempt for Mr Keenan was apparent to anyone in the courtroom, even though it did not always survive in translation.[62]

Comyns Carr's conclusions about the prosecution case as a whole were pessimistic. They had been outwitted by many of the Japanese in the dock. '[M]ost of the defendants have simply danced round the set of incompetence put up against them, with probably damaging propaganda effects', he wrote miserably to London.[63]

*   *   *

The prosecution's problems did not make things much easier for the defence. The accused had been allocated both Japanese and American counsel – the latter unfairly described by MacArthur as 'shysters'[64] – who together mounted a spirited defence of the accused. But they operated under severe restraints. As well as the predictable problems of coordination and language, they lacked for funds, translators, checkers, typewriters and clerical staff. They had difficulty tracking down evidence and witnesses. And they had to contend with William Webb, who was dismissive of defence motions and intolerant of defence arguments, which he often deemed to be Japanese 'propaganda'. (The Canadian judge, Stuart McDougall, was privately critical of Webb's high-handed attitude: when the defence presented a pre-trial motion attacking the jurisdiction of the court, he noted with disquiet that the motion was curtly dismissed for reasons 'to be given later'.[65])

Court rulings were often arbitrary. Traditional rules governing evidence and procedure, which are designed to safeguard the rights of the defendant, simply did not apply at Tokyo – the charter explicitly declared that the tribunal 'shall not be bound by technical rules of evidence'.[66] In 1947, for example, the New Zealand judge, Harvey Northcroft, mentioned that the court had demanded that defence witnesses submit affidavits before their appearance on the stand. This was an 'unusual proceeding,' he admitted, 'but the trial is unusual'.[67] Although this measure was ostensibly intended to save court time, it also conveniently gave the prosecutors advance notice of defence testimony. On another occasion, Hirota Koki's lawyer, David Smith, was in the process of questioning a witness when Webb declared that the defence should restrict questions to matters already raised by the prosecution – a ruling that gave the latter *carte blanche* to set the trial agenda. Smith was horrified, and said that he took exception to 'undue interference' in the examination of a witness. Webb took umbrage at this 'offensive statement' and when Smith refused to apologise, barred him from court.[68]

Some discussions had a distinctly Alice-in-Wonderlandish air about them. Webb once observed that he had absolutely no idea what kind of evidence was acceptable on a day-to-day basis, because he had no idea how many judges would be present at any given time. 'Sometimes we have eleven members; sometimes we have had as low as seven', he observed,

> And you cannot say, I cannot say, that on the question of whether any particular piece of evidence has probative value you always get the same decision from seven judges as you would get from eleven. . . . You cannot be sure what decision the court is going to come to on any particular piece of evidence. . . . On the other day in court on an important point I know the decision would have been different if a Judge who was not here was present.[69]

At one point, all the problems bearing down on the defence appeared to have become so pressing that some judges suspected that there would be 'complete breakdown'. The New Zealand judge, Harvey Northcroft, predicted that in the event of a collapse, the defence would claim that 'either that they cannot go on with, or they are being prevented from presenting their defence, leaving the case to be concluded with a declaration to the world that the trial had been unfair'.[70] However, it is more than likely that the defence also exaggerated their difficulties in order to play for time. In 1947, the French prosecutor, Robert Oneto, wrote to the Quay d'Orsay in Paris explaining that the defence had taken full advantage of 'la procédure anglo-saxonne', which did not impose time limits on the presentation of the case. 'As memories of the war fade, the public, in particular the American public, loses interest in the trial', he observed. Consequently, 'time is working in [the defence's] favour, and it seeks by all available means to prolong the debate in order to ensure lighter sentences for the accused'.[71]

*   *   *

Two and a half years and 48,412 pages of testimony later the trial finally came to a close on 12 November 1948. The court found the Japanese leaders guilty of waging wars of aggression and war crimes, and condemned to death seven defendants, including Tojo Hideki. Sixteen more were given life sentences. No defendant was acquitted. Two of the condemned defendants tried to bring an appeal before the United States Supreme Court, but, to the relief of the Allies, the court decided that it did not have the right to rule on their cases. Meanwhile, the Americans turned loose another group of 'Class A' suspects, who had been imprisoned since August 1945 awaiting a proposed second trial. No-one wanted a repeat of the Tokyo Tribunal, which was widely seen as a political failure.

The final judgement brought to the surface the deep schism that had opened up on the bench as the trial had progressed. Fairly early in the proceedings, William Webb had prepared a draft judgement and submitted it to his fellow judges. This draft did not meet with their approval, and at that point, the judges split down the middle. A revealing report by the French prosecutor, Robert Oneto, indicates that 'five other judges under the direction of the Canadian' took things into their own hands and began to 'prepare their own project'. This breakaway faction was initially made up of the Canadian, Stuart McDougall; the American, Myron Cramer; the British judge, William Patrick; the New Zealander, Harvey Northcroft, and the Filipino, Delfin Jaranilla. After careful vetting, two more judges were then invited to join this faction, turning it into a majority. These were the Soviet, I.M. Zaryanov, and the Chinese judge, Mei Ju-ao. Oneto reported that these seven 'majority' judges henceforth began to meet separately, excluding from their ranks the four 'minority' judges – the Australian, William Webb; the Indian, Radhabinod Pal; the Dutchman, Bernard Röling, and the Frenchman, Henri Bernard. At the end of the trial, the will of the majority prevailed, and their draft judgement 'necessarily' became the judgement of the tribunal.[72]

What was the cause of this extraordinary split? As we shall see, the judges divided over the fundamental question of Japanese war guilt, with the 'majority' faction taking the harder line over the tribunal's right to dispense punishment. Three of the 'minority' judges issued formal dissents from the judgement, while the fourth, Webb, submitted a 'separate opinion' on aspects of the trial.

The schism was starkly illustrated by the judge's votes on the sentences. One of the judges told Associated Press journalist, Frank White, that the bench was split over the death sentences, passing most by a far-from-resounding majority of seven to four, reflecting the majority and minority faction votes. Not only that, White reported, but one defendant, Hirota Koki, was sent to the gallows on the strength of just a single vote, five to six. The bench was also divided over the method of execution, although it eventually settled on hanging rather than shooting.[73] Western governments were extremely unhappy about this being leaked to the newspapers. The British mission in Tokyo thought that it would 'add to the existing confusion in Japanese minds and may create suspicion that the guilt of the accused was not clearly established and that the legality of the trial was not above question'.[74]

While he formally supported the majority verdict, Webb's 'separate opinion' – which surprised many, obviously – questioned some aspects of the trial. The tribunal should not have imposed death sentences, he wrote, not least because the Emperor, whom he described as the 'leader in the crime', had not been granted immunity from prosecution. 'The outstanding part played by him in starting as well as ending [the war] was the subject of evidence led by the Prosecution', he argued, 'But the Prosecution also made it clear that the Emperor would not be indicted.' That decision was their prerogative, he said, but a British court would have taken into account that a ringleader had been granted immunity.[75] London officials were unimpressed by Webb's reference to English court practice: 'It is unfortunate that he should . . . have decided to express opinions about the Emperor, which can only cast doubt on the equity of the trial over which he has presided', E.J.F. Scott noted.[76] Douglas MacArthur was furious, and accused Webb of 'playing cheap politics' by appealing to anti-Hirohito sentiment in Australia.[77]

The Indian judge, Radhabinod Pal, dropped an even bigger bombshell. He rejected the authority of the tribunal in its entirety, setting out his arguments in a 1,235-page document which he later published in Calcutta, pointedly illustrated with photographs of the devastation and injuries wrought by the atomic bombs. He argued that the colonial powers had no right to judge an Asian government, and that they had committed war crimes equal to those of Japan, if not worse. The bombing of Hiroshima and Nagasaki, for example, was an act that was 'the only near approach to the directives of the German Emperor during the first world war and of the Nazi leaders during the second world war'.[78]

The Indian judge's approach was that of a legal purist who wished to uphold pre-existing international law against Tokyo-style legal innovations. He wrote:

> In my judgment . . . it is beyond the competence of any victor nation to go beyond the rules of international law as they exist, give new definitions of crimes and then punish the prisoners for having committed offences according to this new definition. This is really not a norm in abhorrence of the retroactivity of law: It is something more substantial. To allow any nation to do that will be to allow usurpation of power which international law denies that nation.[79]

Thus, Pal argued, 'A trial with law thus prescribed will only be a sham employment of legal process for the satisfaction of a thirst for revenge.'[80]

Pal was a complex character. Although he was fiercely anti-communist, he also harboured a bitter hatred of colonialism, as his conduct throughout the trial clearly shows.[81] His Asian nationalism was entirely typical of Indian sentiment at the time. In his home city of Calcutta, for example, anti-British feeling was so strong that in 1942, the Inspector General of Police in Bengal had privately admitted that 'if the Japanese attempted an invasion of Calcutta they would be received with garlands by a large proportion of the population and . . . many of the police themselves would join in the welcome'.[82] Many years later the Dutch judge, Bernard Röling, recalled that,

> The Indian judge . . . really resented colonial relations. He had a strong feeling about what Europe did in Asia, conquering it a couple of hundred years ago, and then ruling and lording over it from so far away. That was his attitude. So this war of Japan to liberate Asia from the Europeans, the slogan 'Asia for the Asians', really struck a chord with him. He had even been involved with the Indian Army that fought with the Japanese against the British. He was every inch an Asian.[83]

The Canadian judge, Stuart McDougall, noted with distaste that Pal had travelled to Tokyo with the express purpose of 'torpedoing' the judgement.[84] But officials back in London took Pal's views seriously because they sensed that his protest against Allied justice was, of all the judgements, probably the most accurate reflection of the public mood in Asia at the time. So it proved. Reports confirmed that the Indian press and public opinion warmly supported the substance of Pal's dissent, in spite of the fact that the nation had sustained large numbers of war casualties and prisoner-of-war deaths at the hands of the Japanese.[85]

The two other 'minority' judges – the Dutch judge, Bernard Röling, and the French judge, Henri Bernard – also dissented from the verdict, and questioned the harshness of some sentences. Bernard's dissent was anodyne compared to that of his fellows, but ten days later he issued a more powerful and heartfelt document, which is still on file in the French Foreign Ministry archives in Paris. 'I ask you, honourable Gentlemen . . . if this justice that has been served to the condemned Japanese generals, diplomats and political men, is really the Justice that we want to show as an example to the historians of future generations', he wrote. He pleaded for generosity toward the condemned on Christian grounds: 'Human lives do not belong to man but to God,' he wrote, 'and it seems to me that we have no right to kill a human being in cold blood.' He concluded:

> There is war. And nothing else. War is a violent means to attain one's goal. Whoever wins a war benefits by it and there is nobody to send him before a court. Whoever loses, as Brennus said three centuries before our era, 'Vae Victis': woe to the defeated.[86]

In December 1948, the two halves of the human rights project – building the peace, and expunging old sins – came together, with the acceptance of the Universal Declaration in Paris on 10 December, and the hanging of seven Japanese leaders at Tokyo on 23 December. The tribunal had been presented as an act of justice rather than of war, but occasionally officials let slip that it was, after all, the final blow against a vanquished enemy. 'The executions,' wrote E.J.F. Scott in the Foreign Office, 'complete the defeat of the Japanese.'[87] *Vae Victis.*

*   *   *

While the Tokyo assize was in progress, the political map of the world was being redrawn. Old allies became new foes; while old foes became new allies. By the end of the trial China was deemed to be the new Asian menace, while Japan was being groomed as the United States's most important anti-communist ally. The Korean War solidified the new alliance between the old enemies, and in 1952, the Americans brought their occupation of Japan to a close. Yet the imprisoned war criminals continued to be a source of friction. The Japanese were no more contrite about the war than the Germans, and they tended to sentimentalise the plight of those still held in Sugamo Prison. Campaigns for their release were not the slightest bit defensive – indeed, many were run by government officials. Even the Japanese royal family made clear their continued interest in the issue: in 1953, a British diplomat attending a cocktail party hosted by the Canadian Embassy reported that Prince Takamatsu had button-holed a guest and had 'volubly' urged the release of war criminals.[88]

In November 1952 the Japanese authorities asked the prosecuting powers to agree to the release of the war criminals. Some Western governments were in two minds about this request. In Britain's case, a row seems to have broken out between the Foreign Office (which was mindful of the views of survivors of the prisoner-of-war camps) and the British Embassy in Tokyo (which wished to remove all obstacles to better relations with the Japanese). Embassy minutes contain dark allusions to the fact that the Foreign Office's Japan and Pacific Department 'did not enjoy the confidence of the embassy as regards the handling of war criminal cases'.[89] Tokyo Ambassador Esler Dening's comments seemed to bear this out. 'HMG [is] activated by political motives', he argued, namely, to 'satisfy the spirit of revenge of a limited number of Britons'. He continued,

To my own mind the only useful purpose of punishment [of] international crimes is to discourage their repetition in the future. I do not believe for one moment that this is in any way whatsoever achieved by punishments inflicted unilaterally by the victor on the vanquished, while on the other hand they do create and are creating in the vanquished a sense of injustice and grievance which can be and is being exploited by our enemies. But it is idle to say this to the Foreign Office . . . and I conclude with the observation that we shall probably have cause to regret the attitude adopted by HMG.[90]

History's verdict on the tribunal is no kinder than Dening's. The assize is often presented as the Nuremberg that failed. This was not just because Tokyo was victors' justice, or legally defective – Nuremberg shared those flaws – but because it operated at a different time and in different circumstances. Nuremberg was convened while the façade of Allied unity was still just about intact; Tokyo was held as it was breaking apart. Nuremberg was convened in Western Europe, where nations had regained their independence; Tokyo was held in Asia, where nations were still agitating for freedom. William Webb tried to banish the Cold War from his courtroom, but he was battling against impossible odds. The time for prosecuting the Second World War had passed, and new conflicts were already underway.

*　*　*

President Truman rarely aired misgivings about the bombing of Hiroshima and Nagasaki, but he was known to be touchy about the subject. One of Truman's biographers, David McCullough, describes, for example, how he recoiled from an encounter with Manhattan Project leader Robert Oppenheimer:

Robert Oppenheimer came to see him privately, and in a state of obvious agitation said he had blood on his hands because of his work on the bomb. For Truman, it was a dreadful moment. Oppenheimer's self-pitying 'cry-baby' attitude was abhorrent. 'The blood is on my hands', he told Oppenheimer.

'Let me worry about that.' Afterward he said he hoped he would not have to see the man ever again.[91]

The matter came up again one evening in January 1953, in the final month of his Presidency, when Harry Truman hosted a 'stag dinner' for Winston Churchill and some of his closest confederates: Secretary of State Dean Acheson, General Omar Bradley, Robert Lovett, and Averell Harriman. The atmosphere was convivial, and the conversation and champagne flowed. Then Churchill turned to Truman, and growled:

> Mr President, I hope you have your answer ready for that hour when you and I stand before Saint Peter and he says, 'I understand you two are responsible for putting off those atomic bombs. What have you got to say for yourselves?'[92]

The party froze. Robert Lovett tried to parry the question with another: 'Are you sure, Prime Minister, that you are going to be in the same place as the President for that interrogation?' Churchill sipped his champagne and said, 'Lovett, my vast respect for the creator of this universe and countless others gives me assurance that he would not condemn a man without a hearing.' 'Oyez! Oyez!' cried Dean Acheson, sensing a little diversionary entertainment in the offing: 'Mr Bailiff, will you empanel a jury?' Each of Truman's guests chose a figure from history: Bradley nominated himself as Alexander the Great; others, Julius Caesar, Socrates and Aristotle. Churchill rejected the role of Voltaire because the Frenchman was an atheist, and Oliver Cromwell because the roundhead did not believe in the law. Then, as the President's daughter, Margaret Truman, recounted in her 1973 biography of her father, Acheson summoned George Washington.

> That was too much for Mr Churchill. He saw that things were being stacked against him. 'I waive a jury,' he announced, 'but not *habeas corpus*.' They ignored him and completed the selection of the jury. Dad was appointed judge. The case was tried and the prime minister was acquitted.[93]

This account does not explain why this jury of peers absolved Churchill. Perhaps they sensed that their own hands were dipped in blood. Or perhaps they reasoned that it did not matter anyway. After all, even in real life tribunals, no one ever punishes a victor.

FOUR

Cold Fronts

On 15 October 1948, Britain's representative on the UN's Third Committee, the Labour MP Christopher Mayhew, made one of the most important speeches of his life. After limbering up with a series of remarks about the perils of totalitarianism, he launched into an attack on the use of forced labour in the USSR. The Soviet Union, he said, 'has instituted a slave system recruited from among its own citizens which in scope has no parallel in history'. He continued,

> Mr Chairman, if the great body of evidence on Soviet Forced Labour, that is now available to us has any meaning at all, it means that there exists in Soviet Russia a monstrous system of oppression, which makes a mockery of the claim that that country is a democratic or a socialist state. It bears out the truth – that for democrats, socialists and working men and women the world over Soviet Russia provides not an example, but a deadly warning.[1]

Mayhew's speech was delivered with conviction, but it was by no means spontaneous. In fact, the 'anti-Soviet speech', as it was dubbed in one official note, had been knocking around the Foreign Office for nearly a year.[2] It dated back to around November 1947 when the American Federation of Labor, aiming to embarrass the Kremlin, had urged the UN's Economic and Social Council (ECOSOC) to ask the International Labour Organization (ILO) to carry out a global survey of forced labour. In London, the Interdepartmental Human Rights Working Party had decided to go along with this motion, despite the prevalence of such practices in Britain's own colonies. It therefore instructed Paul Gore-Booth, head of one of the Foreign Office's UN departments, to write a 'rousing anti-Soviet speech' on the subject. This Gore-Booth did, fully aware of the double standards at work. '[T]he only way to tackle a speech of this kind,' he noted, 'is on the very broadest lines and with superb disregard of any minor motes in our own colonial eye.'[3]

Although the Western powers had little evidence to go on at this stage (the gulag was not revealed until later) Gore-Booth clearly warmed to his task, and even managed to implicate the leader of the Soviet's UN delegation, writing,

May I recall that in 1931 a leading Soviet authority spoke of 'mass projects employing those deprived of liberty'. Lest I should seem out of date in quoting a 1931 phrase, may I add that this authority was none other than Mr. V.M. Molotov. . . . [H]e spoke with evident pride of 'mass' projects and, without attempting to guess at this stage how many forced or slave labourers this implies, I can only suppose that in a country of great extent and big ideas like the Soviet Union it must have been a great many.[4]

When Gore-Booth had completed the speech, the Foreign Office sent it to the Ministry of Labour for comment. One of its officials wholly agreed that it was 'wise to fashion our thunderbolts in leisure here in order to have them ready to throw should a suitable opportunity arise'.[5] The speech was returned to the working party, which approved it on 27 January 1948. At the same time, the Colonial Office produced a back-up brief on forced labour in the colonies in case the matter arose in the United Nations. It explained that 'compulsory labour' there was in no way similar to forced labour behind the Iron Curtain. For one thing, it 'only' applied to eight colonies. For another, such duties – labour on public works and porterage for officials – were 'not onerous' and paid at standard rates. All in all, it bullishly concluded, 'His Majesty's Government have nothing to hide or to be ashamed of.'[6]

When Christopher Mayhew finally found the right moment to deliver the speech, the British delegation was gleeful. The telegram home commended his 'strong and detailed attack on forced labour in the Soviet Union on the lines of the IRD brief'. (The last was a reference to the recently established semi-secret Information Research Department, responsible for Foreign Office Cold War propaganda warfare).[7] Mayhew recalled that his uninhibited invective had surprised the committee, and that while some delegates were delighted, others were shocked. Eleanor Roosevelt, said Mayhew, 'was warmly supportive but complained with some justice that I should have forewarned her'.[8] The speech certainly registered with John Humphrey, head of the Secretariat's Human Rights Division, who wrote in his diary that day that,

Just before closing time, Mayhew of the United Kingdom relieved himself of the strongest anti-communist blast that I have ever heard in the Third Committee, or indeed any of the organs with which I deal. It is true that he had been provoked; but he paid his debt with compound interest.[9]

The British noted that the speech had 'certainly stung the Russians', and anticipated that they would reply in strong terms.[10] It had, and they did. A few days later, Alexei Pavlov rose and denounced the 'quislings and traitors' who had provided the statistics so carefully husbanded by the Information Research Department. According to a British summary, Pavlov said: 'All Mr Mayhew's figures were to be found in the book written by the traitors Dallin and Nicola Evsky.' He continued:

Estimates of twenty million, forty million and eighty million forced workers could all be found in this book, but that was absurd since it would mean that in whole areas, the entire male population must be in camps.

Pavlov concluded:

. . . if Mr Mayhew's statements were true, how could the Soviet Union have won the war and carried their flag to Berlin . . .[11]

The Cold War contest was by now being recast in the elevated morality of human rights, and the United Nations and its satellite agencies became the most important arena for the ideological struggle. The Americans embraced the issue of forced labour, harrying the Soviets in ECOSOC and the ILO. It was clear from a 1949 State Department position paper that they believed they had found the Soviets' human rights Achilles' heel:

[I]t appears that the USSR is peculiarly sensitive to the accusations of forced labour. Posing as it does as the champion of an allegedly oppressed proletariat, stories of huge Nazi-like concentration camps in the USSR have forced the Communist Party into an unconvincing defensive in many countries, such as France, where the contest for the support of workers in extremely keen. Hence those [Americans] responsible for 'cold war' propaganda are eager to pursue discussion of the subject wherever opportunity exists.

In 1951, the United States succeeded in persuading ECOSOC and the ILO to set up an Ad Hoc Committee on Forced Labour under the leadership of Sir Ramaswami Mudaliar of India. When this committee appealed for information, the Americans made the best of the little that they had. On the one hand, they held the Anders Collection of release passes and affidavits collected from Poles interned by the Russians between 1939 and 1941. And on the other, they had access to the statements of a hundred or more former labour camp inmates – Germans, Japanese, escapees and defectors – gathered by US intelligence in the years since the war. Interestingly, the State Department decided to use a non-governmental organisation, the International Confederation of Free Trade Unions, to hand over material from the Anders Collection, because it thought it would look better coming from a non-official source with a declared interest in labour issues. The government, meanwhile, would present the debriefing statements.[12] This early, calculated collaboration between officialdom and an NGO on a human rights issue would later become commonplace.

In 1953, the ad hoc committee produced a 621-page document condemning, among other things, practices behind the Iron Curtain. The Americans thought it was a propaganda godsend. Here was an 'impartial but unequivocal' report from an apparently neutral source about forced labour in the 'Communist orbit'.[13] (They ignored the report's coverage of similar practices in Southern Africa, and the colonies and protectorates of Portugal, Belgium, Britain and Australia.) They relished the prospect of deriding the USSR's claims to being a worker's paradise in the General Assembly, and recommended that their delegation

> put heavy reliance upon the conclusions of the UN–ILO Committee, and should commend the Committee, and particularly its Indian Chairman, for their fearless objectivity and impartiality. At the same time the delegation should point out that additional work needs to be done both as regards the collection of additional information (the report does not extend to forced labour in Communist China . . .) and any further steps to be taken by the United Nations to combat the evil.[14]

Meanwhile, the Soviets stonewalled. They returned documents on forced labour to the UN Secretariat, accompanied by a letter perversely explaining that they were 'unexamined' because they contained 'slanderous fabrications concerning the Soviet Union'.[15]

The United States accelerated its anti-Soviet offensives, especially after the outbreak of the Korea War. A report produced by officials in Washington in about 1954 entitled 'Propaganda in the United Nations' set out the somewhat cynical motives behind their human rights initiatives:

> Since 1949 we have undertaken certain policies determined in large part by propaganda considerations – introducing or encouraging UN action on items which while sincere in the sense that we could live with them and even profit greatly if they were carried out, were introduced with the primary purpose of winning Cold War propaganda advantages with little or no expectation that their ostensible purpose would be achieved directly or within a reasonable time.

These offensives included condemnatory resolutions on 'Failure of USSR to repatriate POWs' and 'Observance of Human Rights and Fundamental Freedoms in Bulgaria, Hungary, and Rumania' as well as 'our initiative in exposing through ECOSOC forced labour conditions in the Soviet system'. Yet at the same time, America's propaganda campaigns against repression were carefully calibrated to avoid alienating allies or repelling the Third World. As the report noted, 'we have avoided condemning some of our friends (South Africa, eg) for deprivations for which we have unhesitatingly condemned the Soviets', while 'soft-pedalling . . . Soviet anti-Semitism because of anticipated Arab hostility' in the General Assembly of 1952.[16]

These set-piece battles may have satisfied the participants, and, to a very limited degree, audiences at home. But the evidence suggests that the debate on forced labour did little to capture the hearts and minds of onlookers from the Third World, the ostensible target of such posturing. Some officials such as James Green, deputy director of the State Department's Office of UN Economic and Social Affairs, were aware of this problem. '[T]he fact that all the debates have seemed to be a "cold war" operation on the part of the great powers,' he observed, 'has seriously limited the appeal of this subject to the Near Eastern and Asian members, and to some extent the Latin Americans.'[17] After the row between Christopher Mayhew and Alexei Pavlov, the delegate from Mexico, far from being inflamed with righteous anger, instead wearily appealed for a truce.[18]

When General Dwight Eisenhower assumed the Presidency in early 1953, he stepped up the tempo of the Cold War offensive, establishing the Operations Co-ordinating Board to streamline Cold War psychological warfare. The Board's paladin, former *Time* vice-president Charles Douglas 'C.D.' Jackson agreed with Eisenhower's hawkish UN Ambassador, Henry Cabot Lodge, that the organisation was particularly fertile ground for even greater propaganda efforts against the Russians. They collaborated closely on one operation – dubbed the Lodge Human Rights Project – to blitz the United Nations with information about Soviet abuses. Jackson worked behind the scenes with the State Department's intelligence unit, formulating tactics and stacking up 'juicy, 500-word, newsworthy excerpts' and 'three or four sizzling press releases a week'.[19] Lodge, meanwhile, spearheaded the offensive at the UN's new headquarters at Turtle Bay, New York, aiming to 'reveal to the world that the Soviet Union is on the morally wrong side of every great issue'.[20]

Among these initiatives was the ambassador's 1953 attempt to persuade the General Assembly to denounce the communists for atrocities against blue helmet POWs during the Korean War. Although the timing was poor (most prisoners had already been exchanged after the Armistice), the propaganda angle, said C.D. Jackson, was 'dramatic and understandable by the dullest schoolboy'.[21] Lodge's lurid tales of 'death marches' and *Manchurian Candidate*-style brainwashing elicited a response from the Soviet delegate, who denied the allegations but also refused to accept a Red Cross investigation, thus enhancing the credibility of the charges. The General Assembly passed a vague motion against the ill-treatment of POWs, naming no names, but anti-communists were rapturous. Senator Joseph McCarthy's sidekick, Roy Cohn, witch-finder general of the Grand Jury hearings against suspected American 'subversives' working in the UN, rang Lodge to congratulate him.

*   *   *

Eleanor Roosevelt joined the Cold War crusade while she was at the peak of her fame as the doyenne of human rights. Like many American liberals of her time, she had misgivings about aspects of the Truman Doctrine and opposed McCarthy's witch-hunts. But her commitment to the anti-Soviet cause was unswerving.[22]

In September 1948, at the height of the Berlin Blockade, Roosevelt delivered a keynote address at the Sorbonne on 'The Struggle for the Rights of Man'. The title was predictable, given her leadership of the Human Rights Commission, but the content served purely Cold War ends. The idea of using her as a weapon against the Russians originated earlier that year during a meeting attended by Secretary of State George Marshall and John Foster Dulles, leader of the US delegation to the UN General Assembly. Dulles wanted to use human rights as his 'theme song' at the forthcoming assembly in Paris, but he also wanted to parry the anticipated Soviet attacks on the United States without appearing to engage in an outright propaganda war. It was decided that the best way to establish the rights motif, while stealing a march on the Russians, was to get Roosevelt to deliver a State Department-drafted speech before the assembly debates got going.

When Marshall floated the idea with her, she said that she was 'ready to go along with her part of it'. As he wrote to Dean Rusk, head of the Office of UN Affairs, in August,

> I told Mrs Roosevelt that I did not want her embarrassed or her statement weakened by having it in a form that was quite evidently State Department affair rather than Mrs Roosevelt [sic], that while we wanted certain points presented, I regarded it as very important that it be entirely in char[acter] with Mrs Roosevelt and in her language. She said that if Mr Dulles had any suggestion s[he] would like to hear what they are. . . . She was thoroughly in sympathy with the idea . . . and commented on the fact that the Russians in pra[ctically] every Committee established clever basis for prop[aganda, and] that we must find some way of meeting this effect[ively].[23]

Durward Sandifer set to work writing her speech, while the American Embassy in Paris orchestrated the event. René Cassin, who fixed the invitation from the Sorbonne, assured embassy officials that the evening would be suitably high-powered, presided over by either the Prime Minister or the President of the National Assembly or 'some other high personality'. Ambassador Jefferson Caffery cabled Washington that in turn, Cassin (or his political superiors) sought assurances that Roosevelt's speech 'will not be concerned with immediate burning political issues before Assembly'. It is not clear whether Cassin was referring to the UN's *General* Assembly, the anticipated forum for a showdown between America and the Soviet Union over the Berlin blockade, or the *French* Assembly, the regular venue for slanging matches over Nato. Whichever it was, an embassy official smoothly assured the Frenchman that the speech would be devoted to human rights and the 'basic US position on all aspects of question' – not exactly a lie, but a disingenuous response given the State Department's anti-Soviet intent.[24]

The Sorbonne address, presided over by Paul Ramadier, the Minister of National Defence, and attended by 2,500 grandees from the French political and cultural scene, passed off exceptionally smoothly. Embassy staffer, William Tyler, recapped the highlights:

> When the Secretary of State and Mrs Roosevelt entered the room, the whole audience rose and there was vigorous and sustained applause for two or three minutes. Throughout the evening, an atmosphere of sympathy and interest was very marked and Mrs Roosevelt was repeatedly interrupted by applause as she delivered her speech in excellent French and with extreme graciousness of manner. The speaker departed at times from the prepared text in order to illustrate a point with illustrations from her own experience. These improvisations went to the heart of the audience and were most effective. The audience was particularly delighted when Mrs Roosevelt said that she thought she had reached the limits of which human patience is capable when she brought up her family, but that since she had presided over the Commission on Human Rights she had realised that an even greater measure of patience could be extracted from an individual.[25]

Roosevelt's intention was not just to entertain, but also to admonish. Turning her fire on the Soviet Bloc she said,

> The Declaration has come from the Human Rights Commission with unanimous acceptance except for four abstentions – the USSR, Yugoslavia, Ukraine and Byelorussia. The reason for this is a fundamental difference in the conception of human rights as they exist in these states and in certain other Member states in the United Nations.

She continued,

> We must not be deluded by the efforts of the forces of reaction to prostitute the great words of our free tradition and thereby to confuse the struggle. Democracy, freedom, human rights have come to have a definite meaning to the people of the world which we must not allow any nation to so change that they are made synonymous with suppression and dictatorship.

She went on,

> The field of human rights is not one in which compromise on fundamental principles are possible *[sic]*. The work of the Commission on Human Rights is

illustrative. The Declaration of Human Rights provides: 'Everyone has the right to leave any country, including his own.' The Soviet Representative said he would agree to this right if a single phrase was added to it – 'in accordance with the procedure laid down in the laws of that country'. It is obvious that to accept this would be not only to compromise but to nullify the right stated. This case forcefully illustrates the importance of the proposition that we must ever be alert not to compromise fundamental human rights merely for the sake of reaching unanimity and thus lose them.[26]

Roosevelt's attack on the Soviet Union, which also stressed the superiority of American over Soviet conceptions of human rights, clearly spoke to the fears of her French audience, who were horrified by the looming presence of the French Communist Party, and tormented by the Cold War convulsions in neighbouring Germany. Durward Sandifer was delighted by the way things had gone – Roosevelt had played her part to perfection.[27]

The Soviets responded to the Sorbonne speech – 'crammed with well-worn anti-Soviet phrases' – with an article in the *Literaturnaya Gazeta* entitled 'The Unbecoming Role of Eleanor Roosevelt' (and here translated by the US Embassy in Moscow). Her 'senile weakness for loquacity,' wrote the author, G. Petrov,

has recently been combined with the special anti-Soviet itch, which gives no rest to such American 'peace-makers' as Dulles and [US Ambassador to UN, Warren] Austin. At times it is difficult to distinguish where the Democrat Eleanor Roosevelt begins and where the Republican Dulles ends.[28]

*   *   *

The Human Rights Commission was an important theatre of the Cold War, and Roosevelt, encouraged by her ever-present aides, exploited her position as chairwoman in order to pursue the anti-Soviet line. John Humphrey, for one, was dismayed. On June 1949, for example, the commission was scheduled to discuss new articles submitted by the Soviet Union dealing with economic and social rights – rights opposed by the United States. She declared that the new articles would be have to be discussed *en bloc* and that there would be no vote; she also made proposals that would have denied Pavlov his rightful place on the speakers' list. Pavlov protested that the new articles *should* be put to the vote, and won a vote among delegates confirming that this was the case. Humphrey described the ensuing wrangling:

It was before this [commission] vote that I told Mrs R that in my opinion Pavlov was right. In spite of the vote, however, Pavlov was in fact by one procedural trick after another prevented from exercising his right which had, moreover, been confirmed by the Commission. It was a dishonest, scandalous business. To what extent is Mrs R personally responsible? She is, of course, blindly anti-Soviet and perhaps does not realise that she is often unfair. The real culprit is [US advisor, James] Simsarian who is taking advantage of her. The latter incidentally accused me of being interested and favouring the Soviet view. I retorted: 'Yes, I receive my instructions straight from Moscow.' I must add, however, that in the afternoon he apologised.[29]

Humprey recalled another incident that took place during the row over whether Communist China should be recognised by the United Nations. In the commission, the Soviets called for the removal of deputy chair Chang Peng-chun on the grounds that he was a representative of the 'Kuomintang'. In response, Roosevelt read out a State Department-prepared statement ruling them out of order. John Humphrey was angered by this: 'That was the chairman's privilege, but it was quite improper to give the impression that she had been so advised by the Secretariat', he wrote in his diary. 'I wished I could have warned her that some people thought the chair was being exploited for political ends.'[30]

Clearly disenchanted, Humphrey recorded in 1949 another example of her Cold War partisanship.

Here is a story about Mrs Roosevelt that her biographer will not mention. Having been invited to speak tomorrow at the Human Rights celebration in Carnegie Hall she submitted a script of her speech today to the Radio Division. Notwithstanding the fact that she is to speak as Chairman of the Commission of Human Rights and at an official UN function the last part of her proposed speech was an attack against communism and a thinly veiled attack against a group of member states. On representations being made to her she agreed to modify her speech. I wonder whether she herself feels that she is working for peace as she says. She has contributed largely to the growing hate in this country of the USSR and she is making of the Declaration a weapon with which to fight that country in the cold war. That it may be legitimately so used I do not deny; but one is entitled to expect something more constructive from the person whom public opinion has made a symbol of human rights.

Humphrey then adds, 'Incidentally, I find her book, *This I Remember*, very bad.'[31]

*   *   *

The commission worked on the human rights covenant throughout the early years of the Cold War. At first, State Department officials advanced strong arguments in favour of a legally binding treaty. They believed that the United States was the crucible of liberty, and that rights were a gift to be bestowed on others. 'Our record is something to which we can point with pride; the records of most other member nations fall far short of the standard we have set', declared the authors of a 1947 position paper. They also argued that as a self-declared international exemplar, the Americans should produce a treaty with teeth, because one riddled with holes would 'not fulfil any very useful purpose'. Yet in time, Washington's commitment to the covenant ebbed away, as domestic lobbies led by anti-communists seeking a withdrawal from the United Nations, and conservatives opposed to the extension of civil rights, singled it out as the worst kind of Red-backed 'globaloney'.

One of the first indications that Washington was getting cold feet about a treaty appeared in late 1947, when Under Secretary of State Robert Lovett, looking over his shoulder at the Senate, instructed Roosevelt to prioritise the declaration over the covenant. The latter 'should not be pressed' because, he argued, 'The United States does not wish to see members of the United Nations enter into a convention unless they intend to observe it in good faith.'[32] Six months later, his position had softened slightly, although he was still anxious to set out ground-rules for American involvement with the project:

> The basic position regarding the Covenant is that it should be limited to civil rights. . . . A second basic point is that a general limitation provision should be substituted for the listing of specific limitations with respect to each right. . . . An additional point implicit in the detailed papers is that the rights should be in general accord with the Constitution and law of the United States. This latter point is for your guidance and is not intended to be used as an argument in the Commission.[33]

Thus armed, US delegates began to lay down the law. The Soviets had by now gained themselves a reputation for obstruction,[34] but the Americans proved to be equally adept at filibustering, submitting endless amendments, and generally making a nuisance of themselves. This posturing frustrated those who were still wedded to a binding human rights treaty, such as Britain and France. Britain, which envisaged the convention as a 'code of conduct of the élite' conforming to their own law,[35] were often as critical of their American allies as their Russian foes in this respect. As a Francis Rundall, head of the Foreign Office's UN Economic and Social Department, noted in 1948, 'The main stumbling block in the Commission is the United States, whose ideas (owing to their Constitutional difficulties) are quite different from ours.'[36]

During 1948 the Americans made their first attempt to secure a 'general limitation' clause, which would have enabled them to set out qualifications and limitations on the entire covenant, rather than spelling them out on each article. When they failed to get it, they started to make life difficult. British delegate Geoffrey Wilson grumbled:

We are not making very satisfactory progress at the Drafting Committee, largely because of American insistence on dragging in their general limitation clause at every possible and impossible opportunity. This generally gives rise to utter confusion and I sometimes suspect that it is premeditated rather than accidental.[37]

The Americans twisted arms outside commission meetings too, threatening to load down every article with qualifications if they did not get agreement to a general limitation clause. As Ambassador Warren Austin cabled Washington, 'Arguments which have impressed doubtful members have been enumeration of masses of new justifiable limitations on specific rights which have not heretofore been thought of.'[38] The British braced themselves for a deluge of US-inspired qualifications: 'In the case of some articles', the British Embassy in Washington warned the Foreign Office, they had 'already thought of no fewer than thirty limitations'.[39]

This was on top of a long list of loopholes and opt-outs already attached to each article in the covenant. By May 1948, the 'arbitrary arrest' article was already struggling under the weight of nineteen qualifications. The basic article read:

1. No one shall be subjected to arbitrary arrest or detention.
2. In consequence, no person shall be deprived of his liberty save in the case of . . .

Seven qualifications had been added at a previous stage: 'reasonable suspicion of having committed a crime', 'non-compliance with the lawful order or decree of a court', 'a person sentenced after conviction', 'detention of persons of unsound mind', 'parental or quasi-parental custody of minors', 'unauthorised entry into the country' and 'aliens against whom deportation proceedings are pending'.[40]

But this was not the end of it, for commission members, including the Americans, added twelve more, each of which cast an interesting light on the national preoccupations of the time. These were duly set down in the UN record as the following:

1. Arrest and detention of persons suffering from serious contagious disease (Netherlands, United Kingdom, Norway)
2. Arrest and detention of alcoholics (Norway)
3. Arrest 'flagrante delicto' (Brazil) . . .
4. Arrest for the purpose of removal from one province to another (Union of South Africa)
5. Arrest for the purpose of removal of persons other than aliens (Union of South Africa)

6. Arrest of witnesses in order to bring them before a court (Union of South Africa) or for their protection (United States)
7. Detention of children in need of care (Union of South Africa)
8. Arrests for breach of military discipline (Chile . . .)
9. Arrest in civil cases usually involving wrong-doing (fraud, etc), in the commencement of an action (United States . . .)
10. Arrest as a means of satisfaction of a judgement in such actions or by way of punishment in such cases (United States . . .)
11. Detention of persons listed under Article 8, paragraph 3 of the Geneva draft of the Covenant (this relates to the class of persons who may be subjected to forced or compulsory labour in connection with military or emergency service, etc) (United States . . .)
12. Detention of enemy aliens (United States . . .)[41]

Governments invariably tread very carefully when it comes to drafting treaties because sovereignty issues are involved. In August 1950, John Cates, an American delegate to ECOSOC, wrote to Durward Sandifer that

> The general attitude of almost all members of the Council may be characterised as one of extreme caution. This caution seems to spring either from the feeling that the Draft Covenant, while a worthy effort, is far from being the type of document which may be placed before governments for ratification; or from a feeling that 'the time is not now' for consideration of a document as important as the Covenant given the world security situation; or from a rather firm belief that a covenant on human rights is undesirable.[42]

Given these views, it is hardly surprising that the draft covenant approved by the commission earlier that year was so riddled with loopholes that there was barely any treaty left. Indeed, it offered far fewer guarantees than those offered by the American Bill of Rights. One article of the draft, for example, was an all-purpose escape clause absolving governments from the responsibility of upholding the rights of free expression, fair trial and peaceful assembly during a state of emergency – the very time such rights were most needed. The draft also placed wide restrictions on the exercise of specific rights. 'Freedom of thought, conscience, and religion' was subordinated to such broad exemptions – namely, 'limitations as are pursuant to law and are reasonable and necessary to protect public safety, order, health or morals, or the fundamental rights and freedoms of others' – that it could hardly be described as freedom at all.[43]

*   *   *

The early fifties saw a significant shift in American thinking. Initially, officials had seen human rights as something they would impose on others. Now, they also began to see them as something that others might impose on them – not directly (as erroneously claimed by conservatives), but indirectly, through the weight of global opinion. Washington's defensive response to international attacks on Jim Crow shows how sensitive they were to Cold War stimuli. Recognising that racial discrimination undermined America's reputation in the Third World, and left it vulnerable to attack from the Soviet Bloc, it took steps to put its house in order by initiating the campaign to end segregation.[44] At the same time, however, officials were forced to respond to an increasingly powerful alliance of domestic groups opposed to desegregation and other liberalising measures.

Under these conflicting pressures, cracks began to open up in American foreign policy-making circles over human rights. Early in 1951, Eleanor Roosevelt went to lunch with a former Policy Planning Staff member, Joseph Johnson, who suggested that the delegation should ease off on the covenant.[45] Unsettled, she passed this opinion on to Durward Sandifer, who dismissed it as 'a minority view – although one held by an influential and vocal group'. He also expressed his disagreement with the views of another official, Peter Stewart, who, he wrote, 'over-estimates the comparative importance of the . . . "re-examinists" . . . who either oppose the completion of the Covenant or would pursue such dilatory tactics . . . as to make it unlikely that it would ever be completed'. Sandifer reassured Roosevelt that in his own opinion, 'we would lose far more in international position and prestige by relaxing on the Covenant to the extent that Mr Johnson advocates than we will from the possibility of the Senate ultimately refusing to approve the document'.[46]

Despite Sandifer's reassurances, America's interest in the covenant *did* decline. At the same time, the Third World's interest and lobbying power increased, which meant that a range of new proposals – often deemed 'objectionable' by Washington – were finding their way on to the agenda. The Americans were especially agitated by the introduction of clauses which targeted South Africa or the colonial powers; or which tried to compel the United Nations to give effect to economic and social rights which they considered to be long-range, if not impossible, objectives. An irritated James Green complained that the commission had been adding 'completely unsatisfactory articles, like the new ones on marriage, incitement to violence, and non-self-governing territories', while they had been subtracting articles favoured by Washington 'out of pique or procedural confusion'.[47]

In February 1952, American officials, calculating that a treaty incorporating economic rights would never survive the Senate, succeeded in breaking the covenant into two. Thenceforth, one covenant would cover familiar political and civil rights, while the other covenant would cover the more controversial economic, social and cultural rights.

This did not solve their problems, however, because they were then confronted with the new challenge posed by Article One – asserting the right of peoples to self-determination – which was inserted at the start of both covenants at the insistence of the General Assembly. This addition was 'real trouble', Cassin wrote, because it had a 'collective and political character which puts it outside the normal competence of the Commission'.[48] A leading member of the US delegation bristled at the implications of self-determination: 'Are the Aleuts of our own Territory of Alaska . . . to be permitted to determine whether they continue to be administered by the United States or are to join their kinspeople in Asiatic Russia?' As for colonial peoples: 'It is of course not the view of this Government that the people of the Trust Territory of the Pacific Islands should be consulted at present as to whether or not they would like to continue their association with the United States.'[49]

Worse, US delegates had no success in erasing a sentence from Article One that promised signatories 'permanent sovereignty over their natural wealth and resources'. These eight words were seen as a green light to Third World governments aiming to nationalise industries without compensating foreign companies and as a red rag to corporate America. Perhaps they were unlucky with the timing of their opposition to this clause, which had been championed by Chile, the leader of the Third World countries on the commission. As the French delegate René Cassin observed, 'If the right to dispose of resources had been addressed after the treaty between the United States and Chile on the subject of copper, the Chilean delegation would have been less uncompromising.'[50]

The reaction of the West Europeans to the self-determination article was another headache for the Americans. James Green spelt out the negative implications:

> The Commission had proceeded, quite deliberately, to include provisions regarding self-determination, which will obviously make it impossible for the other seven administering powers to sign the Covenants – an act of irresponsibility that reflects the high emotion of this so-called technical body.[51]

The West European nations were already clearly disillusioned with the negotiations. In 1950, they had signed their own European Convention on Human Rights – a limited document which was designed to assert Western values against Eastern communist ideology without committing signatories to anything more than was set out in their own national statutes. Consequently, their interest in the UN covenants, which represented the different and, they thought, dangerously radical, interests of the Third World nations, rapidly receded. By 1952, James Simsarian disconsolately reported that Britain and Belgium would have been happy to cynically 'let the present article on self-determination help sink the ship'.[52] The question was, would the United States go down with it too?

* * *

Senator John Bricker, who led the final assault on America's participation in the UN's human rights programme, took the issue out of the administration's hands. He was an unlikely figure to assume such a prominent role. The towering, silver-haired Republican governor of Ohio was once described as one of the few Senators who actually looked the part, but his stature was seemingly unmatched by substance. A sympathetic portrait in *Life* conceded that although Bricker may have been Ohio's 'favourite son', he did not really 'set the political horizon on fire'.[53] Other profiles were harsher. 'Little record exists that Bricker has ever said anything worth more than thirty seconds of consideration by anybody', wrote John Gunther in his forties bestseller *Inside USA*. For good measure, Gunther added that, intellectually, Bricker was 'like interstellar space – a vast vacuum occasionally crossed by homeless wandering clichés'. Furthermore, he was 'the man who . . . puts his foot in his mouth every time he opens it'.[54] The political commentator Eric Goldman was even blunter: Bricker was 'neanderthalic'.[55]

Nevertheless, Bricker's domestic legislative assaults on the human rights covenants and the President's foreign policy prerogatives during the early fifties were not easily dismissed. Although no isolationist (at the end of the war he backed a global role for the United States), he was dead against entangling treaties.[56] His campaign for greater Congressional control over foreign policy caused untold aggravation to two US Presidents. The Democrat Harry Truman once jokingly admitted that he had promised his wife a treasured ceremonial sword if she would 'kick Bricker in the ass'.[57] The Republican Dwight Eisenhower confided to his press secretary that, 'If it's true that when you die the things that bothered you most are engraved on your skull, I am sure I'll have there the mud and dirt of France during [the Normandy] invasion – and the name of Senator Bricker.'[58]

John Bricker launched his campaign against the UN programme in July 1951 with a resolution designed to 'bury the so-called covenant on human rights so deep that no one holding high public office will ever dare to attempt its resurrection'.[59] This first resolution died in its pigeonhole, but he was undeterred. Over the next three years, Bricker and other Senators, working hand-in-glove with a conservative coalition led by the American Bar Association, proposed a series of constitutional amendments which aimed to halt US involvement with the covenant (a threat to 'life, liberty and *property*') and rein in the President's treaty-making powers.[60]

The spectre of national betrayal and suspected communist subversion cast a heavy pall over Washington in the early fifties, with conservatives claiming that Truman had sold America out to Stalin, Mao and the UN. Bricker's amendments struck a chord with Cold Warriors and opponents of the civil rights movement, who feared communist-inspired meddling in the nation's affairs, and with legislators who thought that the White House enjoyed too much of a free hand in the conduct of foreign policy. The British Ambassador in Washington, Roger Makins, accurately summarised the forces driving the campaign:

> The incentive for this move arose out of opposition to the United Nations conventions on human rights, the rights of women and genocide; but it was also aimed originally at President Truman who, it was thought made too liberal a use of executive agreements which, unlike treaties, are not subject to the ratification of the Senate. . . . The issue is thus bound up with Congress's traditional jealousy of the Executive branch, and support for it on Capitol Hill is due in part to Congress's determination to regain the pre-eminent position it lost during the Roosevelt régime.[61]

The new President, Dwight Eisenhower, initially handled the issue with kid gloves, to avoid antagonising his own party. Even so, the strength of support for Bricker's campaign was extremely troubling, and he fretted about the 'complete readiness of the Republican Party to tear us apart' over the issue.[62] When the coalition tabled another amendment in early 1953 declaring its opposition to any international agreement which would 'supervise . . . rights of citizens of the United States', it gained the support of sixty-four Senators, including forty-five of the forty-eight Republicans. The party leadership was well and truly boxed in. As the issue ground on, Eisenhower could barely contain his frustration: 'I'm so sick of this, I could scream', he privately admitted.

> The whole damn thing is senseless and plain damaging to the prestige of the United States. We talk about the French not being able to govern themselves, but we sit here discussing a *Bricker Amendment*.[63]

But Eisenhower's failure to take the battle to his own supporters contributed to the impasse. While the Bricker coalition was fighting against the covenants, Bricker's opponents were not actually fighting *for* them.[64] Instead of standing up for human rights on their merits, they chose to fight on the coalition's terms, by arguing that diplomacy, security and the Presidency – in short, matters pertaining to American sovereignty – would be compromised by the amendments. As a consequence, Congress came close to seriously undermining presidential powers.

While the White House agonised, the State Department opposed any Bricker-appeasing retreat from the human rights programme. In February 1953, the Assistant Secretary of State for UN Affairs, John Hickerson, wrote a report making the case for their participation in the drafting of the covenants. American leadership on rights was a 'significant factor in the cold war', he argued.

> It has helped to bring into focus the basic differences between the countries aspiring to greater freedom on the one hand, and those under the control of totalitarian Communism on the other. It has helped to strengthen the ideological basis for common action on the part of the free nations and for greater unity among them.[65]

He warned that if America refused to support the covenants, it would weaken its leadership of the United Nations, and would be 'exploited to the full by countries hostile to the United States, and particularly [by] the USSR'.[66]

But Hickerson was over-ruled. In spring 1953, Eisenhower reluctantly decided to throw the Brickerites the bone of the covenants in order to maintain his own command over foreign policy. And so, on 6 April, Secretary of State John Foster Dulles publicly reversed his previous support for the human rights enterprise when he informed the powerful Senate Judiciary Committee that the USA would not become a party to them. Two days later in Geneva, the Eisenhower-appointed successor to Eleanor Roosevelt, Mary Pillsbury Lord, told the Human Rights Commission that her government would not ratify the covenants because, she said, 'The climate of world opinion does not yet seem favourable.'[67] Delegates were rocked by America's sudden abdication. It was a 'bombshell', said the new Egyptian chairman, Mahmoud Azmi.[68] The Uruguayan complained that their defection 'made discussion of the Covenants rather academic'; the Indian that it 'knocked the bottom out of the Covenants'.[69]

Commission members rightly interpreted the withdrawal as a straightforward capitulation to Bricker, because, despite American denials, their actions suggested a sudden policy reversal under duress. When Mrs Lord proposed three face-saving human rights 'action programs' as a substitute for the covenants – annual reports, global surveys and an advisory service – it was apparent that these ideas had been thrown together in a hurry. (British delegation leader, Percy Pell, mischievously pointed out that he had spotted 'precisely the same proposals' in a recent pamphlet by the 'Carnegie International Foundation [sic] for Peace'.) At a meeting held to discuss the 'action programs', disgruntled delegates were in no mood to give the Americans an easy ride, and took sly pleasure in keeping them from their beds until one o'clock in the morning with deliberately long-winded objections.[70]

'We all felt that, during the first week, we had fallen off a very high cliff and, after being a bit stunned, we had to begin to climb slowly back again',

James Green wrote to Durward Sandifer. Those State Department officials who had advocated withdrawal had finally got what they wanted, but he was still not persuaded that it was the right thing to do:

> During the past several years, as you well know, Ben Cohen, Joe Johnson, Pete Stewart and Len Meeker have all advocated exactly the kind of approach which the new Administration has just taken. I had always opposed their point of view on two grounds: first, since the Department in general and Mrs Roosevelt in particular were completely committed to the Covenants, we had the bear by the tail and could not let go; and second, because . . . the majority in the United Nations are determined to stretch the Charter by resolution and to embarrass the western powers whenever it serves their purpose to do so. I have great concern that we are in for increasing trouble year after year in the Commission now that we have focused their attention on things other than the Covenants. I only wish that we could have followed the more subtle British and Soviet technique of playing along with the Covenants to the exclusion of everything else.[71]

The deeper implications were dissected at leisure. A British commentator, Maurice Cranston, dryly observed that,

> Mrs Lord's announcement was more than the Communists had ever hoped for. It at once profoundly damaged any hopes of the United Nations being used to enforce human rights and made America responsible for that damage.[72]

*   *   *

The end came for Bricker himself when the Senate buried his amendment in 1954. But there was one final, comic twist to the drama. A less brawny Brickerite motion, proposed by Democrat Senator Walter George, was still before the Senate in March, and needed a two-thirds majority to pass. Various Senators arrived in the final minutes of the vote, causing its fate to teeter on the balance. In the dying moments, the score settled at sixty 'Ayes' to thirty 'Noes'– exactly the number needed for the resolution to stand. The administration strongly opposed it, and Vice President Richard Nixon, presiding, scowled around the chamber. Then the glass doors flew open. Senator Harley Kilgore, a West Virginia Democrat who had previously voted against all the previous Bricker amendments, staggered in. He was somewhat the worse for drink, and, according to the gossip, aides had either flushed him out of a local drinking den, or woken him from a boozy slumber in his office.[73] This crucial vote now rested in his shaky hands. *Time*, which knowingly ascribed Kilgore's unsteadiness to an 'influenza attack', reported that

Sick, drowsy with medicine, Kilgore stared groggily at Nixon. . . . Nixon said nothing. The Senate sat, gripped in silent suspense. Washington's Democratic Senator Warren Magnuson jumped up. Asked he, in a time-delaying tactic: 'Mr President, how am I recorded voting?' The clerk studied the list and reported what everyone already knew – Magnuson was recorded against the resolution. The few seconds gave Kilgore the time he needed. He nodded at Nixon. 'The Senator from West Virginia', called Nixon. 'Mr Kilgore', called the clerk. Said Kilgore, 'No.'

The Senator's vote pushed the final tally to thirty-one to sixty, and the resolution fell, preserving White House foreign policy prerogatives by a single vote. The last Brickerite motion had been sunk in the last minute by a man summoned from a barstool. Afterwards, *Time* reported, 'Harley Kilgore got up, trudged off the floor and went home to his sickbed.'[74] Bricker was beaten, except in one important respect. It would be another twenty years before Americans took human rights to heart once again.

FIVE

Colonial Concerns

As the Cold War drove America out of the human rights arena, it drew the Western European nations in. They banded together in an anti-communist alliance, the Council of Europe, and created their own equivalent of the covenant: the European Convention on Human Rights. Britain was the first nation to ratify it, but ministers, including one-time Labour Foreign Secretary, Ernest Bevin, had had their doubts about the enterprise. 'If you open that Pandora's Box you never know what Trojan 'orses will jump out', Bevin said of the Council of Europe.[1] And so it proved, with a Trojan horse called Cyprus.

When Whitehall announced in 1953 that it was going to extend the European Convention to its colonies, the rightwing *Daily Express* dutifully stooped to the occasion. Under the sub-heads: 'Good for hot-heads' and 'Bad for Britain' it lambasted the Council of Europe as 'a farcical institution, run by a lot of cranks'. It added that

> Certainly this ridiculous declaration will give encouragement to all those who make a sport of besmirching Britain's Colonial Administration. Any malcontent or trouble-maker from the Colonies can now go trotting off to air his grievances at Strasbourg.[2]

This was untrue – colonial inhabitants were denied the right of petition – but why let a fact ruin a good story?

On the left, meanwhile, the *Daily Worker*, organ of the Communist Party of Great Britain, argued that it was pure hypocrisy to extend the convention to colonies where emergency laws denied human rights. At the press conference held to announce the extension, its correspondent demanded to know

> Whether under the article about the right to trial all persons arrested without charge or trial in Malaya, Kenya and British Guiana would now be either promptly released or brought to trial? Whether the article guaranteeing freedom of association (which specifically mentions trade unions) meant that the bans on the Pan-Malayan Federation of Labour, the Malayan Communist Party and the Kenya African Union would be lifted? Whether Article 10 guaranteeing the freedom to receive and impart information without interference by public authority and regardless of

frontiers meant that the *Daily Worker* could now send a correspondent to British Guiana, Malaya, Kenya?

The Colonial Office spokesman replied that under Article 15, nations were able to opt-out of the convention during public emergencies. When the *Daily Worker* reporter suggested that it was 'so much poppycock', the spokesman tartly responded, 'I did not say that.'[3]

* * *

In 1953, anti-colonial sentiment was at its peak. But while Europe's other major colonial powers stonewalled, Britain accommodated. By extending the convention to most of its colonies, it hoped to neutralise Third World criticism and gain political credit for its actions at home.[4] The benefits seemed substantial, the risks minimal. Under opt-out terms negotiated by Britain on ratification, her subjects did not have the right to petition the European Human Rights Commission, which administered the convention, nor bring complaints before the proposed European Court. Furthermore, the convention contained two loopholes. Article 15 allowed derogation 'in time of war or other public emergency threatening the life of the nation'.[5] And Article 63(3) allowed nations to act 'with due regard . . . to local requirements' in the colonial territories. Although Whitehall realised it would have to modify some repressive colonial laws, it was confident that it would be able to smooth out these rough edges to the satisfaction of Strasbourg.

Yet events in Cyprus, one of Britain's most important colonies, soon proved that this confidence was misplaced. In the fifties, Cyprus was the 'indispensable' strategic key to its Middle East policy, operating as a Mediterranean intelligence listening-post and a military staging area for the defence of the vital oil route through the Suez Canal. In Whitehall's view, independence was out of the question. British intransigence fuelled Greek Cypriot intransigence, and in the mid-fifties, the rightwing Greek officer, George Grivas, formed EOKA (National Organisation of Cypriot Combatants) to fight for *enosis* – unity with Greece. While Britain was gearing up for intervention in the Middle East (culminating in the Suez invasion) Grivas's militias mounted a hit-and-run campaign against its forces on the island. The colonial authorities took a hard line, calculating that if EOKA could not be turned, it had to be broken.

In 1955, Whitehall installed Sir John Harding as the new governor of Cyprus and declared a state of emergency. Harding awarded himself sweeping new powers to bring the *enosis* movement to heel. Those caught using weapons would be hanged; those found possessing weapons faced life imprisonment; large numbers of people were arrested and interned without trial; the press was heavily censored; collective punishments were imposed;

political leaders were exiled; demonstrations were banned, curfews were declared. A young English barrister, Peter Benenson, visited the colony, and was horrified by the suspension of ordinary legal procedures for dealing with arrests and imprisonment:

> When I first arrived in Cyprus, in October 1956, the entire Greek Cypriot Bar was inundated with complaints against the authorities. I have seen a queue of anxious parents at the chambers of the present Ministry of Justice so long that it stretched outside the front door. The authorities insisted that the Greek lawyers were mischievously inventing allegations of violence. To prevent them talking to their arrested clients, they were refused information as to their whereabouts. Independent Greek doctors were denied access to prisons or prison hospitals. Regulations were passed permitting the Government to hold arrested persons administratively in close confinement for 16 days without charge. . . . In these circumstances the Government could have scarcely expected anything else except that the rumour of torture should grow, until it swept like a cloud across to mainland Greece.[6]

Greece advanced its own global campaign for *enosis* by seizing on the issue of human rights. In 1956, Athens complained to Strasbourg that the British colonial administration on Cyprus was breaching the European Convention by imposing collective punishments, whipping adolescents, and illegally deporting and imprisoning people. Furthermore, it suggested that there was no 'threat to the life of the nation'. (This threat permitted derogation from the convention under Article 15, and was used to justify emergency measures.) The European Commission on Human Rights agreed to investigate – the first time that it had ever taken up an interstate complaint. It was also the first time that any supra-national human rights body had sat in formal judgement of a member of the Big Five.

The Foreign Office, which received news of the complaint in May 1956, was jolted into action. The Greek charges were serious. For example, how was Britain to justify the whipping of adolescents? If they were to shrug off the Greek criticisms of corporal punishment, they had to prove that whipping was neither uncommon, nor uncommonly brutal. Sir John Harding cabled the Colonial Office with chapter and verse of Regulation 75(2) of the Cyprus emergency powers, which dealt with the whipping of males beneath the age of eighteen for such crimes as unlawful assembly and disorderly conduct. The rule stated that the punishment, not to exceed twelve strokes, was administered with a 'light rod, cane or birch' (a photograph in the file shows a half-metre rod[7]). Furthermore, the rule specified that the trousers were removed; that the strokes were inflicted on the bare buttocks; that a medical officer carried out a prior examination; that a police officer 'not below the rank of Inspector' watched the punishment; and that a parent or headmaster could also be present.[8]

Harding admitted that Cypriots saw whipping as humiliating and perverse. At an English public school, he explained, beating 'is generally accepted as a normal form of punishment by the person to whom it is administered, and also by the boy's parents'. However in Cyprus, whipping 'is almost universally regarded by the boys and their parents as a most undignified and degrading form of punishment'.[9] (Harding did not comment on the brutality of the act.) The punishment was administered to teenage boys on a regular basis on Cyprus, and a Colonial Office report counted 101 whipping sentences in the year up to July 1956. By comparison, corporal punishment was used sparingly against adult males on the island, and only for more serious offences. These included sex offences such as rape, 'defilement' of a girl under thirteen or 'unnatural offences' (one sentence in the years 1952 to 1954); or revolts against the prison authorities such as mutiny, attempted mutiny or violence towards a prison officer (one sentence in 1952).[10]

In an attempt to prove that the practice was widespread, the Foreign Office sent a circular to its overseas missions and other government departments asking questions about corporal punishment abroad, such as, '[W]hat kind of instrument is used?' and 'Is the culprit clad or partially clad?'[11] The results offered them little comfort. They discovered that most West European nations not only eschewed corporal punishment but also considered it to be barbaric. It was even banned in Franco's Spain, where, the embassy reported, the practice was 'regarded with horror'.[12] (A 1954 Home Office survey confirmed that corporal punishment was not used in any West European country 'either as a punishment which may be imposed by the order of a court or as a punishment in a penal institution, except in Finland where it is used in the State reformatories for children'.[13]) Not only that, but most countries *outside* Europe also prohibited the practice. For example, it was forbidden in most nations of Latin America, and in most states of the USA (except Delaware and Virginia). The few places that did commonly practice corporal punishment were Britain's white former colonies, such as South Africa, Australia and Canada.[14]

While Whitehall was digesting the implications of the Greeks' complaint to Strasbourg, the Athens government began to attack on new fronts. In August 1956, its permanent representative at the United Nations, Christian Palamas, presented UN Secretary-General Dag Hammarskjold with a sheaf of testimonies alleging torture and mistreatment by the British security forces in Cyprus. The inhabitants of the village of Frenaros complained that troops had forced male villagers to lie in a freezing muddy field overnight, and that they had vandalised houses and mutilated sheep. The young women's Orthodox Christian association, Evangelismos, of the town of Pedoula complained that a parade had been broken up by soldiers using clubs and rifle butts. And a medical certificate affirmed that a teenage boy, who said he had been beaten around the head while wearing a 'steel helmet' in Omorfita prison camp, had suffered massive bruising.[15] A Foreign Office official reading those testimonies responded wearily. 'We are asking the CO for ammunition to answer these charges', he minuted, so that it could be shown that they were just 'a tissue of fabrications and misrepresentations'.[16]

The British colonial authorities were adamant that brutality against Greek Cypriots was the exception, and that if 'bad apples' were discovered within their ranks, they were immediately punished. The Greek government and EOKA, meanwhile, counter-claimed that British brutality was endemic and sanctioned from the top. Files at the Public Record Office at Kew suggest that brutality was random, but more common than Whitehall cared to admit.

One widely discussed case was that of Captain Gerald O'Driscoll and acting Captain Robert Alexander Craig Linzee, both of whom were court-martialled in April 1956.[17] That case was presented either as the punishment of bad apples, or as the tip of the iceberg, depending on political allegiance. O'Driscoll was, according to interrogation and other reports, a stocky 36-year-old Scotsman and longstanding member of the Intelligence Corps, who was at the time attached to the first battalion of the Gordon Highlanders. The War Office described him as being engaged in 'special duties' in Cyprus that included 'interrogation of persons arrested and detained as a result of operations against terrorist organisations'.[18] Linzee was a six-foot 25-year-old from Belfast, who served as the first battalion's intelligence officer in both Malaya and Cyprus, and had worked closely with O'Driscoll in Cyprus.[19] When they faced court martial, the Cyprus chief-of-staff, Brigadier G.H. Baker, wrote in their defence that they had been responsible for successful actions around Lefka and Troodos, and that they had shown 'a complete disregard for their personal safety' in an 'extremely dangerous' job. As proof of their effectiveness, he also mentioned that Athens Radio had denounced them both as 'traitors'.[20]

Two reports about the case – written by Sir Frederick Gentle, the Judge Advocate General (JAG), and the Deputy Judge Advocate General (DJAG) for the Middle East – describe how Linzee and O'Driscoll subjected Christos Constantinou, a Greek Cypriot tailor, to a terrifying and painful ordeal. On 12 January 1956, the DJAG records, Constantinou and Andreas Koronides were arrested and transported to Aberdeen Camp in the vicinity of Xeros, where the first battalion of the Gordon Highlanders was stationed.[21] Constantinou was locked in a room with a chain hanging from the ceiling, which, the JAG noted, Linzee claimed had previously been used to 'tether prisoners'.[22] O'Driscoll started to question Constantinou and, in the process, allegedly punched him in the face. At the court martial, O'Driscoll was acquitted of this charge.

Having failed to extract any information from Constantinou, O'Driscoll left the room, and an army private joined them. The JAG states that according to the evidence, the soldier 'punched and slapped' Constantinou. Linzee then ordered the prisoner 'to be stripped, or to strip, to the waist'. He then 'struck him on the back or shoulder blade with a chain which had been hanging on a rafter' while the soldier held him. Constantinou said he was struck eleven times; the soldier said six times.[23] The DJAG asserted that when Linzee was cross-examined about the assault he tried to shift the blame away from himself, saying that he had a 'grave suspicion' that the soldier may have inflicted Constantinou's injuries while he was out of the room.[24] The tribunal found both Linzee and O'Driscoll (not present but implicated in a 'common design' to use force to extract information if necessary) guilty of this assault. The assault verdict against O'Driscoll was not confirmed.

Two days after their arrest, Constantinou and Koronides appeared before a magistrate and complained that they had been beaten up. Meanwhile, they were visited by the accused, who asked the prisoners to write statements saying that they been treated with 'respect, kindness and carefulness'.[25] The DJAG report noted that an investigating police officer, Inspector Raymond Reynolds, described these testimonies as 'not being worth the paper they were written on'. The DJAG added that, 'it is difficult, in the circumstances, to quarrel with that description of their value'.[26] (Constantinou's statement was nothing more than a few scrawled sentences on a flimsy scrap of paper.[27]) The DJAG also recorded that Doctor Diomedes Isaias was summoned to examine the two Cypriots and found injuries on both men, including oval marks on Constantinou's back consistent with assault using a chain, as well as evidence of 'severe manhandling'. A week later, the two men were also looked over by an army medical officer, Captain James Williamson RAMC, who 'substantially confirmed' Dr Isaias's assessment.[28]

Once it became clear that the authorities were pursuing the complaint, O'Driscoll and Linzee convened a meeting at Platres where they reportedly conspired with accomplices to pervert the course of justice. After that, there were various attempts to pressurise accusers and witnesses to water down evidence of the beatings. The DJAG notes, for example, that the soldier tried to persuade Constantinou to tone down his complaint but was unsuccessful. Then O'Driscoll paid Constantinou a visit, and persuaded him to alter his evidence, but he had less luck with Dr Isaias and Inspector Reynolds. O'Driscoll denied that he had approached either Constantinou or Isaias, and tried to establish his whereabouts at the time of these meetings by claiming that he had, in fact, been with his Turkish driver. The court did not believe his alibi, because, the DJAG observed, 'He stated that he spent six hours with this driver discussing the latter's job, but had to admit that he could not speak Turkish nor could his driver speak English.' At the end of the trial, the judge found the accused guilty of assault (the verdict against O'Driscoll was not confirmed) and of conspiracy to pervert the course of justice, and sentenced them to be cashiered. This was later modified to dismissal from the Army.[29]

In July 1957, Greece complained to the European Commission a second time, this time accusing Britain of torture. This is always a grave allegation, but was especially so in 1957, the year that marked the high-point of the controversy over French torture in Algeria. Athens submitted forty-nine examples of alleged maltreatment. A sub-commission appointed by the European Commission ruled that twenty-nine cases merited further investigation. In response, Whitehall sent Hilary Gosling, a former Crown prosecuting counsel in Cyprus, back to the colony in January 1958 to construct a defence against the twenty-nine allegations. At the same time, they set out to expose the Greek charges as a political ploy designed to strengthen the case for *enosis*. A Foreign Office letter to the British Embassy in Athens outlined this strategy: 'it is our intention to discredit the Greek case by showing that these allegations are all part of a cynical and highly organised "smear" campaign directed against the Security Forces in Cyprus'. To this end, it asked the embassy to dig up Greek press reports showing 'reckless and irresponsible charges. . . . The more extravagant they are the better'.[30]

A fortnight after his arrival in Cyprus, Hilary Gosling wrote to the Colonial Office about his preliminary findings. Of the cases, there were some incidents that he thought were 'entirely fabricated' by people fearful of 'retaliation or ignominy' because they had given information to the security forces. There were also cases where 'trivial occurrences have been magnified into acts of deliberate brutality'. And there were, by Gosling's estimate, two cases in which 'the complainant has been roughly treated' (although he was quick to add that, 'as in other cases we are faced with a strong tendency by complainants and their witnesses to exaggerate to the point of lying').[31] This information provided the basis of Whitehall's defence strategy: if they could cut down the number of cases from twenty-nine to just two, and persuade the sub-commission that Britain was being smeared, they could thus 'point to the absurdity of the whole Application'.[32]

Throughout this imbroglio, the Foreign Office took careful soundings of commission members' attitude to the Cyprus question. They had gleaned inside information that some were 'sickened by the Greeks' behaviour', but that others would only accept the British case if it was 'driven home with a sledgehammer'.[33] They also solicited assessments from their diplomatic missions in Europe. The Greek representative on the commission, Constantin Eustathiades, would 'probably regard the Greek application as a purely political stunt in which his only duty is to play for his side'.

The 'idealist' Irmgard Fuest of the Saar would be inclined to be 'rather theoretical and sentimental' about Cyprus. The West German Christian Democrat, Adolf Susterhenn, was expected to make 'no bones about his dislike of our policy in private'. The 'impetuous, obstinate' former Prime Minister of Iceland, Hermann Jonasson, was deemed to be an anti-colonist '[l]ike all Icelanders'. And even though Denmark's Professor Max Sørensen had spent part of the war in London and 'understands British ways', his support was not guaranteed.

All was not lost, though. The Foreign Office was confident that it could rely on the support of Turkish representative, Muvaftak Akbar, who made cautious public statements but would be unlikely to 'depart from the well-known Turkish thesis on Cyprus'. Sture Petren of Sweden was a 'friendly person of judgment and integrity' whom it hoped would emulate his government's sympathetic stance. Georges Pernot of France, a right-wing Senator of 'unimpeachable conservative views', was expected to be 'well-disposed towards harassed colonial powers'. The Foreign Office also thought it could count on the backing of the Italian Christian Democrat, Francesco Dominedo, who, though 'garrulous and rather ridiculous', was believed to be 'probably basically friendly to us'.[34]

These assessments were soon put to the test. The sub-commission declared in 1957 that it intended to travel to Cyprus to assess for itself whether there was sufficient unrest 'threatening the life of the nation' to justify British emergency measures. Whitehall did not relish its role as the subject of the investigation – another first – but with the Greek complaint pending, it did not want to give the impression that it had anything to hide. In the event, the mission restricted itself to assessing the general situation rather than delving into individual complaints. The British therefore decided to submit to the probe with as much grace as they could muster. In January 1958, the delegation led by Sørensen (Denmark) and accompanied by Waldock (United Kingdom), Eustathiades (Greece), Susterhenn (Federal Republic of Germany), Crosbie (Ireland) and Dominedo (Italy) set sail for Cyprus.

The investigation began with a low farce, rich in symbolism, revolving around the governor's representative in Limassol, Gordon Williams, and the sub-commission's Italian representative, Francesco Dominedo. On 13 January 1958, Dominedo's boat finally docked in Limassol's outer harbour after being delayed by heavy seas. Williams braved awful weather as he travelled by launch out to the SS *Messapia* to formally greet the Italian representative and to convey him back to dry land. When he boarded the ship, however, Dominedo was not there to accept his greetings. In fact, an embarrassed member of the delegation's secretariat, a Mr Vis, explained, Dominedo was still lunching with the captain, and had declined to make an appearance before he had finished. Williams kicked his heels for half an hour, doubtless fuming over the breach of diplomatic protocol. When the unapologetic Dominedo finally appeared he announced that he had been unable to come earlier because he had been engaged in 'operation luncheon'.

Williams did not record for posterity what happened between him and Dominedo on the trip back to the shore, although he noted that the Italian's behaviour was 'extraordinary' and obviously 'intended to show to everyone that he was master of the party'. When they landed, Dominedo spied Williams's car and told Vis in French: 'I will not travel in any car flying the British flag' (it was explained that the car was not intended for him). Williams disapprovingly reported that Dominedo made a great effort to 'ingratiate himself' with customs officers and workers; and unhappily concluded that, 'by this morning most people in Limassol will know that the Governor's representative was purposely insulted by a member of the Sub-Commission'. The worst thing about the whole affair, he said, was that the Italian had done it all on purpose. 'I regret to have to tell you that I fear Mr Dominedo's behaviour was premeditated,' he wrote, 'and that in my opinion he set out to show that he was a member of an international organisation which was above Great Britain'.[35] There was the rub. Back in London it was agreed that Dominedo's behaviour had been 'infantile and ludicrously self important', but it was decided to let the matter drop.[36]

Worse followed. In the course of a whistle-stop tour of hearings and visits around the island, the sub-commission visited Pyla detention camp. There, their British minder, K.J. Neale, got wind of the fact that delegates had quizzed the camp commandant about the mistreatment of prisoners. Neale saw this line of enquiry as a breach of their mandate, and immediately halted the hearing. He confronted delegation leader Max Sørensen and demanded to know whether they had solicited information about brutality from other witnesses as well. Sørensen was 'obviously greatly discomfited' (the new governor of Cyprus, Sir Hugh Foot, cabled home) and admitted that they had received such evidence, but what could he do? The Dane did not want to inhibit witnesses from making complaints, and he had problems controlling some of the other delegates, 'especially the Greek'. Neale retorted that this activity was 'not satisfactory' because Britain had been 'subjected to a scurrilous campaign of lies on atrocities'. He insisted that Sørenson stick to his brief.[37] London braced itself for more bad news from Strasbourg.

It never came. The controversy blew over when Greece dropped complaints against the United Kingdom as part of the 1959 Zurich settlement on Cyprus. The sub-commission's report was not released to the public. Britain was spared the embarrassment of being brought to book. It had been a close run thing though, and it forced officials to consider whether to withdraw its colonies from the protection of the

European Convention. A debate about this started in the Foreign Office in 1957. J.A. Thomson, who was in favour of the colonies' withdrawal, warned that other European nations (perhaps 'a Communist Government in Iceland') might haul Britain over the coals for colonial misdemeanours.[38] But S.G.J. Cambridge, who was against withdrawal, countered this view. He wrote:

> The Convention has for some time now been regarded as the crowning achievement of the Council of Europe and (I quote) one of the first major statements of the 'European idea'. With such high-flown sentiments around, we should expect the criticism of our action to be even more impassioned than it might otherwise have been.

Then, his clincher argument:

> . . . such criticism would come at a time when we want as much European goodwill as we can get for the success of the Free Trade Area Negotiations. I submit that our temporary embarrassments over Cyprus are not worth jeopardising these.[39]

The discussion continued in the Colonial Office. Many high officials considered themselves to be enlightened advocates of colonial development, and displayed a keen awareness of the anomaly of bestowing a human rights convention on colonies governed, by definition, by inequality and lack of freedom. As J. Buist wrote:

> Colonial governments are not 'democratic', as that word is usually understood – I take it that the S of S's ultimate responsibility to Parliament is not sufficient to guarantee 'democracy' – nor do 'democratic societies' exist under colonial rule.[40]

Another official, Henry Steel, listed all the options they had regarding the convention in the colonies – withdrawal from the convention, flouting the convention, or relying on the 'public danger' loophole. Then he added, apparently straight-faced: 'There is also, I suppose, the course of adhering strictly to the Convention and refraining from doing what we want to do.'[41]

In one of the lengthier contributions to the debate, E.C. Burr recognised that although Colonial Office officials 'may not very much believe in these Conventions', the issue was not going to go away.

> I think it behoves us to look at our general policies in regard to these human rights, and I think it is not unfair to say that in a number of cases these policies are anything but liberal. For reasons which are satisfactory to us we detain people, control the holding of meetings, hinder freedom of movement

and do a number of other things which we roundly condemn when any other State does them. As I say, we are always able to justify these things to ourselves in terms of preservation of public order and orderly political development and a variety of other expressions, but the question is, I think, posed whether we are right in doing all these things and whether we would really lose much if we allowed the Human Rights Convention to have its full effect.[42]

Yet like other colonial officials, Burr could only fumble for an answer to this question.

*   *   *

Repression in the British colonies was brought into shuddering focus by an horrific event at the Hola prison camp at the height of the war against Kikuyu ('Mau Mau') insurgents in Kenya. On 3 March 1959, Kenyan guards, operating on British instructions to force their prisoners to work, clubbed to death eleven Kikuyu men for refusing to dig irrigation ditches. In the shocked parliamentary debate that followed the massacre, the Conservative's Colonial Secretary, Alan Lennox-Boyd, defended the policy of forced labour:

Experience has shown, time after time, that unless hard core detainees can be got to start working, their rehabilitation is impossible. Once they have started working, there is a psychological break-through and astonishing results are then achieved.

At this point, Sydney Silverman MP interjected:

Who told the right hon. Gentleman that? Stalin?

Hansard does not record whether Christopher Mayhew MP, one-time scourge of Soviet forced labour, was in the chamber at the time.[43]

The same year, the French government seized the entire edition of a book called *La Gangrène*, published by Les Editions de Minuit, which reproduced the statements of Algerian detainees who had been horribly tortured by the French internal security forces at the Direction de la Surveillance du Territoire headquarters in Paris in December 1958. A few months later, the London publisher, John Calder, published an English-language version of the same book – *Gangrene* – which also included accounts of torture and murder in Kenya.

Peter Benenson, by now president of Justice, the British lawyers' human rights organisation, contributed an eloquent foreword to *Gangrene*, in which he compared the brutality and repression of French-run Algeria to that of British-run Kenya. On the use of torture in Paris, he wrote:

It seems almost unbelievable that somewhere in what has long been regarded as the most highly-civilised city in the world, there should be a room where officers of the French Republic deliberately suspend naked young Algerians over a spit slung between two tables, and proceed to discharge spasms of electric current through their sexual organs.[44]

But he warned people against being too complacent about the United Kingdom's human rights record. 'British readers may be tempted to object that Algeria and Kenya are not parallel cases', he observed: 'The essential difference between Algeria and Kenya . . . is that on the British side there has never been any attempt to justify the use of violence.'[45]

*   *   *

A year later, when Benenson read that two students had been gaoled in Portugal for the 'crime' of toasting freedom, he did not just turn the page. He was moved to act. Why not campaign for the release of prisoners like these? With the help of influential friends – barrister Louis Blom-Cooper, advocate Sean MacBride, Quaker Eric Baker – he launched the campaign for 'Amnesty' for political prisoners in the *Observer*, which ran a big feature on 28 May 1961. Amnesty declared that it would henceforth 'work impartially for the release of those imprisoned for their opinions' and 'seek for them a fair and public trial'. The *Observer* piece showcased 'forgotten prisoners' from around the world: the Romanian philosopher, Constantin Noica; the American 'friend of the Negroes', Reverend Ashton Jones; the Angolan poet, Agostino Neto; the Archbishop of Prague, Josef Beran; the Greek communist Toni Ambatielos; and the Primate of Hungary, Cardinal Mindszenty.

Following the blueprint set out in the *Observer*, the new campaign would henceforth operate under guiding principles that reflected the pacifist and apolitical leanings of the founder members. It would petition on behalf of 'prisoners of conscience' – those gaoled for peaceful resistance, rather than violent opposition – using the simple, moral power of letter-writing to secure their release. And it would rise above the Cold War's political fray by being avowedly impartial and non-ideological, and by taking cases in equal measure from the East, the West and the Third World. Benenson warned that political allegiance was anathema because 'campaigns in favour of freedom brought by one country, or party, against another often achieve nothing but an intensification of persecution'.[46] But official documents tell a different story. They show that the organisation's leadership, unknown to its members, was at times strongly partisan, and perfectly willing to back actions and accept support from one country – Britain.

The story begins a year after its founding, when an Amnesty delegation was invited to a meeting with Foreign Office Parliamentary Under-Secretary Peter Thomas to discuss the European Convention. This encounter was something of a coup for the fledgling organisation, and it took advantage of the opportunity to urge Harold Macmillan's Conservative government to allow people to petition the European Commission and take cases to the European Court. The distinctly pro-British and anti-communist cast of the delegate's arguments was striking, given Amnesty's avowedly impartial stance. One delegate, Colonel Gerald Draper, argued that Britain's support of the two articles would 'deprive our enemies of a possible propaganda point', and thus set an example to nations which (Thomas quoted) 'had not yet learned to give human rights their full value'.[47] He also stated that, 'Our record was so good in relation both to the preservation of freedom in our own country and to granting freedom to dependent territories that we deserved a better reputation.'[48] Thomas responded that this difficult issue 'must be left to the political judgement of Her Majesty's government', but his interest had been piqued – these people were clearly patriotic, indeed, really rather conservative.[49] Amnesty was talking his language.

Over the next year or so, Foreign Office officials kept a careful eye on the organisation, and were pleasantly surprised by what they saw. Here was a group of respectable professionals who upheld human rights while actively resisting radical influences. (Amnesty's 1964–5 report noted with satisfaction that 'those who thought that they were joining a mass demonstration in favour of freedom in its widest anarchical sense . . . [and] those who saw this movement as a weapon to be added to the armoury of their own political cause' had dropped out.[50]) Amnesty International, as it was by now known, was the perfect humanitarian riposte to the more radical demands of Third World nationalists, Stalinist fellow travellers and New Left intellectuals. Here was an organisation with which Whitehall could do business.

Business began in 1963, when the Foreign Office gave the campaign its formal blessing as a body that 'provided humanitarians with an organisation free from Communist exploitation'. It despatched a circular to its overseas missions explaining that Amnesty International was henceforth to be a regarded as a body that deserved *'discreet support'*. 'Discreet' was the operative word, because public endorsement would seriously undermine its credibility. The circular also stressed that the organisation should remain 'independent' in the sense that the British government would in no way be responsible for its activities, 'some of which might from time to time embarrass us'. This new arrangement marked an important milestone in the relationship between a Western state and the youthful human rights movement.[51]

Amnesty's 1963–4 annual report detailed the comings and goings of a small and rather homespun operation. That year, with an income of just £4,000, it had dispatched 'several' parcels of clothes to Spain, and sent £90 a month to prisoners' families in South Africa.[52] It raised some money by selling postcards and biros, but the report gloomily informed members that there was 'no guarantee of our solvency next year'.[53] It celebrated Human Rights Day at St Bride's Church in Fleet Street, where 'Miss Jacqueline du Pre kindly played a cello piece by Bach, and Cy Grant and the Reverend Pere Duval each sang and played their guitars.'[54] The report also noted that Benenson had travelled to South Africa, and that Sean MacBride, head of Amnesty's International Executive, had travelled to Spain. That year MacBride was also appointed secretary-general of another human rights body, the International Commission of Jurists, which 'has led to closer cooperation between the two movements'.[55] This link would later prove to be significant.

Official documents show that during this period, Peter Benenson began to cooperate more closely with the Foreign Office and the Colonial Office. Britain was in the process of withdrawing from its colonies, and advice from someone sensitive to human rights concerns was welcomed. He was granted regular audiences with senior ministers. In return, previously closed doors opened to his organisation.

Benenson thrived on his privileged status and was full of useful pointers. In 1963, for example, he wrote to Lord Lansdowne, the Colonial Office Minister, about an Amnesty proposal to install a 'refugee counsellor' in the Southern African British protectorate of Bechuanaland to deal with refugees fleeing across the border from South Africa. Although Dr Verwoerd's regime was notoriously brutal, Benenson was at great pains to stress that this project was not intended to provide shelter to active opponents of apartheid. 'I would like to re-iterate our view that these [neighbouring British] territories should not be used for offensive political action by the opponents of the South African Government', he wrote. 'Indeed,' he added, 'it is a matter of importance that Communist influence should not be allowed to spread in this part of Africa, and in the present delicate situation, Amnesty International would wish to support HMG in any such policy.' Lansdowne, one of the last Conservative ministers to preside over Britain's shrinking empire, would doubtless have been gratified to hear this.[56]

Amnesty backed up its words with deeds. The Colonial Office was at that time under heavy fire at home for their hounding of two self-proclaimed communists, Jack and Rita Hodgson, who had sought shelter in Bechuanaland after escaping house arrest in South Africa. When they arrived in the territory, the Hodgsons refused to obey the territory's draconian ban on all political and trade union activity, and tried to foment a strike at Bechuanaland's sole 'industrial' site, the local abattoir. In response, the authorities quarantined them in the Kalahari Desert and then deported them to Britain.

Before the Hodgsons' expulsion from Bechuanaland, a delegation of representatives from Amnesty, the Anti-Apartheid Movement, the African National Congress, and members of all major political parties, appealed to the Colonial Office to effect some kind of compromise. After all, its treatment of the Hodgsons was embarrassingly reminiscent of that meted out to them in South Africa. But behind the scenes, Benenson was more in sympathy with the Bechuanaland authorities than with the communist Hodgsons. 'I have made further enquiries [o]n this case, and would say privately that I am quite satisfied that it was in the best interests of the population of the Protectorate that they should be asked to leave', he wrote to Lord Lansdowne. Amnesty had communicated their 'present views' to the International Commission of Jurists, and, as a result, the latter had 'agreed to withdraw [the case] from any further publications to the United Nations'.[57] By this means, the Hodgsons' plight was effectively frozen off the human rights agenda.

While Benenson was busy cultivating Whitehall's senior officials (and they him), Amnesty was tying itself in knots over the African National Congress prisoner, Nelson Mandela. The organisation had taken up his case before, but when he was gaoled again in 1964, this time for sabotage, many members felt that Mandela should be dropped as a 'prisoner of conscience' because he had used violence. At the same time, they felt uneasy about forsaking him during his life sentence on Robben Island. Eventually, an assembly was convened at Canterbury. The leadership argued that 'Amnesty International would be applying a double standard if it insisted that the police and prison authorities abstain from any act of violence or brutality yet maintained that those on the other side should be allowed to commit such acts and yet be unpunished.'[58] This argument was accepted by the membership. Delegates voted overwhelmingly against giving the 'prisoner of conscience' tag to anyone involved in violence, and Mandela was dropped.[59]

Amnesty was active in Southern Africa in the early years. In 1963, Benenson wrote a report entitled *Now in the Future is it Peace or War?* about the plight of refugees fleeing from South Africa to the British territories. Amnesty's vaunted reputation for factual accuracy got off to a slightly shaky start – as the High Commissioner pointed out, he had wrongly stated that Basutoland was a protectorate, when it was in fact a colony.[60] Aside from such errors, though, Whitehall was pleased with his largely positive conclusions about colonial policy. Benenson meanwhile sent a secret 'annex' to this report to four people: Conservative Prime Minister Alec Douglas Home, Labour leader Harold Wilson, Liberal leader Jo Grimond, and, for reasons unexplained, to Christopher Barclay, the head of the Information Research Department (the Foreign Office's propaganda warfare section). In this annex, he assessed the scope of South African incursions into neighbouring territories, and the strength of the opposition to the regime.[61]

If Benenson's report on South African refugees was well received in government circles, another, written by Amnesty representative Lieutenant-Commander Michael Cunningham in 1965, was not. Cunningham reported that refugees were not made welcome in the British territories of Bechuanaland, Basutoland and Swaziland. Not only did they face the threat of kidnap by members of South Africa's Special Branch who crossed borders unmolested by the local police, but they also faced the hostility of the white population, which was suspected of dynamiting a newly constructed refugee transit centre at Francistown.[62] These claims were impossible to deny, and the colonial authorities reacted defensively. The Bechuanaland police commissioner heatedly repudiated charges that his force was 'prejudiced' against refugees.[63] Other officials simply attacked Cunningham. He 'tries to impress everyone with his importance', reported the Francistown district commissioner, but 'information supplied by him is usually inaccurate . . . and he is generally a nuisance'.[64] The Basutoland resident commissioner attributed Cunningham's allegations of police harassment to a 'bibulous evening in local hotel bar' where he happened to encounter 'some senior African members of BMP [Basutoland Mounted Police]'.[65]

Decades later, it is hard to weigh the truth of these claims. Nor is it possible to gauge the effectiveness of Cunningham and other human rights advocates. Although undoubtedly brave, one suspects that many were innocents abroad, attempting to patrol treacherous terrain armed with nothing but a wallet full of cash, a cultivated English accent, and a sense of moral outrage. Some were gulled. In January 1964, for example, Amnesty (which had a policy of assisting 'genuine' refugees rather than anti-apartheid activists, and emphatically not those engaged in armed struggle) unknowingly evacuated a planeful of Pan African Congress members on a flight paid for by the aid charity War On Want. A report circulated by the Colonial Office dryly noted that the group were in fact 'going north for sabotage training'.[66] The same year, a senior British official vented his frustration over the well-intentioned but chaotic efforts of the non-governmental organisations on his patch:

> [I]s it not about time the refugee organisations put their own house in order? . . . Could they not come together and produce a single integrated executive . . . staffed by people who are both dedicated *and* efficient? The perpetual bickering about who represents whom, and the rivalries and documents such as [Amnesty's] do nothing towards helping the unfortunate refugees, and in the collective mind of this country create a misguided but very human feeling that it could stand the refugees if it weren't for the Cunninghams.[67]

*   *   *

In late 1964, Benenson asked the Foreign Office to help him to get a visa to Haiti, the desperately poor Caribbean nation saddled with the bloody regime of President 'Papa Doc' François Duvalier. This request set off a train of events that strained Amnesty's relationship with Whitehall.

Haiti discouraged visitors, but the Foreign Office threw its weight behind Benenson's entry application. They cabled their representative, Alan Elgar, in Port-au-Prince to remind him that 'we support the aims of Amnesty International and would like to give him any help we can'.[68] They did not need to add that a critical Amnesty report might wrong-foot the Americans, who backed Duvalier and rivalled British influence in the Caribbean.[69] The trip had to be handled with caution, however. Benenson was to travel under his own name but with a false identity (it was assumed that the Haitian authorities would be unaware of his connection with Amnesty). His cover story was that he was an artist, interested only in painting the streets and markets of Port-au-Prince.[70] This fiction was important because it gave Benenson a chance to talk to the victims of the regime without attracting the attention of Duvalier's murderous Ton Ton Macoutes. It also disguised official British backing of an Amnesty investigation – provided, of course, that Benenson wrote his report anonymously or under a pseudonym. As the Minister of State, Walter Padley, reminded him before he left, 'We shall have to be a little careful not to give the Haitians the impression that your visit is actually sponsored by Her Majesty's Government.'[71]

Benenson arrived in Port-au-Prince in January 1965. He painted most mornings and interviewed Haitians when he was able to. Alan Elgar made himself useful by introducing the 'painter' to prominent members of the expatriate community, such as the American Ambassador, the Canadian *chargé d'affaires*, and 'a number of reliable people in the business community'.[72] (Benenson later commented that the ambassador was the only 'apologist' for the Duvalier regime that he came across during his stay.[73]) His true identity remained a secret for the weeks he was there. As Elgar reported home, 'I did not tell anybody of his connexion with Amnesty International and neither did Benenson except, on the last day, the representative of the Shell Company here.'[74]

But Benenson's garrulousness got the better of him on the way home. In Paris, he called a press conference about his trip to Haiti, and, in what he foolishly assumed to be an off-the-record briefing, he revealed his 'painter' cover story. The resulting press coverage ruined the breakfasts of a good many Foreign Office officials. *The Times* named him as the Amnesty representative who had travelled to Haiti, and the *New York Times* elaborated on his disguise: 'He obtained his entry visa as an "artist" and circumvented restrictions on internal travel by a ruse.'[75] The Haitians and the Americans were bound to put two and two together and realise that Britain had formally backed the entry of an Amnesty investigator. Elgar sent a strongly worded complaint from Port-au-Prince. 'I was really shocked by Benenson's antics as I thought he had, when he was here, more discretion and commonsense.'[76] The British mission was expelled from Haiti several months later.[77]

On his return to London, Benenson was carpeted by a furious Walter Padley at the Foreign Office. He apologised and handed over a *mea culpa* letter for Alan Elgar. 'Please believe how utterly miserable I feel to have caused you so much annoyance', he wrote. (No mention was made of the 'annoyance' of those Haitians imperilled by contact with him.) But while he was keen to patch up relations with Padley, he placed most of the blame on a perceived breach of faith by the newspapers. 'I really do not know why the *New York Times*, which is generally a responsible newspaper, should be doing this sort of thing over Haiti', he complained. 'I can only suppose that some of the editorial staff are rather indignant about the present regime on the island and are using every opportunity to shake the US administration into action.'[78] Exactly what Benenson had imagined *he* was doing in Haiti, if not to highlight repression, stimulate indignation and shake politicians into action, one can only guess.

Yet this incident was just a curtain-raiser for the drama that followed. In 1966, Amnesty's Swedish branch sent Dr Selahuddin Rastgeldi to investigate allegations of torture in the Southern Arabian colony of Aden. There, the conflict between the British authorities and the Adeni nationalist movement was balanced on a knife-edge. A state of emergency had been declared, and the Ras Morbut interrogation centre had acquired a fearsome reputation for maltreating suspects. Rastgeldi's investigation was likely to embarrass Harold Wilson's Labour government, which had a case to answer for its colonial policies. But it also placed enormous pressure on Amnesty's London leaders, who wobbled under the strain of their divided loyalties. Should they defend Britain or Rastgeldi? In the event, they tried to do both.

The British authorities gave Rastgeldi a glacial reception when he arrived in Aden on 28 July 1966. His meeting with the High Commissioner, Sir Richard Turnbull, was tense. He recounted that,

> Upon mentioning the word[s] political detainees the High Commissioner answered 'There are no political detainees in Aden.' I produced a list of 164 prisoners with the dates of their arrests which I had been supplied with in Cairo and asked the High Commissioner if all these prisoners, without exception, were terrorists. Then came the next remarkable answer: 'How can we know? We cannot produce any evidence against these people as no one is willing to witness against them.' I . . . asked if the British Authorities could supply me with reasonable evidence of terrorism by individual detainees. His answer was categorical: 'All these people are either terrorists or associated with terrorism. . . .'[79]

Turnbull flatly denied Rastgeldi's request to visit prisoners, and the visitor was swiftly returned to his hotel in an official car. On this trip he was asked to sit in the front seat next to the driver. 'A soldier holding a machine gun was placed in the rear to defend me against the terrorists who could give me "a shot in my neck".'[80] The Amnesty representative spent the remainder of his trip collecting the testimonies of those who had been in Ras Morbut interrogation centre.

In the period preceding and following Rastgeldi's investigation, Turnbull contended that it was impossible to relax the regime at Ras Morbut because there was no other way of collecting intelligence. As Whitehall was well aware, his was an embattled regime dealing with a hostile population. A special branch police unit had been decimated by assassinations, and 'while our movements and intentions were being conveyed to the opposition by a thousand willing tongues, no news was being brought to us', he wrote.[81] As a result, the British had been forced to fall back on a single source of information: that extracted by interrogation.

Did the British use torture? The official files have been pruned of the most sensitive information, but they nevertheless provide interesting glimpses of life behind the massive, sound-proofed walls of Ras Morbut. Turnbull admitted that the rulebook had been torn up. Suspects were usually held incommunicado; their families kept in ignorance of their whereabouts in the period after arrest ('Incidentally even Rochat' – the Red Cross investigator in Aden – 'has not dredged this one up', Turnbull confided). They were often held in undesignated places of detention such as guardrooms (a breach of a decree that, he warned the Foreign Office, could be 'a lawyer's beanfeast').[82] They were routinely subjected to the humiliating ordeal of being stripped naked, and the disorientating experience of being hooded – a procedure which, Turnbull conceded, 'may in popular imagination be regarded as maltreatment'.[83]

Furthermore, scores of prisoners protested that they had been beaten up during their detention. Even if one accepts the authorities' claim that they were all lying for partisan ends, it is nevertheless clear that the Ras Morbut interrogation centre, and the Al Mansoura prison to which they were usually transferred, were dangerous places to be. In a period of just six months, from August 1966 to February 1967, prison officials investigated complaints from fifty-one prisoners or former prisoners. The following cases were typical. Haider Abdullah Hussein Audhali said that he had been struck in the face with a rifle butt, but three soldiers said that the cut had been caused by 'the end of the detainee's bed falling off' (no further investigation).[84] Ahmad Muhammad Haidan said that he was kicked, burnt with cigarettes and made to lie on a wet floor, but investigators said that he was 'hysterical' and suicidal (case closed).[85] Nasser Ahmad Bin Uthaiman Ba Bakri said that he had been pushed against a wall while hooded, but a corporal stated that he had simply '[struck] his head on a pillar' (case closed).[86] Salih Salim Bin Uthaiman Ba Bakri and Muhammad al Abudi Ahmad both complained that they were kept awake for long periods, but the authorities concluded that this was probably due to the unavoidable clanging of the prison's steel doors (cases closed).[87] Abdul Alim Ali Muhammad Baidara said that he was forced to carry stones and jump a bar with a sandbag on his shoulders, but a commandant alleged that he 'is having psychiatric treatment' (no further investigation).[88] Muhammad Ali Abdullah said that he had been hit with a chair, but, while noting his 'tendency to faint during the first few days of his interrogation', investigators ruled that there was no substantiation (case closed).[89] Muhammad Said Farah had sustained injuries to the knees and the wrist, but investigators decided that the detainee was probably 'attacked by his fellow detainees' (no further investigation).[90] Said Ali Hassan said that he was punched, kept awake and forced to work day and night: investigators noted that he was a 'hardened and indoctrinated terrorist', and that it 'may well have been that his behaviour in the Centre was such as to try the patience of the guards so much that they may have treated this detainee with more severity than usual' (case closed).[91]

The British government itself believed it had reason to be concerned about Ras Morbut. As a senior official in the Prime Minister's Office rather cautiously remarked to a colleague at the Ministry of Defence, 'The Prime Minister is inclined to the view that . . . there is apparently prima fac[i]e evidence of irregularities (to put it no higher) at the interrogation centre.'[92] As a sop to Amnesty and parliamentary critics, the Foreign Secretary George Brown sent barrister and Liberal Party MP, Roderick Bowen, to investigate procedures for dealing with reports of torture – but not specific allegations. Bowen stuck scrupulously to this evasive brief and produced a report that exonerated everyone bar a few officials accused of sins of omission, and 'three [unnamed] men' who had worked as interrogators at Ras Morbut. He did, however, quote a damaging memo from the health services director to the Deputy High Commissioner in Aden. It said that

> The injuries sustained by detainees brought from the Interrogation Centre indicates that their interrogation was assisted by physical violence. . . . I should be grateful if the allegations of physical violence which were substantiated by bruises and torn eardrums, etc, could be investigated.[93]

Bowen's report triggered two more investigations, which respectively examined the sins of omission and the 'three men'. In the latter inquiry, the military investigated the military and whitewashed a whitewash by concluding that there was insufficient evidence to bring anybody to court for their actions.

While these inquiries were creaking into action in late 1966, the chairman of Amnesty's Swedish section, Hans Goran Franck, put a threatening shot across British bows by writing a letter to Prime Minister

Harold Wilson outlining the results of Rastgeldi's investigation. 'Dr Rastgeldi has gathered reliable information on the practice of torture in the British interrogation centres in Aden', Franck stated, including: 'Undressing the detainee and letting him stand naked during interrogation . . . forcing the prisoner to sit on a pole entering his anus . . . hitting and twisting his genital organs . . . extinguishing cigarettes on his skin . . . keeping him in filthy toilets with the floor covered with faeces and urine.'[94] The letter enclosed testimonies from people who said that they had been tortured in Ras Morbut. One described the experience of a senior civil servant, Adel Mahfood Khalifa:

> At the [Ras Morbut] gate as I went through I was hit and abused by soldiers. The big fellow who threatened me previously hit me on my back. Revolvers were kept at my back and the back of each of those who were arrested with me. At about 5am I was taken into a cell where I was forced to strip off my clothes completely under duress and I was completely naked. I was then asked to open my mouth and I was hit in the mouth by the large man. I was then beaten up by him and another soldier until I fainted and I was not even asked a single question. Cold water was then thrown at me. . . . I was continuously beaten at nerve points and at sensitive parts of my body. . . . I stayed in Ras Morbut for eight days. During this time I was also hit on the untouchable parts of my body with a stick. I was also threatened that a stick will be put in my anus. . . .[95]

The government's response to such allegations was swift and emphatic. 'Mr Franck,' Foreign Secretary George Brown wrote to the Prime Minister, 'is known to have fellow-travelling tendencies. . . . His letter is couched in very slanted, not to say, offensive, terms'.[96]

Amnesty publicly released the Franck letter on 20 October, but Rastgeldi's report took longer to see the light of day. Although he had made his trip to Aden in July 1966, his report was not issued until December. Why? According to co-founder Eric Baker, Benenson and Amnesty general secretary Robert Swann met George Brown on 29 September, and indicated that they would hold up publication of the Rastgeldi report if the Foreign Office 'made concessions about procedure which would ensure that no such incidents could recur'.[97] In another version of events, Benenson claimed that Swann, whom he by then suspected of being a secret service plant in the organisation, suppressed it.[98] Yet a memo by Lord Chancellor Gerald Gardiner to Harold Wilson in November suggests that both claims were wide of the mark. A single extraordinary sentence in Gardiner's minute indicates that if anyone was responsible for holding up the report, it was Benenson. Gardiner wrote: 'Although very much pressed by their Swedish branch, Amnesty held the Swedish complaint as long as they could simply because Peter Benenson did not want to do anything to hurt a Labour government.'[99]

When Rastgeldi's report, citing the same examples of brutality as the earlier Franck letter, finally appeared, an outcry against Amnesty ensued. George Brown publicly denounced its 'wild allegations' during a Commons speech.[100] Meanwhile, the Wilson government tried to discredit Rastgeldi through the press. Officials summoned journalists to 'non-attributable' briefings and told them that the Swedish envoy was biased and anti-British. They claimed that he naturally sided with people from the Middle East because he was of Kurdish extraction, and that he was in the pocket of Egyptian President Gamal Nasser because he had stopped off in Cairo on his way to Aden. Benenson complained about the tactics being employed by 'unidentified officials',[101] while others protested that Rastgeldi had only visited Cairo to collect contacts (and to convey to the non-pacifist Adeni exile community Amnesty's abhorrence of violence).[102]

*   *   *

The final detonation in the Amnesty saga was triggered in spring 1967 by events involving the International Commission of Jurists (ICJ). This elite organisation, founded in 1952 to uphold human rights by legal means, was a progeny of the Central Intelligence Agency. During the early decades of the Cold War, it was financed by the CIA and the Ford Foundation, and directed by members of the Ford-funded Council on Foreign Relations.[103] Complex funding arrangements were set up to disguise the ICJ's links with its covert American patron. From 1958 to 1964, the CIA funnelled $655,000 through two 'dummy' foundations, the Borden Trust and the Beacon Fund, to the 'real' MD Anderson Fund, which passed it on to the CIA-backed American Fund for Free Jurists Inc, later known as the American Council for the International Commission of Jurists.[104] This body in turn directed funds to the ICJ.[105] When CIA money fell short, the Ford Foundation made up the shortfall.

In the fifties, the ICJ began to sprout national sections abroad, including the British section – Justice – founded by Peter Benenson and chaired by Hartley Shawcross. In the sixties, Amnesty's Sean MacBride also took up the post of ICJ secretary-general. The cross-fertilisation between Benenson's human rights organisations and the ICJ rebounded on all in March 1967, when the American magazine *Ramparts* published an exposé of the CIA's use of 'dummy' foundations to finance the US National Student Association.[106] The papers picked up on the story, and it was soon revealed that the CIA had used 'dummy' funds and the American Fund for Free Jurists Inc to finance the ICJ. Sean MacBride denied that he had any knowledge of the original source of this money.

Within days, a similar funding scandal broke over Amnesty's head, directly implicating Peter Benenson. A twenty-year-old student, Polly Toynbee, now a *Guardian* columnist, had worked for the organisation as a volunteer. In March 1967, she contacted the press with evidence suggesting that Amnesty was being covertly funded by the British government.

Toynbee had travelled to Nigeria and Rhodesia with the organisation in 1966. On the Nigeria leg of the trip, she had acted as secretary to the Amnesty representative, Sir Learie Constantine, who was petitioning for the release of political leaders. The party also included Michael Cunningham, who, she observed, always seemed to have 'an enormous amount of cash on him'. If she had envisaged a vigorous campaign for the release of prisoners she was disappointed:

> We stayed at the Federal Palace Hotel, outside Lagos. . . . We sat around doing nothing but drinking, eating enormous meals and entertaining the Press. It was like a businessman's expense-account outing. We must have spent an enormous amount, but we never achieved anything. We never saw anyone important. We just got vague assurances that the prisoners were all right.[107]

Toynbee then travelled on to Rhodesia, where Ian Smith's white supremacist government had some months earlier declared its unilateral independence from Britain, and then proceeded to lock up and execute black political leaders. Amnesty's operation seems to have been as unfocussed and as well-funded as it had been in Nigeria.[108] During the six weeks she spent in Salisbury, Toynbee and other volunteers sent money to detainees' families and tried to arrange legal aid for prisoners. Again, money was no object ('I could go to the bank and pull out £200 at a time . . . there was no one to check up'). Rumours circulated about the source of all this cash, and when Benenson arrived on a flying visit, Toynbee tackled him about it. 'At first he told me not to ask such questions,' she said, 'But then he admitted that the money was coming from the Government, and he told me it had been very hard to get.'[109] When she asked about strings attached, he assured her that the question was irrelevant because he would in any case 'act according to what the Government wanted him to do'.[110]

Toynbee and other volunteers were expelled from Rhodesia in March 1966, and when she left she carried with her a bundle of Amnesty correspondence which she said she had found abandoned in a safe. It contained thinly coded letters written in early 1966 from Benenson's address to Robert Swann and others then working in Rhodesia. These appeared to indicate that Amnesty had asked someone in Harold ('Harry') Wilson's government for money; that Amnesty had provided a budget assessing amounts needed 'based on [detainees'] actual family need'; and that 'Harry' had paid up in late January 1966.

> *January 12:* The only news of any import comes from Harry. He's giving us the money we asked for, so I think it reasonable for you to work on the basis

that you have the whole of that £2,000 from the World Council of Churches for family relief.

January 15: He will be bringing another piece of paper from Harry like the one you collected in Brighton.

January 20: Harry's present has arrived so all is now well. Cunningham should reach you in about a week's time with part of the present.

February 1: According to my calculations you have £2,000 at Jack Grant and the better part of £1,000 from each of Bernard and Michael. . . . You can if you need have another £1,000 on 15th February.

February 2: What with North Hull [Labour had won this by-election on 27 January, raising their wafer-thin majority from 3 to 4] . . . Harry's financial problems apparently have been solved, and he's in a generous mood.[111]

When these excerpts were published in the press in March 1967, Amnesty's head office flatly denied knowledge of the payments. Benenson told a different story, claiming that the government *had* provided secret funds, but that they were a direct gift to prisoners and their families in Rhodesia rather than a donation to Amnesty.[112] Yet a private letter from him to Gerald Gardiner, written two months before the Toynbee revelations, reveals another scenario: that the government had asked a third party – Charles Forte, the owner of the catering and hotel chain – to donate £10,000 to the work. 'I had been led to believe that these moneys were paid by Mr Charles Forte', Benenson wrote, adding that in return 'it was not altogether unlikely that the name of such a well-known caterer would appear on a future honours list', he added.[113] Interestingly, Charles Forte's autobiography records that in 1970 he received a letter 'out of the blue' from Harold Wilson's office offering him a knighthood for 'the financial help I had given to various charitable and cultural enterprises'. He did not mention Amnesty or Rhodesia in this context.[114]

Whatever the truth of the matter, Benenson got cold feet about the money provided for the Rhodesia operation and wanted to return it. He wrote that, 'rather then jeopardise the political reputation of those members of the Government involved in these secret payments, I had decided to sell sufficient of my own securities to repay the secret donor, Mr Charles Forte, out of my own pocket'. It is not clear why he suddenly became so anxious to repay this very large sum. Perhaps he had an inkling that the government's involvement in the Rhodesia project was about to be exposed, to the detriment of it and himself – as indeed happened shortly after. His only explanation at that time was that 'The object of this not inconsiderable donation was to clear the record so that it could be said that the money sent for succour to HM loyal subjects in Rhodesia came from a . . . private person with a known interest in the cause, who did not object (as Mr Forte did) to the fact of his donations becoming public.'[115]

Benenson was equally keen to rid himself of Foreign Office funds provided for other human rights organisations he was involved in. These were Justice, the ICJ off-shoot, and the Human Rights Advisory Service, which he had set up in January 1966, and which was also active in Rhodesia.[116] Benenson wrote:

> There are also in being two sums of money advanced to me in 1965 by the Foreign Office – £3,000 for any purpose I selected within the ambit of the Human Rights Advisory Service and £2,000 for any purpose within the ambit of Justice. Both these sums were banked by me and have not been spent. In my view, under present circumstances it would be better if the money went back whence it came as soon as practicable.[117]

What are we to make of this letter? It states that 'members of the Government' were 'involved in these secret payments' to 'HM loyal subjects in Rhodesia', probably using funds provided by a third party, Charles Forte. It also says that the Foreign Office had given funds to Justice and the Human Rights Advisory Service. Amnesty is not mentioned in this connection. As we have speculated, Benenson may have feared a scandal over his organisations' covert links with the Wilson government. He also expressed his disappointment at its handling of issues close to his heart: 'It may be asked why I ever accepted these payments if I now wish to return them. The answer is that at the advent of the Labour Administration I believed on the evidence of my friends' record and their public declarations that they would set an example to the world in the matter of human rights. . . . Alas, such an example has been set, but it is not a good example.'[118]

*   *   *

At the height of the 'Harry letters' controversy, Amnesty official Stephanie Grant approached the recently renamed Foreign and Commonwealth Office for a strange favour. She asked if she could use the diplomatic bag to send an urgent letter to their representative in Salisbury, G.C. 'Jack' Grant, explaining to him the scandal that threatened to destroy the organisation. As she indicated, Benenson had travelled to Aden in November 1966 during the Rastgeldi affair, and had returned to Britain a changed man.

> . . . Peter Benenson has been levelling accusations . . . which can only have the result of discrediting the organisation which he has founded and to which he dedicated himself. All this began soon after he came back from Aden, and it seems likely that the nervous shock which he felt at the brutality shown by some elements of the British army there had some unbalancing effect on his judgement. He came back to England in November, resigned from the Presidency of Amnesty on the grounds that its offices were bugged and its mail opened, and publicly announced that he could no longer live in a country

where such things were tolerated – or even engineered – by the Government. We have no proof either way whether these particular charges of bugging were founded, though during our criticism of the Government over Aden I personally feel it was very possible. But the way in which he made them – with maximum publicity – did then suggest that he was under very great nervous strain and needed a long period of rest.

As a consequence of Benenson's actions the Amnesty executive had disassociated itself from him: 'You will imagine how difficult and unpleasant this has been', she wrote.[119]

Had Benenson suffered a nervous breakdown after Aden, as Grant seems to suggest? That would certainly explain some of the more paranoid sections of his correspondence of the time.[120] At the very least, it must be surmised that he experienced a profound moment of truth on his trip to the Middle East, where he may have realised that the British authorities were indeed torturing political prisoners. But before dismissing his judgement as skewed, we should also consider his impassioned yet apposite comments about the government's handling of Aden, written in the letter to Gardiner after his return:

> During many years spent in the personal investigation of repression . . . I never came upon an uglier picture than that which met my eyes in Aden on 12th November 1966, over two years after the Labour government came to office. It is no exaggeration to say that I was physically sick[ened] not only by the deliberate cruelty and affronts to the human dignity of the Arab population. . . . Parliament has now been told direct and deliberate untruths three times running in answer to questions about the publication of the reports of the International Committee of the Red Cross relating to Aden. Furthermore, very recently, the Foreign Secretary was used to misinform Parliament by describing Dr S. Rastgeldi's report as 'wild allegations'. . . . [H]aving been to Aden and carried out my own investigations, I think that there is to say the least a strong possibility that some if not all the rather horrifying allegations are correct. . . . [T]hose Arabs who have suffered – some of whom have lost the balance of their mind – should be compensated. It is only when this has been done, and when some steps have been taken to withdraw the allegations made against Dr Rastgeldi . . . that the situation will begin to be restored.[121]

In March 1967, representatives of Amnesty's European and American groups gathered at a conference in Elsinore, Denmark. Under the gloomy ramparts of Kronborg Castle, the setting for Shakespeare's *Hamlet*, chairman Sean MacBride issued a vituperative written attack against the movement's founder, pointedly referring to Benenson's 'ill-health' and 'unilateral initiatives'. Benenson did not attend, but he submitted a resolution demanding MacBride's resignation on the grounds that the CIA had funded the American Council for the International Commission of Jurists. Foreign delegates, especially from the wealthy (and, it should be added, government-subsidised[122]) Swedish branch, were far from impressed by this face-off between the two human rights heavyweights. After the conference, Benenson faded from the scene to take up farming in Buckinghamshire. The organisation's leadership passed to a caretaker, Eric Baker.

The honeymoon between Amnesty and the British government was at an end. Amnesty vowed that in future, it 'must not only be independent and impartial but must not be put into a position where anything else could even be alleged'.[123] In May 1967, the Foreign Office sent its missions a circular revising its 1963 instructions about the organisation: 'For the time being our attitude to Amnesty International must be one of reserve', it cautioned, adding that, 'Much will depend on the personality of the future Director-General.' Official support for the body was suspended, and 'reference to Amnesty International in the Appendix . . . (which lists organisations which deserve discreet official support), should be deleted'.[124] But this was not the end of the relationship.

Martin Ennals took over the leadership of Amnesty in 1968. As a new broom, he was expected to restore the organisation's credibility and reputation for impartiality. Before he took over, he had been a leading light in the National Council for Civil Liberties, a body once described in official circles as 'communist-dominated'.[125] He was seen as more of a radical than Benenson, but there was a rapid mending of fences with the Foreign Office. Like his predecessor, Ennals was soon mixing with government ministers and civil servants. Not long afterwards, the topic of money was raised once more.

It might be imagined that after the previous controversy, Amnesty had learnt its lesson about the perils of soliciting funds from government. This was not the case. In December 1968, Martin Ennals met Minister George Thomson at the Foreign and Commonwealth Office (FCO) to discuss the plight of political prisoners in Rhodesia. He was anxious to reassure Thomson that his organisation still backed official policy there, and told him that 'Amnesty would be more than willing to take . . . advice or respond to requests for help.' The FCO minutes then record that he broached another matter:

> Mr Ennals then raised the question of HMG making a financial contribution towards the work which Amnesty and one or two other organisations were doing in Rhodesia to help the families of those in restriction and detention. He understood that in the past the British government had given help in this way through informal channels, but unfortunately this assistance has ended when Amnesty's connection with HMG had been made public as a result of

internal dissensions *[sic]* in the organisation. Mr Ennals said that in his opinion, the affair had been very badly handled at the time by Mr Benenson. He personally did not either then or now feel that help of this kind in any way infringed Amnesty's independence.[126]

This minute not only arouses further suspicion that Amnesty had received money from the government 'through informal channels' for its work in Rhodesia.[127] It also shows that Ennals was insensitive to the issues that such transactions raised. Once again, an Amnesty leader requested money for the support of detainees' families in Rhodesia, the very thing that had caused such a furore after Toynbee's publication of the 'Harry' letters. Unlike many of the organisation's members, Ennals clung to the belief that government assistance did not compromise the independence of an avowedly non-partisan organisation. Not only that but, just like his predecessor, Ennals declared his unqualified support for official British policies – this time in Rhodesia – to the extent that he was prepared to 'take advice' from the FCO and respond favourably to 'requests for help'.

In the event, officials were unenthusiastic about the proposal and turned Ennals down, saying that money was tight.[128] There were various reasons for this, relating to the circumstances of prisoners in Rhodesia, and the claims of other charities. Perhaps they also calculated that at that time, a financially independent – yet sympathetic and loyal – Amnesty was more useful to a government than an Amnesty tainted by 'discreet support'. Money or no money, the organisation would continue to play a useful role, operating as eyes and ears abroad, and as a sounding board at home.

Under Ennals's stewardship, Amnesty grew into one of the most influential human rights groups in the world. When it was awarded the Nobel Peace Prize in 1977, the *Guardian* reported that Ennals was so concerned to preserve its reputation for incorruptibility that

> To avoid the embarrassment of accepting funds from governments or major corporations, Martin Ennals's . . . rule is that he holds up each pound note to the light.[129]

*   *   *

After twenty years in the doldrums, human rights was back in fashion again across the Atlantic, as a reaction against the foreign policies pursued by the Republican administration. By the time Amnesty had won its Nobel Prize, a new American President, Jimmy Carter, had made the rights issue the centrepiece of his government's policies.

SIX

Carter's Crusade

During the dog days of the Nixon presidency in 1974, Deputy Secretary of State Robert Ingersoll sent a revealing memorandum to Henry Kissinger, about a pressing issue. '[V]iolations of human rights abroad are becoming an increasingly urgent problem', he wrote. His concern was surprising, given the State Department's adherence to *realpolitik* at that time. But as it turned out, the problem that concerned Ingersoll was not torture or murder abroad, but the pressure being brought to bear on the administration by political opponents at home. 'Congress is beginning to insist that military and economic aid be reduced when authoritarian regimes with which we are identified commit violations', he said, warning that, 'if the Department did not place itself ahead of the curve on this issue, Congress would take the matter out of the Department's hands'.[1] Human rights were back in town after two decades in the wilderness.

The renewed interest in the issue grew out of the poisoned soil of Chile and Vietnam. Shortly after the US-backed overthrow of Salvador Allende's government in 1973, Democrat Congressmen began to agitate for bans on US aid to repressive regimes. They contended that Washington's patronage of despots had ruined its credibility: Donald Fraser observed 'a loss of respect among democratic forces abroad, and the growing disillusionment of the American public'.[2] As well as reacting to this immediate crisis, they were also responding to the breakdown of the foreign policy consensus during the Vietnam war.[3] They thus proposed to shift the focus away from the East–West struggle that provided the *raison d'être* for such damaging relationships, and to redeem the nation's reputation by mounting a global campaign against abuse. Like John Bricker's campaign of the fifties, these activists sought to wrest control of foreign policy from the White House. This time, though, the boot was on the other foot, with human rights being kicked onto the agenda, rather than off it.

In 1973, Fraser and other Congressmen held a series of hearings on conditions within countries receiving American aid; and, the following year, they published a report pointedly entitled *Human Rights in the World Community: A Call for US Leadership*. This was accompanied by a flurry of law-making activity. In 1973, they passed a 'sense of Congress' resolution denying military and economic assistance to governments that interned political prisoners – in other words, Chile and South Vietnam. In 1974 anti-détente hawks Henry Jackson and Charles Vanik initiated the Jackson–Vanik amendment that denied normal trade status to any 'non-market economy country' restricting immigration – namely, the USSR. In 1975, Democrat Tom Harkin sponsored an amendment denying economic assistance to dictatorships unless it benefited needy people.[4] In a pattern that would become familiar, this was backed by a coalition of liberals (concerned about America's image) and conservatives (intent on reducing overseas aid). As the House Republican leader, John Ashbrook, argued, '[W]e ought to cut off these give-aways generally, but until this House is more enlightened in our own self-interest, we should at least cut off aid to repressive regimes'.[5] Human rights had become the flag of convenience for politicians of every hue.

The State Department, pushed by Congress, began to install bureaucratic machinery to deal with the issue. In 1974, the sole full-time human rights officer attached to the International Organizations Bureau was promoted, and embassies were instructed to report back on political prisoners. But a Carter-era official, Roberta Cohen, observed that the impact of these early initiatives was 'minimal'. The new Office of Humanitarian Affairs under James Wilson usually 'side-stepped the issue of human rights and focused its attention almost exclusively on the Vietnam refugee problem'.[6] (Wilson himself was best remembered for entreating Congressmen not to create more human rights laws, and for his role in denying the Peruvian radical Hugo Blanco a visa.[7]) Not only that, said Cohen, but State Department reports on abuses in Argentina, Haiti, Indonesia, Iran and Peru were censored.[8] (An official from the department's East Asia Bureau later divulged that such reports were produced 'just to satisfy liberals on the foreign aid committees'.[9]) The cosmetic nature of these initiatives was obvious: one study published in 1979 observed that 'the human rights officer is little more than a new title tacked on to that of the previous labour officer'.[10]

Although precious little may have changed in practice, the bandwagon continued to gather speed, driven both by Congress's desire for greater leverage over affairs abroad, and the administration's own search for credibility at home. In 1975, President Gerald Ford backed the inclusion of human rights provisions in the Final Act drawn up at the East–West conference at Helsinki. The following year, Henry Kissinger – who in 1974 had admonished the US Ambassador in Chile for broaching human rights issues with Pinochet's military staff ('Tell Popper to cut out the political science lectures'[11]) – started giving political science lectures himself. During the 1976 Organization of American States conference in Santiago, Kissinger roundly denounced the hosts, claiming that 'the condition of human rights has impaired our relationship with Chile'. He added:

Human rights are the very essence of a meaningful life, and human dignity the ultimate purpose of government. A government that tramples on the rights of its citizens denies the purpose of its existence.[12]

His oratory was greeted with a stony silence at the conference, and with faint praise in Washington (few had forgotten how Kissinger had helped to install General Pinochet's bloody regime three years earlier). But if Americans disliked the messenger, they were learning to like the message.

*   *   *

The disgrace of Richard Nixon exposed the cynicism and corruption of politics inside Washington's Beltway, and tainted all machine politicians by association. Enter Jimmy Carter, the soft-talking 'peanut farmer' from The Plains, Georgia. The contrast between Jimmy and Tricky Dicky was both dramatic and deliberate. Carter was a moral man, although not overbearingly evangelical (lest he scare off the Catholic vote). One of his campaign slogans, 'A New Morality', spelt out the message that here was a politician with a higher calling. Once he hit the election trail, though, a more complex character began to emerge. 'Certainly there is the smile, the courtly southern charm, the flattering intensity with which he talks', said a 1976 *Time* profile, but, it added, there was also the 'almost total humorlessness and an implacable quality to the pursuit of all his goals'. The profile continues:

> Trying to reassure an audience in Green Bay, Wis, that he was not dangerously ambitious, Carter pointed out that he had not always wanted to be President. Said he, in all seriousness, 'When I was at Annapolis, the only thing I wanted to be was Chief of Naval Operations.'[13]

The pundits watched in fascination as saintly, ambitious Jimmy set out on the long road to the White House. If he got there, would he really practice what he preached?

The answer was yes, and no. Carter's record on human rights is patchy. He embraced the issue rather late in the day – far later than either Congress activists or Republican incumbents. As Arthur Schlesinger, former special advisor to President Kennedy, wrote in *Foreign Affairs*:

> It is not altogether clear how Carter personally came to human rights. The phrase does not appear in the chapter on foreign policy in his memoir, *Why Not The Best?* (1975). . . . On occasion, indeed, he seemed to be moving in the opposite direction. He criticized not only the Helsinki Agreement but the whole philosophy of intervention.[14]

The Democratic Party had been deeply divided over foreign policy throughout the Vietnam War, and the sulphurous atmosphere lingered in 1976.

At meetings to decide the election platform, human rights was one of the few areas of common ground between the party's liberal and conservative camps. Yet no one seemed to have spotted its potential for uniting the party. There was the usual horse-trading between George McGovern's people, who wanted to condemn right-wing dictatorships, and Henry Jackson's people, who wanted to denounce communist dictatorships. (They finally accepted the deal proposed by rightwinger Patrick Moynihan: 'We'll be against the dictators you don't like the most . . . if you'll be against the dictators we don't like the most.'[15]) Meanwhile, Carter's team seems to have been somewhat periphal to the discussion. They 'were at best neutral,' Moynihan recalled, 'giving the impression of not having heard very much of the matter before and not having any particular views'.[16]

By the start of the presidential race, the pointers to Carter's later campaign were already discernible. However, he adopted a pious tone on foreign as well as domestic matters, contrasting his own patriotism and compassion to the amorality of the Ford-Kissinger ticket. In particular, he expressed his concern about covert actions in Cambodia, Chile and Angola, and argued for more exemplary conduct abroad. Not that he was unique in this respect. Almost every presidential hopeful, from Morris Udall to Ronald Reagan, proposed some kind of 'moral' foreign policy – indeed, it was precisely this cross-party consensus that created the surge of interest in human rights. As a Carter advisor interviewed by Elizabeth Drew in 1977 observed

> There was a genuine feeling even before the campaign that the previous Administration didn't care very much about human rights. At another time, that might not have mattered so much. Eisenhower didn't, either. But we were coming out of Vietnam. . . . There was a widespread feeling that we would like to get our bearings again. Watergate. Chile. The inquiry into the CIA's role in assassinations. There was the feeling that there was no moral underpinning to our government. That created a vacuum, and an environment where this issue would be very important.[17]

Carter first referred directly to human rights during his acceptance of the Democratic nomination in July. Through the autumn, though, he failed to really distinguish himself from the President on foreign affairs; rather, he adopted the negative tactic of belittling Ford by casting him as Kissinger's lap-dog. He clearly needed a more positive policy to put forward, and human rights edged back into the picture. After a few dry runs, he raised the issue during a televised debate with the President in October, in which he accused the Republicans of 'supporting dictatorships [and] ignoring human rights'.[18] The press did not take much notice. The only big story that night was Ford's famous blunder, when he chopped the air with his hand and declared: 'There is no Soviet domination of Eastern Europe, and there never will be under a Ford Administration.'[19] In the event, the economic recession and his pardoning of Nixon were enough to sink his Presidency. Jimmy Carter won the election by a whisker.

Human rights may not have played a crucial role in the victory, but they were set to play an important role in the new administration. Carter had promised Americans a fresh start, and the need for positive policies was now more pressing than ever. In the months that followed, the Democrat inner circle tentatively felt its way towards human rights. Party pollster Patrick Caddell reported that it pushed all the right buttons with the electorate and, significantly, that it appealed to both liberals and conservatives.[20] As well as its public appeal, it also addressed burning sectional concerns, by uniting the powerful factions within the Democrat Party, morally out-flanking the Republicans, and pre-empting Congress activism on the issue. The Cold War appeared to be on the wane, and anti-communism was losing its purchase. Here was another big idea that had the beauty of being unifying and morally satisfying. It also had the welcome advantage of being cheap. A human rights crusade was the perfect post-Vietnam, post-Cold War, recession-era antidote to the American malaise. It was, in short, an idea whose time had come.

*   *   *

'Our commitment to human rights must be absolute', Jimmy Carter announced in his January 1977 inauguration speech.[21] A few days later, he received a letter from Andrei Sakharov complaining about Moscow's persecution of Soviet dissidents. It presented a perfect opportunity to kill two birds with one stone. Carter could display his commitment to the full, while using rights as a shiny new stick with which to beat the old enemy. So he sent an open letter back to Sakharov pledging that America would 'promote respect for human rights not only in our country but also abroad'.[22] The wording was bland, but the Kremlin was furious, and strongly denounced Washington for meddling in its affairs. Although surprised by the vehemence of the response, Carter toughed it out, in public at least. When the Soviets banished Associated Press correspondent George Krimsky from Moscow, he made light of it, quipping at a press conference: 'When the AP reporter was expelled from Moscow, I had a first thought to retaliate by expelling the AP reporter from Washington.'[23] Instead, he banished the Tass representative, Vladimir Alekseyev.

Throughout the first month of the administration, the State Department shot off human rights broadsides in every direction – against the Czechs for arresting those who had signed Charter 77; against Ian Smith's white minority government in Rhodesia; and against Idi Amin for his rule of terror in Uganda. Sanctions were announced too – against Argentina, Uruguay and Ethiopia (but not strategically important South Korea, stressed Secretary of State Cyrus Vance). These actions were intended to establish the government's *bona fides*, and to steal a march on Congress. Officials were at pains to stress that the campaign was not a voyage on to uncharted ground, but a return to tradition. As one official, Charles Maynes explained, the new government was 'simply asking that the United States return to that period of forward, balanced and determined leadership in the field of human rights that we associate with Eleanor Roosevelt'. Americans liked what they heard, and Carter garnered plaudits from across the political spectrum. Civil libertarians and moral re-armers, Jews and Southern Baptists, baby-boomers and war veterans, immigrant groups and labour unions were all smitten, for a while at least.

So too were fellow politicians. Liberal George McGovern and conservative Barry Goldwater both congratulated the President for his stand, as did Henry Kissinger – a calculated act of magnanimity in defeat. (After 'the traumas of Vietnam and Watergate', he wrote detachedly, Carter had given Americans 'a renewed sense of the basic decency of this country, so that they may continue to have the pride and self-confidence to remain actively involved in the world'.[24]) The pundits also embraced the new credo. As the commentator Ronald Steel wrote in June 1977:

> The good grey liberals on the *New York Times* love it; so do the Friedmanites on the *Wall Street Journal*. Senator Henry Jackson thinks it's made in heaven, and the hitherto-ignored members of Amnesty International hope that at last it may be coming down to earth. The hawkish neo-conservatives at *Commentary* and the dovish leftists at the *New York Review* have found one issue on which they can agree on – almost. Who can bad mouth human rights? It is beyond partisanship and beyond attack. As a political issue, it's the international equivalent of the environment.[25]

Success spurred the Carter team on. They had more or less stumbled on the issue during the election campaign, and although they lacked a grand strategy, they made the most of every opportunity that came along. One foreign policy official admitted that the campaign was both makeshift and driven by domestic politics:

> I know there was no specific planning for a particular human rights campaign or program, such as it is. I think then fate intervened – happenchance things, letters – that blew the issue up unexpectedly. I'm persuaded they were not part of a deliberate attempt to seek out opportunities, but they drew such enormous attention and acclaim – especially from the right. That was useful. It gave the President manoeuvring room.[26]

Human rights improved America's self-image, and engineered consensus where none had existed before. Its beauty was that it was all things to all people.

Those on the left embraced the issue as a harbinger of progressive change, while those on the right saw it as a return to core values. And both believed that the USA was the keeper of the flame. In effect, they subscribed to the latest version of American exceptionalism. Indeed, Carter had referred to this ideal when he stated in his inaugural address:

> Ours was the first society openly to define itself in terms of both spirituality and of human liberty. It is that unique self-definition which has given us an exceptional appeal, but it also imposes on us a special obligation, to take on those moral duties which, when assumed, seem invariably to be in our own best interests.[27]

Many in the administration were inclined to view human rights in fairly conservative terms, and so, apparently, were many citizens. Carter's chief of staff, Hamilton Jordan, acknowledged the issue's traditionalist appeal in a memo to the President when he wrote that, 'Of our numerous foreign policy initiatives, it is the only one that has a broad base of support among the American people and is not considered "liberal"'. Consequently, they used it to sugar the pill of less popular initiatives – especially the Strategic Arms Limitation Treaty (SALT) with the Soviet Union, which was opposed by many on the right. 'With Panama and SALT II ahead of us, we need the broad-based, non-ideological support for our foreign policy that human rights provides', Jordan noted. Thinking along the same lines, National Security Advisor Zbigniew Brzezinski and public liaison official Anne Wexler later recommended that Carter hold a 'White House event on human rights' in order to 'offset the emphasis that will be placed on SALT'.[28]

The magic wore off when human rights was overtaken by concerns about inflation and the price of gasoline.[29] But that did not matter, because the campaign had already served its purpose – washing away the stench of dirty wars and dirty linen, and restoring the credibility and resolve of the elite. Some politicians got a new lease of life: Vietnam-era retreads like Cyrus Vance, former Secretary of the Army, and Zbigniew Brzezinski, formerly of the State Department's Policy Planning Council, slotted straight back into power. More importantly, morale picked up in ruling circles. After the long horror of Vietnam, the unconscionable revelations about Chile, and the self-disgust engendered by Watergate; human rights restored their *esprit de corps* and appetite for leadership.[30] When Carter's aides spoke of losing the underpinnings of '*our* government' and finding '*our* bearings', it is apparent that as well as searching for solutions to the problems that faced America, they were also finding the solutions to the problems that faced the Americans who ran America.[31]

*   *   *

Trouble started when the State Department tried to turn political oratory into working diplomacy. The administration had some hazy notions of reclaiming the moral high ground internationally, and strengthening relations with progressive elements in the Third World. But there was no clear directive from the White House on how to proceed, and many officials were not persuaded that public castigation was more effective than traditional 'quiet diplomacy'. Although senior people were keen to show that they were 'on board' during the first months of the government,[32] the policy received a more critical reception on the regional desks and in embassies abroad. Stanley Heginbotham, Foreign Affairs Division chief of the Congressional Research Service, testified that there was only 'a relatively thin layer of support' for it in the department, and that there was often 'strong opposition' at the working levels.[33] As the senior Democrat Arthur Schlesinger put it: 'Had the new President confided the idea to the State Department for analysis, there very likely would have been no human rights campaign at all.'[34]

In the seventies, many diplomats were professionally immune to the charms of human rights. 'Taken in a foreign minister's baggage on a world tour, they might, as I once heard one of them say, spoil the whole trip', wrote the historian, R.J. Vincent.[35] Diplomacy is, above all, about communication – and communication means accommodation, often with those less fastidious about civil liberties than one might wish. Within the global 'freemasonry of diplomacy', as Vincent calls it,[36] everybody from the loftiest ambassador to the lowliest third secretary seeks the common ground. The embassy's guest-books and the high commission's framed photographs of His or Her Excellency shaking hands with the Minister and toasting the General are testimony to a *modus operandi* of glad-handing and keeping the channels open. Morality was generally left to its own devices, lending credence to the old Foggy Bottom saw: 'The bureaucrat is seldom seen, without a pen – or with a dream.'[37]

In marked contrast to this ethos, human rights advocacy breeds discord. At the very least, it causes defensiveness and embarrassment. At worst, such advocacy threatens important interests such as trade pledges and arms deals, security alliances and credit arrangements, landing rights and sea lanes. And even if one government persuades another to release prisoners or commute sentences, little kudos is gained, because publicising a success usually alienates the transgressor. As Vincent observed:

> The foreign policy professionals are not then excited about human rights. They might favour them in principle, but shrink from dealing with practical cases of their violation. They prefer standard-setting. They are happier that this is done in multilateral rather then bilateral diplomacy. . . . When forced to take up a particular case, they prefer acting behind closed doors to conducting

it in public, and they place great stress on the efficacy of 'quiet diplomacy', making use of their professional skills to go to the limits of the possible.[38]

When Carter promised to place human rights at the heart of his foreign policy, he was not viewing the issue through a diplomat's eyes. Murmurs of dissent were soon heard in the State Department. There were fears that public denunciations might upset allies and squander years of quiet endeavour. In 1977, the Assistant Secretary for Inter-American Affairs warned that aid cuts to Argentina and Uruguay would 'produce widespread resentment and alienation', thus wasting efforts 'dating back to and beyond the Second World War'.[39] Others grumbled that they didn't want to 'have their clients beat up on'.[40] At Foreign Service Institute training courses, some officers dubbed the policy 'moral imperialism'; and others thought it would be harmful to more important goals.[41] This scepticism was echoed in wider political circles. After Congress banned military credit to Brazil on human rights grounds, the conservative Roger Fontaine, who later served under Reagan, began a *Foreign Policy* opinion piece with the words: 'The dust has begun to settle, and in the distant haze I see the smoking ruin of a special relationship.'[42]

Diplomats occasionally flatly refused to play the human rights game. When Malcolm Toon, the US Ambassador in Moscow, was asked why he had not invited the dissident Andrei Sakharov to the embassy's 1978 Fourth of July reception, he retorted: 'My job is to get along with the Soviet government.'[43] Others obeyed the letter but not the spirit of their instructions by appointing unsuitable personnel as human rights officers (it was suspected that some were CIA operatives working under new cover[44]). Even the majority, who suppressed their qualms and got on with the job nevertheless harboured doubts about the durability of the policy. One observer wrote that the issue was not conveyed as a 'serious matter of concern' abroad because many officers saw it as 'a fad'.[45]

The administration soon realised that if human rights diplomacy was going to make its mark, the machinery needed to be strengthened. Carter appointed the former Mississippi civil rights activist, Patricia Derian, to spearhead the policy. She was soon promoted to Assistant Secretary for Human Rights and Humanitarian Affairs, and her office was upgraded to a bureau, with a staff of about twenty. But despite this enhanced status, there was no disguising that fact that her operation was pretty small beer. Its budget was minuscule, and it had to battle for amenities taken for granted by other desks, such as access to diplomatic cable traffic. As soon as it tried to make its voice heard above competing trade, defence and political interests it became embroiled in what one official described as 'bureaucratic warfare of the most intense sort'.[46] To remedy this, the Christopher Group, run by Deputy Secretary Warren Christopher, was set up to mediate in disputes and coordinate strategy across the various departments (State, Defense, the National Security Council and others).

Patricia Derian pursued her job with commitment and aggression. She told officials that 'if they wanted a magnolia' to decorate foreign policy, 'they should get someone else'.[47] She was a trenchant critic of 'clientitus' and she excoriated officials who counselled support for dictators (the Shah's supporters within the bureaucracy were denounced as 'retrogressive fascists'[48]). In 1980, she took on Jeane Kirkpatrick, the doyenne of Reaganite foreign policy. 'What the hell is "moderately repressive,"' she demanded to know from her, 'that you only torture half the people, and that you only do summary executions now and then?'[49] Detractors denounced Derian's abrasiveness, which was undeniable, and her amateurishness, which was probably unfair (in public she toed the party line like a true pro).

Clashes between her bureau and others were inevitable, and there were plenty, especially in the first years of the administration. As well as meeting resistance from the State Department's desks dealing with Latin America, East Asia, and Africa, Derian's fledgling outfit also managed to cross swords with those dealing with West Europe, business matters, and politico-military affairs. (An officer from the latter 'cursed with considerable vigor' when asked about the Human Rights Bureau, an observer recorded.[50]) Brian Atwood, a former staffer, recalled,

> [W]e were trying to establish human rights and the realm of law as something we ought to be hearing about. There was perhaps no larger battle than the one that was fought in the bureaucracy. And I want to tell you that it was quite vicious.[51]

Derian's cause was not helped by the fact that the policy was widely perceived within the bureaucracy as being incoherent and *ad hoc*. The administration made little attempt to codify it, and, to make matters worse, the inter-departmental Christopher Group judged each case on its merits rather than against predetermined principle. This confusion enabled opponents to resist her bureau's blandishments.

Terence Todman's Latin America Bureau, which aimed to maintain workable relations with the juntas, was one notable antagonist. Derian's staff was especially disquieted by its propensity to minimise repression in client states in order to evade human rights sanctions. Stephen Cohen, one of Derian's deputies, related how it tried to play down the scale of 'disappearances' in Argentina:

> [They] argued that, at most, hundreds of individuals had been summarily executed by security forces. As the evidence became incontrovertible that the

number was actually 6,500 or more, the bureau shifted gears and argued that only Marxist terrorists were the victims. When it was documented that most of the victims were neither Marxists nor terrorists, the bureau maintained that the abuses were the work of local military commanders whom the ruling junta was struggling to control.[52]

Arms exports to Latin America were another flashpoint. In May 1977, the two bureaux went head to head over whether the US company Colt should be allowed to export replacement M–16 rifle sling swivels (connecting sling to rifle) to the Nicaraguan National Guard. When Derian and Mark Schneider pointed to reports of its brutality, Wade Matthews of the Latin America Bureau criticised them for peddling 'feel good' symbolism. On that occasion, the Christopher Group ruled in Derian's favour, but not for human rights reasons: the National Guard could do without their new sling swivels because at the time, they seemed to be holding the line against the Sandinistas.[53]

Meanwhile, Terence Todman did his best to maintain cordial relations with client regimes in Latin America. On a visit to the Dominican Republic in late 1977, he claimed that the State Department was encouraged by 'recent evidence that the [regional] trend away from democracy may be ending' and cited General Pinochet's vague promise of reform in Chile.[54] And in El Salvador in early 1978, Todman offered succour to the authorities when he said that 'terrorism and subversion are the major problems confronting the people of Latin America'.[55] The Human Rights Bureau, along with liberal Congressmen and NGOs, were infuriated by such pronouncements, and mounted a campaign to have Todman removed from his post. He dug his own grave in February 1978 when he publicly aired his misgivings about the stress on human rights. 'We must avoid holding entire countries up to public ridicule', he said, and stop 'believing that only the opposition speaks the truth'.[56] He was clearly out of step with the administration's thinking, and was soon given a new post in Spain.

There were also bruising confrontations between the Human Rights Bureau and Richard Holbrooke's East Asia Bureau. One official described relations between the two as hardly better than chaotic during 1977, and still with 'many rough edges remaining', during 1978.[57] The latter's attempts to conceal repression in Asian states aggravated Derian's staff. Stephen Cohen recalled, for example, how it claimed that reports of abuses in East Timor were grossly exaggerated, despite evidence that 100,000 or more Timorese had died at the hands of the Indonesian Army. When such white-washing over-stretched credulity, the East Asia Bureau fell back on the argument that American security interests would be damaged by human rights measures. Thus, it once proposed that instead of condemning

President Marcos's brutality, Washington should *treble* military aid to the Philippines to preserve its Clark and Subic Bay military bases.[58]

The tensions created by the policy were occasionally replicated in diplomatic posts abroad. The conflict that took place within the walls of the US Embassy in Buenos Aires in 1977, at the height of the 'dirty war', was a case in point. In February, Cyrus Vance announced that he intended to halve Argentina's security assistance programme for human rights reasons. General Jorge Rafael Videla's government responded that it had no intention of accepting aid under that programme anyway. Meanwhile, the embassy became the site of a clash between Allen 'Tex' Harris, a political officer appointed to report back to Washington on government abuses, and Ambassador Raul Castro.

Prior to Harris's arrival in Buenos Aires, diplomats had turned a blind eye to the fate of 'the disappeared' – those Argentines kidnapped and usually murdered by the junta. The journalist, Iain Guest, reported that

> There was only one entrance into the embassy compound, and it resembled a round piece of cheddar cheese with a slice cut out of it. That was as far as the distraught relatives got before they were turned away. The official policy was to 'cut 'em off at the cheese.'[59]

Tex Harris, now president of the American Foreign Service Association, reversed this policy by welcoming those with grievances, and using the information he received to build up damning dossiers on the disappearances. 'At first, my telling of this story to the US government was applauded by embassy personnel, from Ambassador Raul Castro on down.' But their attitude changed when it became apparent, Harris claimed, that US actions towards Argentina were 'no longer to be based on Ambassador Castro's recommendations, but on the behavior of the Argentine government'. This was overstating the case – otherwise, why maintain diplomats on the ground? – but Castro doubtless felt squeezed by the new orthodoxy emanating from Washington.

Sparks really began to fly when senior staff tried to water down and delay Harris's reports back to Washington. 'A classic battle began with the front office trying to put a more favourable "spin" on my human rights reporting', he recounted:

> As it became more difficult to report the full details of human rights abuses in diplomatic telegrams, I used airgrams, memoranda of conversations and official-informal letters – none of which required front-office clearance – to send the facts to Washington by classified air pouch. My major confrontation with senior embassy officials came when one of my letters, which had been copied to Ambassador Castro, was withdrawn from the diplomatic pouch, and I was requested not to send it. The information in that letter resulted in

the cancellation of a multi-million-dollar US government loan guarantee to a major American corporation to provide turbine technology to a front corporation owned by the Argentine Navy.[60]

Harris says he was nearly fired for insubordination. But the culture within the diplomatic service was beginning to change.

*   *   *

The problems over human rights decreased in the second half of the Carter presidency, when the warring parties were forced to reassess their priorities. The bureaucracy evolved clearer working principles, advocating rights where it would be advantageous, and delineating areas where they would not considered. (Countries understood to be off limits on security grounds included China, South Korea, Taiwan, Vietnam, Saudi Arabia, Egypt and Israel.) As a result, Stanley Heginbotham observed, the Bureau's focus became 'somewhat narrowed'.[61] Yet at the same time, many officials began to get a glimmering of the benefits to be derived from a 'moral' foreign policy. Indeed, as time passed, human rights advocacy began to yield up dividends – some foreseen, other unexpected – which dissolved antipathy among officials, and guaranteed this apparent flash in the pan issue a permanent place in the day-to-day conduct of American diplomacy.

Human rights provided Washington with a medium through which to renegotiate its relations with the Third World, and engage in a more nuanced form of containment. In previous decades, the State Department, Defense, the National Security Council, the CIA and other agencies were preoccupied by the threat of radical insurgency in Asia, Africa, the Middle East and Latin America. They thus operated according to doctrines that prioritised relationships with ruling parties capable of maintaining stability (and developing market-based economies). With the relaxation of the Cold War and the retreat of radical forces, America's apprehension about revolutionary guerrillas dimmed, and its interest in cultivating less repressive regimes increased. Donald Fraser's agitation in Congress signalled the new tack: why support brutal autocracies, losing one's own credibility in the process, when one could make overtures to more popular, non-revolutionary democratic forces?

The State Department was too slow off the mark to shape the opposition movements in Nicaragua and Iran. (In fact, they had no prior contacts with either the Sandinistas or Ayatollah Khomeini, and had to build relationships, such as they were, from scratch.) Determined not to repeat this mistake elsewhere, it overcame its initial reluctance to sour relations with client regimes, and began to put out feelers to opposition parties under the cover of human rights. The aim was to identify with the forces for change, said Secretary Cyrus Vance, 'for those who identify with it will be able to influence its direction'.[62] This strategy soon began to produce positive results. As the Carter-era official Richard Feinberg pointed out in 1981,

> The human rights policy permitted US Embassy officials to associate with opposition elements, for it was their rights that were being monitored. The United States could thereby collect information on a wide range of political factions, while establishing better relations with them. Had these forces come to power . . . the United States should be able to avoid the diplomatic disruptions that can accompany governmental changes.[63]

Another factor that contributed to the change in diplomatic practice was the law, initiated by Congress, which compelled the State Department to produce the annual *Country Reports* on human rights. The first, produced under Ford, covered eighty-two countries, all receiving US aid; after 1979 they were extended to every country bar one – the USA.[64] They invariably made a big splash in Washington: their 'major value', reported Stanley Heginbotham in 1979, 'is not in their utility for foreign assistance policymaking, but rather in the contribution to public and government awareness of human rights problems'.[65] However, as time passed, the requirement to collect information about abuse began to impinge on embassy activity. Officials who may once have been more used to back-slapping government officials at cocktail parties were now compelled to study *samizdats* and cultivate dissidents. The change was most apparent in places where the United States had formerly maintained exclusive relations with the ruling elite, such as Latin America's Southern Cone nations. But it also had an effect in places where contact with the opposition was expected, such as in the Eastern Bloc countries. The academic Charles Gati observed in 1978 that

> While it is true that in the past the Embassy in Warsaw maintained contact with Cardinal Wyszynski of the Catholic Church and other critics . . . these contacts have increased in recent years. While in the past the standard procedure, as I understand it, used to be that opposition elements had to seek out our people in the East European capitals, now it is mutual. . . . So I would say that here is a difference in attitude, yes.[66]

By opening lines of communication with dissidents, the United States was able to exert even greater leverage over foreign regimes. Or, as a 1978 State Department pamphlet coyly explained, contacts with opposition leaders could 'be used to send signals' to ruling parties.[67] Incumbents could no longer assume that they were necessarily Washington's favoured friends. Indeed, America could, and did, demand all kinds of concessions in the name of human rights – even changes of government. When Richard

Holbrooke (who later served as Clinton's UN Ambassador) admonished those who 'sought to . . . undermine governments and change regimes',[68] Mark Schneider of the Human Rights Bureau responded that they were indeed 'pressing to try and see democratic governments and respect for human rights become the norm'.[69] This 'pressing' included decisive interventions in Bolivia and the Dominican Republic, where Washington threatened to terminate aid unless election results were honoured; and in Nicaragua, where it cancelled aid when General Somoza refused mediation in his war against the Sandinistas.

Since then, diplomats have routinely made contact with forces agitating for change. In 1990, for example, the *New York Times*'s Barbara Crossette observed that after a bloody interlude in the war over Kashmir, a beleaguered civil rights group told her that only one diplomat had made the effort to contact them. That diplomat was an American.[70]

*   *   *

Carter abandoned his human rights campaign just as officials were starting to find their feet. The most active phase lasted just a few months – essentially, the honeymoon period of his presidency. Then, for the next eighteen months or so, the administration adopted a more cautious approach. The first indication that the President was cooling down on the issue came in March 1977, just two months after his inauguration. Powerful forces in Congress were troubled by his bullish criticisms of the Soviet Union in the run-up to the strategic arms limitation talks – his main peacemaking aim. So too were senior State Department officials, who advised Cyrus Vance to ease off. To this end, a proposed meeting between Carter and the Soviet dissident Vladimir Bukovsky was slightly delayed – a signal that the White House was backing off without exactly backing down. And he did not reply to a second letter from Andrei Sakharov. But the Soviets were not appeased. When Vance travelled to Moscow, President Leonid Brezhnev made it plain that the SALT II talks were going nowhere until Washington stopped meddling in their domestic affairs.

Faced with a restless Congress and an intransigent Soviet leadership, the administration changed tack. From summer 1977 onwards, it confined its attacks on the Eastern Bloc to the 'Helsinki' negotiations at Belgrade, while shining the big spotlight on the Latin American nations – countries more susceptible to pressure. Still in upbeat mood, it initially claimed that it would improve the human rights situation there by the judicious manipulation of aid. Domestic lobbies reserved their judgement. But the few sanctions that were imposed did not produce the required dramatic changes. The aid involved was small, and the diplomatic costs were high. The affronted governments of Argentina, Brazil, El Salvador, Guatemala and Uruguay all told Washington to keep their hand-outs, and found alternative supplies of arms, development funds and credit, if not from Europe and Israel, then from other US sources. So in 1978 the administration changed direction once more. It stopped talking about halting abuse, and started talking about the need to distance itself from dictatorships. Analyst Lars Schoultz observed that a new buzzword – 'disassociation' – became one of the most frequently used words in the lexicon of human rights officials.[71] This retreat to a policy devoted to brightening America's halo seemed to confirm the self-serving nature of the enterprise.

Public disillusion soon set in. Critics took their first proper bite out of Carter in April 1977 after Congress proposed a bill calling on the United States to use its 'voice and vote' against loans to human rights abusers by international financial institutions. The White House opposed it. And it opposed it for the same reason that Kissinger had once opposed similar motions – because it tied the government's hands. '[W]e have enough law to do what we want to do', said Mark Schneider of the Human Rights Bureau.[72] The journalist Elizabeth Drew listed representatives' reasons for backing the bill against the President, and in the process, illustrated how human rights concerns were driven by self-interest in the legislature as well as the executive. Carter's opponents included:

> liberals dedicated to the cause of human rights and suspicious of the Administration's requests for flexibility, people who wanted to hoist Jimmy Carter on his own rhetoric, people who wanted to strike a pose, people who . . . hadn't thought about it much one way or the other, conservatives (including some on the far right) who are opposed to any form of foreign aid, a few Democrats who represent districts where organized labor is particularly strong and who fear that foreign assistance leads to low-wage imports, and representatives (mainly from the South and the Southwest) who were seeking protection against the importation of palm oil, sugar, or citrus fruits.[73]

After that, the pundits took the line that not much had changed since the bad old days 'BC' (Before Carter). In the years that followed, they queued up to attack the administration for its bad faith and double standards.

Pointing out the inconsistencies in the campaign became a popular pastime in newspapers and on current affairs shows. Each pundit had his or her own axe to grind, obviously. Some accused the administration of attacking the USSR or Chile too much; others, too little. But the overall message – that it was deploying human rights for its own political or economic purposes – came over loud and clear. 'Washington was fearless in denouncing human rights abuses in countries like Cambodia, Paraguay and Uganda, where the United States has negligible strategic and economic interests,' wrote Arthur Schlesinger, but 'a good deal less fearless toward South Korea, Saudi Arabia, Yugoslavia and most of black Africa; increasingly circumspect about the Soviet Union; totally silent about

China.'[74] The USA's policy of flooding oil-rich Iran with arms while cutting security assistance to dirt-poor Nicaragua prompted one wit to quip that nothing would change until American cars 'run on bananas'.[75]

When the administration switched attention to Latin America, most critics concurred that Carter's policy was designed to target the weak – or, as one Congressman put it, 'to kick midgets'.[76] It 'runs the risk of dividing the world into two categories: countries unimportant enough to be hectored about human rights and countries important enough to get away with murder', wrote one commentator.[77] Among those unimportant enough to be hectored about human rights were the United States's client states in Central America, such as El Salvador, Nicaragua and Guatemala. Among those important enough to get away with murder were pillars of American influence abroad, such as Iran, Indonesia and Israel, which remained largely untouched by human rights advocacy, regardless of how many inhabitants lost their lives or their liberty.

Critics also noted that the administration paid lip service, but little more, to the human rights laws enacted by Congress in the period 1974 to 1978. Echoing the view of many advocates, Jo Marie Greisgraber of the Washington Office on Latin America argued that the government had 'acted against the intent of the human rights legislation . . . by stretching loopholes beyond any common sense definition'.[78] In 1982, former bureau official Stephen Cohen penned an article that confirmed what Greisgraber and others had long asserted. Referring specifically to the implementation of Section 502B, the law which banned security assistance to repressive governments, he wrote that the administration

> exhibited a remarkable degree of tentativeness and caution, so that its pursuit of human rights goals was anything but 'single-minded'. . . . Moreover, in some instances, the Carter administration adopted a highly strained reading of the statute which, although not contrary to its literal terms, produced a result contrary to congressional intent. In other cases, the language was simply disregarded, so that decisions violated even the letter of the law.[79]

In a later study, the human rights analyst David Forsythe pointed out that 'even within the Department of State it was not completely clear how section 502B affected executive decisions', and that it was at times 'largely ignored'.[80] The Harkin amendment barring economic assistance to violators fared slightly better: the administration 'occasionally reduced some aid levels . . . [but] did not make these decisions public'.[81] Section 701 dealing with loans by international bodies to violators was upheld, but although the administration either voted against, or abstained on, loan proposals on human rights grounds in the International Monetary Fund or World Bank, all these loans were nevertheless 'eventually approved'.[82]

Carter's campaign was not all posturing, however. There were practical consequences. The administration stopped military aid to Argentina, Bolivia, El Salvador, Guatemala, Haiti, Nicaragua, Paraguay and Uruguay (all Latin American countries, incidentally), and it reduced economic assistance to Thailand, Afghanistan and Morocco – ostensibly for human rights reasons. One might have expected the government to publicise the results of these initiatives, and to capitalise on its achievements. Yet it was surprisingly bashful about the whole thing. While there was plenty of talk about its *efforts* to promote human rights abroad, there was strikingly little analysis of the *effects* of those policies.

At a 1980 hearing, Patricia Derian was uncharacteristically coy about the effects of the policies she espoused. When Stephen Solarz, the chairman of the House Subcommittee on Africa, pressed her to point to 'specific successes', she demurred. '[U]ltimately it is not the United States that brings change in other countries,' she said, 'change comes from within.' Solarz persisted, asking her to list places where 'our actions contributed significantly' to improvements in human rights. She eventually promised to submit this information in writing after the hearing was over – the classic evasion tactic employed by officials under pressure. Predictably, the requested list, compiled at leisure by Derian's staff, carried the disclaimer that the examples given 'are not necessarily attributed to US actions' – thus failing to answer the question that the Congressman had been asking.[83]

Solarz's grilling seems to have rankled because Derian returned to the theme the following month, in a speech before the American Association of University Women at Milwaukee. She said:

> It is hard to take credit for the release of political prisoners, the disappearances that didn't happen, or the would-be refugee who remained at home when freedom was increased. . . . None of us unlocks jails, rewrites laws, or changes practices and traditions anywhere but in out own country. The people on the spot take care of that. So we don't say, 'Attention world, the United States has just achieved a marvellous human rights coup.' It is not the intention of this effort to make us look good. It is not a publicity gimmick or a public relations trick. What it is is an honest humanitarian effort.[84]

The influential House Democrat Dante Fascell was not persuaded by such arguments. A year after this speech, he complained that 'regular, periodic *assessment of results* . . . was lacking in the Carter administration, and made the [human rights] policy unnecessarily vulnerable to criticism'.[85] The latter point reveals Fascell's real interest. He was not primarily concerned in this instance about assessing results in order to curb repression abroad. Rather, he suggests that this failure strengthened the hand of opponents at home. As always, domestic politics ruled.

When the cost became too great, Carter discarded human rights. His noisier diplomatic forays had won few friends abroad, and he was haemorrhaging support on the Hill, where it really hurt. Some lobbies echoed the Commerce Department's line that the policy was thwarting trade and discouraging business; others echoed the Defense Department's line that it was under-cutting important security relationships in a hostile world. All this was nonsense, of course – Carter had sacrificed neither trade nor security to human rights. But it was widely believed to be true, and that, ultimately, was what counted. By the time the Soviets had invaded Afghanistan, the President had abandoned the issue and returned to the unembellished rhetoric of the Cold War.

*   *   *

The long-running feud between Patricia Derian and Richard Holbrooke, Assistant Secretary for East Asia, finally spilled out into the open in 1982, nearly two years after Carter had been ejected from power. Holbrooke threw down the gauntlet during a House Subcommittee hearing on Asia. He argued that when Carter chose to give prominence to human rights,

> some within his bureaucracy interpreted this as a licence to preach publicly or seek to use American pressure to change governments. In the name of human rights, a small but vocal group of people now sought to carry out far-reaching changes in the world structure. Ironically, these same people had been overwhelmingly opposed to our intervention in Vietnam, yet they now advocated deep intervention in the internal affairs of other governments.

This group was arrogant, Holbrooke contended, and highly selective in its moral focus. 'Since their targets were almost without exception regimes of the right which happened to be anti-Soviet,' he claimed, 'it was inevitable that their efforts would in turn become the target of a counter-attack from the right, who accused the entire Carter Administration of seeking to appease the left and abandon old friends.' This group had not only done 'great damage' to the cause of human rights,[86] but – his denouement – they had sought to 'wreck our foreign policy'.[87]

The response from the equally combative Patricia Derian was awaited with keen interest. When she testified at a follow-up hearing a few months later, few were disappointed. After ten long minutes spent assessing human rights diplomacy, she finally rose to Holbrooke's bait. '[I]t is necessary for me to set the record straight in response to a thinly veiled and sleazy attack by a former Carter administration official on "some within the bureaucracy" who were unfortunately his colleagues', she began. She went on to repudiate Holbrooke's 'falsely stated' contention that her bureau had only targeted right-wing regimes. Then she attacked Holbrooke for refusing to speak out about repression in East Asia:

> Efforts to extend the work for human rights improvement to the Communist Government of the People's Republic of China and the right wing Government of Taiwan were stymied time and again by the person who testified that 'we could not, and did not, raise Western concepts such as due process of law' with them. Set to music, the courtship of the People's Republic of China, then and now, is 'Home on the Range' – 'where never is heard a discouraging word'.[88]

Derian was giving as good as she had got, and representatives were eager for more. Jim Leach, a Republican member, tried to draw her out further.

> *Mr Leach:* I must say, though, that I am awfully intrigued with your statement, Ms Derian, partly because I think all of us have an instinct in us that likes gossip. You have certainly la[i]d out some of the dirty linen on the Carter administration. I guess what I would like to ask you is, if Richard Holbrooke's views are so pernicious, how could you conceivably have served under a President who would have named such a villain to high office?
> *Ms Derian:* I assume, Mr Leach, that that is a rhetorical question . . .[89]

This vintage performance by two former officials was a fitting finale to the battle that had raged behind the scenes throughout the Carter administration. But by now, there was a new President, intent on bending human rights to the exigencies of the Second Cold War.

SEVEN

Cold War II

'We are not, as some would have us believe, doomed to an inevitable decline', Ronald Reagan declared at his inauguration, 'We have every right to dream heroic dreams.'[1] The new President believed that the smack of power, rather than the balm of rights, was the cure for America's post-Vietnam malaise. The Cold War was waxing, and the old anti-communist dictators were welcomed back to Washington. Then he appointed Ernest Lefever – an academic who believed the USA had no business exporting human rights – as new chief of the Human Rights Bureau. It was a deliberately provocative move, and it misfired spectacularly.

The irascible Lefever was a conservative Democrat who had opposed Carter's human rights policy, and favored traditional 'quiet diplomacy' for dealing with repression. A pacifist in his early years, he embraced militant anti-communism after seeing first-hand the 'evil of Soviet communism' in Europe.[2] In the seventies, he set up the Ethics and Public Policy Center, a think-tank dedicated to buttressing the 'Judeo-Christian moral tradition' in public affairs, and restoring cordial relations with anti-communist regimes. Human rights advocates were appalled by his appointment, and when his nomination hearing opened before the Senate Foreign Relations Committee on 18 May 1981, the room was packed to the rafters.

The four-day examination was predictably rancorous. Lefever made little attempt to ingratiate himself with those Senators who did not support his nomination; nor they with him. One of the first contentious issues to be raised was his proposal, delivered in testimony a few years earlier, that the United States should delete from its statute book all human rights laws directed at other governments. This comment returned to haunt him, whereupon he claimed that he had changed his mind:

> When I made that broad statement, I goofed. I have made this goof known three months ago, but like in *Romeo and Juliet*, bad news travels faster than good news, and the good news has apparently not caught up with it yet. It is my fervent intention to observe the law of the land.

The tone of his comments jarred, and few were convinced by his apparent change of heart. The Republican chairman, Charles Percy (who personally favoured a moral component in foreign policy), voiced the scepticism of almost everyone in the room, when he posed the rhetorical question: '[H]ave you changed your position, Dr Lefever, because you are up for nomination to the position of Assistant Secretary for Human Rights?'[3]

The Senators also homed in on his relations with the South African government. The press had already suggested that he and his think-tank had received money from a body associated with the Pretoria regime to disseminate favourable propaganda on its behalf. Lefever admitted that he had helped to organise a conference in Washington for the Foreign Affairs Association of South Africa, and that he had been paid to make two speeches, but he denied that he had known that the body was connected to the government. Some Senators may have suspected that he was not telling the whole truth about this, especially after the Democrat Paul Tsongas persuaded him to recall that he had also provided a cuttings service for the same body.[4] Whatever his financial relationship with the South Africans, Lefever was on record as holding views that accorded with those of the regime. As the Democrat Senator Claiborne Pell later commented,

> How can he be credible on apartheid in South Africa, when he has stated that
> – It would be impossible for sophisticated, industrialized white South Africa
> to integrate culturally and politically 10 million largely illiterate Bantu
> without catastrophic consequences?[5]

Many people had protested against Lefever's nomination, but two in particular did him serious damage. One was his brother Donald, a 57-year-old religious pacifist living in Minneapolis, who told the press that Ernest was the wrong man for the job. The *Washington Post* reported that,

> Donald said his basic concern is that the policies of his brother in supporting
> authoritarian regimes in Latin America and elsewhere will tend to repress
> human freedom for many people. He said he rejected the argument that
> authoritarian regimes, unlike totalitarian ones, are only 'moderately
> repressive'. He finally stated, 'If I were nominated for Secretary of Defence, I
> would expect and hope in all good conscience that Ernest would oppose me.'

Lefever retorted that his brother was 'misinformed if he does not realize that I am not enchanted with repressive regimes', but the evidence suggesting links with Pretoria undermined the credibility of this claim.[6]

The other person who contributed to his misfortunes was Jacobo Timerman, a newspaperman who had been imprisoned and tortured by the Argentine junta, and whose release had been secured with the help of Patricia Derian. A week before the hearing, Timerman's book *Prisoner Without a Name, Cell Without a Number* was published in America. Shortly after, the author denounced Lefever's hands-off approach to abuse and warned that he would 'change the title of Assistant Secretary for

Human Rights into Assistant Secretary for Soviet Insults'.[7] Paul Tsongas and Claiborne Pell used Timerman to force Lefever on the defensive. On one occasion Tsongas read an horrific passage from the book about the experience of electroshock torture. Another time, Pell asked him whether he thought the job entailed making personal missions on behalf of political prisoners. Lefever, insensitive to the mood of the hearing, tried to score a political point:

> Senator Pell, I have no desire to be looked upon as a saint or a missionary. I believe my job is rather to help sensitize the entire foreign policy establishment to the concern for human rights rather than play a Sir Galahad role going around the world on personal missions.[8]

During this affair, Robert Bernstein, head of publishers Random House and chair of human rights group Helsinki Watch, hosted a dinner in Washington in Timerman's honour. Tsongas and Pell attended, as did House campaigners Tom Harkin and Don Bonker. According to press accounts, Bernstein, who was due to testify against Lefever the following day, asked Tsongas to find Timerman a seat at the hearing. This was a clever move. By simply sitting silently in the audience, Timerman offered a dramatic rebuke to Lefever's credo (and an irresistible news hook). When Tsongas announced Timerman's presence in the room, chairman Charles Percy contributed to Lefever's mortification by inviting the writer to stand up, which he did, to rapturous applause. Under hearing rules, Timerman was not allowed to speak, but his presence spoke volumes. Afterwards, he held an impromptu press conference in the corridor, where he told reporters that 'quiet diplomacy is surrender'.[9]

After four days, the Republican-dominated Foreign Relations Committee voted down Lefever's nomination by an emphatic thirteen to four: proof, if it was still needed, that rights appealed to conservatives as much as to liberals. The vote was seen as Reagan's first foreign policy reversal. Nearly two decades after the event, Lefever still blames the 'hard left' for his defeat. 'I was a victim of the anti-anti-communism', he claimed in 1998, 'I became the fall guy for the Reagan revolution.'[10] The right-wing academic, Joshua Muravchik, wrote: 'it is hard to avoid the conclusion that . . . President Carter had wrought a lasting change. . . . As the Reagan administration learned the hard way, the idea that the promotion of human rights throughout the world should be an important US goal had taken hold.'[11]

*   *   *

After that fiasco, the administration twisted and turned, trying to shake loose the binds of the Congressionally mandated policy. Conservative Democrat Jeane Kirkpatrick offered one approach to the problem. In a 1979 *Commentary* article 'Dictatorships and Double Standards' – which, incidentally, landed her the job of Reagan's UN Ambassador – she argued that Carter's campaign had punished redeemable 'authoritarian' friends while leaving unscathed intractable 'totalitarian' foes. She later urged the Republicans to turn the screws on the Eastern Bloc while relaxing the pressure on anti-communist allies. (A cartoon of the time showed Reagan proclaiming: 'Look . . . if you can't push human rights in every country, why pick on the fascists?'[12]) But Kirkpatrick's thesis was all too reminiscent of Lefever's approach. Congress bought the anti-Sovietism, but not the pro-junta arguments. The administration needed a more nuanced, and morally convincing approach.

In October 1981, an 'eyes only' memo from top State Department officials William Clark and Richard Kennedy to Secretary Alexander Haig was carefully leaked to the press. It began: 'Human rights is at the core of our foreign policy because it is central to what America is and stands for' – a statement that made advocates sit up and take note.[13] But it also indicated that this change of heart was motivated by expediency. It warned that the issue was 'one of the main avenues for domestic attack' on the administration.[14] Furthermore, 'Congressional belief that we have no consistent human rights policy threatens to disrupt important policy initiatives'.[15] (This echoed Robert Ingersoll in the Kissinger years, who had cynically stressed the importance of being 'ahead of the curve' where Congress was concerned.[16])

The memo was written by Elliott Abrams, the ambitious 33-year-old Assistant Secretary for International Organization Affairs, who, like Lefever and Kirkpatrick, had joined the Republicans from the Democratic Party. He argued that the government should take up human rights to placate domestic critics because (as he stressed, in italics): '*We will never maintain wide public support for our foreign policy unless we can relate it to American ideals and to the defence of freedom.*'[17] Instead of fighting the issue, the administration should co-opt it for Cold War ends:

> While we need a military response to the Soviets to reassure our friends and allies, we also need an ideological response. . . . We desire to demonstrate, by acting to defend liberty and identifying its enemies, that the difference between East and West is a crucial policy distinction of our times.[18]

The White House heeded this advice, and began to construct what Abrams later dubbed 'a "Republican" human rights policy'.[19] As the *New York Times*'s Tamar Jacoby noted, 'It was a brilliant strategy, no more the half cynical, and it almost worked':

> For one thing, it allowed the Administration to strike a pose that was at once assertively moralistic – a quality Kirkpatrick much distrusted – and staunchly

anti-communist. For the President, this was a congenial combination, a welcome release from the cold and calculating Kirkpatrick doctrine. What took the Administration by surprise was just how congenial the new policy also turned out to be to the American people.[20]

As well as proposing a new strategy, Abrams also put himself forward as chief of the Human Rights Bureau. A week later he got the job. His nomination hearing lasted just an hour and a half. The Senators, who had no stomach for another showdown with the President, handled him with kid gloves. In turn, he told Senators what they wanted to hear. When one of them mentioned Jacobo Timerman's book, he agreed that the situation in Argentina was indeed 'terrible and harrowing'.[21]

Yet, in retrospect, the most striking thing about Abrams's testimony was his avowed commitment to truthfulness about repression. '[W]e must tell the truth, ' he said:

In the human rights country reports, we have the statutory obligation to do this. But we have, moreover, a moral obligation. We owe it to people everywhere struggling for freedom to weigh our words carefully and to respect the sanctity of their efforts. If we corrupt the language we use to discuss liberty, we commit a grave offence against all those, including tens of thousands of Americans, who have given their lives to preserve it.[22]

This soon proved to be a hollow promise. A five-year war between Abrams and the human rights groups over falsehoods in government reports was about to begin.

*   *   *

At first, advocates were unsure of what to make of the new bureau chief. By bidding for the human rights job instead of languishing in Kirkpatrick's shadow at his old post, he had shown himself to be a risk-taker. He also had impeccable New Right credentials: former aide to the hawkish Democrats Patrick Moynihan and Henry Jackson; and son-in-law of *Commentary*'s neo-conservative luminaries Norman Podhoretz and Midge Decter. Harvard alumni might have remembered Abrams for his 'Ad Hoc Committee to Keep Harvard Open' during the student strikes of the sixties ('one of my proudest moments', he recalled).[23] Yet liberal critics found it difficult to fault some of his early actions. His support for asylum-seekers from the Soviet-backed Ethiopian regime won praise from the Congressional Black Caucus, his promotion of the rights of trades unions in Poland found favour with labour organisations, and his opposition to the export of shock batons to South Korea earned approval from human rights groups.

The first clues that Abrams might be a Trojan horse for the interests of rightwing dictatorships appeared in his introduction to the *Country*

Reports for 1981. Here, he announced a three-cornered package for the promotion of human rights. Political rights would be pushed, but not economic rights (thus allowing junta-defended inequalities to be overlooked). Rebel violence would be targeted as well as state violence (thus enabling the exaggeration of the former in order to justify the latter). And democracy would be promoted in addition to monitoring repression (thus enabling elections to be hyped, while shifting attention away from abuses).[24] But these motives were not immediately apparent. For a while, Abrams was able to appear to uphold rights, while going easy on 'authoritarian' allies in pretty much the way that Kirkpatrick had counselled. When his bluff was called, he had another tactic up his sleeve: smearing advocates as communist sympathisers.

*   *   *

The American human rights groups were new players on the political scene. Many of them emerged towards the end of the Vietnam War, when campaigns against repression in the Third World seemed to be the logical next step. But the radicalism that had permeated the sixties campaigns had dissipated by the late seventies. The Carter administration had drawn the sting of the New Left by bringing its leaders into government, and enthusiasm for Third World political ideologies such as Ché-style guerrillaism and Vietnamese socialism had turned to disillusionment.[25] The latter-day advocates believed in saving victims, not changing societies. They were humanitarians, and unlike their radical predecessors, they believed that the United States was a potential force for good in the Third World – provided that Washington adopted the correct foreign policies.

The most important group to emerge in the late seventies was the organisation now known as Human Rights Watch. The first Watch committee, Helsinki Watch, was the brain-child of Arthur Goldberg, the Carter-appointed head of the US delegation to the East-West Helsinki review conference at Belgrade in 1977–8.[26] At Belgrade, Goldberg seized the opportunity to denounce the Soviet Union for its human rights violations, to the dismay of his West European allies, and some members of his own delegation, who were concerned about the effect on détente. Goldberg concluded that most West Europeans and Americans were ignorant about the realities of life behind the Iron Curtain, and detected a need for a respectable organisation to increase awareness of Soviet oppression.[27]

On his return from Belgrade, Goldberg persuaded the head of the Ford Foundation, McGeorge Bundy to set up such a group in time for the next Helsinki conference at Madrid.[28] Goldberg's request was especially well-placed. After years of fighting the Cold War in the cultural front, the Ford Foundation was turning its focus towards human rights. McBundy targeted

Robert Bernstein, who was a leading light in the Fund for Free Expression, to lead the new outfit.[29] With Bernstein in the chair, and a $400,000 Ford grant in the bank, Helsinki Watch was born in February 1979.[30]

Like Amnesty International and the International Commission of Jurists, Helsinki Watch was elite-driven from the start. The Ford Foundation was particularly keen to recruit opinion-leaders, and a blue-chip board, drawn heavily from the ranks of the Council on Foreign Relations, was duly convened. One of the organisation's main purposes was to establish contact with dissident groups, and to convey to the Western public their experiences of intimidation, imprisonment and exile. Helsinki Watch's first director, Jeri Laber, a former Slavic languages scholar, threw herself into the task. She travelled frequently to Budapest, Warsaw and Moscow, and she fired off volleys of press releases whenever evidence of brutality was uncovered. Helsinki Watch reports soon acquired a reputation for being the most authoritative on human rights conditions in the Eastern Bloc.[31]

Helsinki Watch came into its own at the Madrid conference, which was held from 1980 to 1983 – a period marked by the death of Afghanistan and birth of Solidarity. In a *New York Review of Books* article published beforehand, Jeri Laber berated a State Department official for suggesting that America approach East–West negotiations in a spirit of cooperation. 'To what end?' she queried. Instead, she said, the United States should 'demand that the Soviet Union and Czechoslovakia release their imprisoned Helsinki monitors as well as countless others being punished for their religious and political beliefs'.[32] In other words, Helsinki Watch was softening the ground for official criticism of Soviet human rights abuses in the way that Goldberg had envisaged.

The organisation was all the more effective in this role because of its exclusive focus on human rights. This set it apart from the diplomats, the émigrés agitating for national and ethnic rights, and the ideologues attached to every anti-Soviet cause. Indeed, its impeccable humanitarian profile did much to enhance the credibility of the Helsinki negotiations as a whole – despite the fact that the process was being bent to the exigencies of the new Cold War.

The Americans had made a point of inviting along to Madrid representatives of thirty US non-governmental organisations as 'public members' of their official delegation (just as they had done at the 1945 San Francisco conference, and for the same reason). Helsinki Watch played a particularly prominent role among these groups. Although just a year or so old at the start of the conference, it hired offices and staffed them with lobbyists armed with briefing papers and press releases. One of the things that set them apart from the crowd was their privileged contacts with two crucial sets of people – Beltway insiders and Eastern Bloc dissidents. They often played intermediary: the US delegation leader, Max Kampelman, commended 'Bernstein, [Orville] Schell, and Jeri Laber' for introducing him to dissidents and émigré groups in the run-up to the conference.[33]

Helsinki Watch, for its part, was delighted by the official attention paid to repression in the Eastern Bloc. In 1981, its vice-chairman Aryeh Neier declared that his group had 'only praise' for the US delegation, which was 'well-informed, forceful, eloquent, persistent and outspoken' in its efforts to promote human rights.[34] Yet at the same time, it was dismayed by the administration's cultivation of brutal anti-communist regimes elsewhere.

This blatantly selective approach was anathema, and, in 1981, Robert Bernstein and Aryeh Neier decided to set up another Watch committee – Americas Watch – to monitor repression in the USA's client regimes in Latin America. As Neier explained,

> We felt that the only way we could be credible in dealing with human rights in the Soviet Union, and not subject to the charge of waging a cold war attack, was if we were even handed and were concerned with human rights abuses in friendly authoritarian countries.[35]

It was a good time to set up the new group, because Washington's relationship with El Salvador was about to move to centre stage in domestic politics.

*   *   *

Ronald Reagan was looking for a war to win without having to fight one, and El Salvador fitted the bill. The anti-communist government's war against the Farabundo Marti para la Liberacion Nacional (FMLN) rebels looked winnable. There was a Cold War angle without the risk of an East–West confrontation. And victory would restore America's battered self-esteem. It was a high-risk strategy, though, and the administration still had to persuade Congress to bankroll the Salvadoran armed forces.

Congress swallowed the line that El Salvador could become 'another Nicaragua', but it was also haunted by the risk of another Vietnam, and alarmed by reports of death squad murders. So in December 1981, it hedged its bets by passing a two-year law requiring the President to certify every six months that the situation was improving in El Salvador as a pre-condition for the release of further aid. While this law clearly placed human rights at the centre of the debate about El Salvador, it was no victory for advocates. Congress had effectively passed the initiative to Reagan, who had no qualms about certifying that repression was diminishing while the regime's death squads were busy slaughtering thousands of people. In November 1983, after four hearings, Reagan vetoed a proposal that would have extended the certification requirement for a further year. The fact that he got a good portion of the aid he had demanded to bankroll the

Salvadoran government, is testimony to the strength of the executive and the incoherence of the House opposition.

Between 10 and 13 December 1981, the Salvadoran army committed one of the worst atrocities of the war, when it slaughtered the entire population of the village of El Mozote and surrounding hamlets. Representatives of the Salvadoran Catholic Church monitoring group, Soccoro Juridico, and reporters Raymond Bonner of the *New York Times* and Alma Guillermoprieto of the *Washington Post* arrived in El Mozote soon after, and they all concluded that a major massacre had taken place. This incident was the first test of Abrams's policy towards a rightwing ally, and provided a blueprint for the battles ahead. Instead of adopting a cold-blooded approach, he and other officials proclaimed their concern about human rights, while simultaneously disputing evidence of abuses. Aryeh Neier watched the strategy unfold:

> Previously it had been 'We [Americas Watch] think this human rights thing is important and you don't think it's that important'. . . . What the Reagan Administration did was embrace the principle of human rights and then conduct warfare over the facts. The fight over El Mozote exemplified this.[36]

To this end, officials claimed that they had found no evidence of a civilian massacre, that the guerrillas had left civilians to their fate, that the massacre may have been a battle, and that the death toll at El Mozote had been inflated. These confident claims were based on a summary paragraph of a single cable from the US Embassy in San Salvador, which was submitted as evidence to a Senate certification hearing in February 1982. The cable's author was embassy staffer Todd Greentree who, it should be noted, had not actually visited El Mozote, but had only circled high above it in a helicopter seven weeks after the killings had taken place.[37] His summary of events was a masterpiece of politically convenient obfuscation, which, with careful sentence construction, even managed to exonerate the Salvadoran Army:

> Although it is not possible to prove or disprove excesses of violence against the civilian population by government troops, it is certain that the guerrilla forces who established defensive positions in El Mozote did nothing to remove them from the path of battle. . . . Nor is there any evidence that those who remained attempted to leave. Civilians did die during the operations, but no evidence could be found to confirm that government forces systematically massacred civilians in the operation zones, nor that the number of civilians killed even remotely approached the number being cited in other reports circulating internationally.[38]

Meanwhile, Abrams cast aspersions on the human rights groups gathering evidence of the massacre. Salvadoran organisations were 'biased' and 'pro-guerrilla', he said,[39] while American groups 'did not have a great deal of credibility with us'.[40] When asked why NGOs and officials had reached such different conclusions about events at El Mozote, he replied with a rhetorical question: 'Do you believe the Embassy, an agency of the United States government, or Americas Watch?'[41]

El Salvador was not the only place where the administration downplayed violations committed by anti-communist allies. After the publication of the 1982 *Country Reports*, Michael Posner of the Lawyers Committee for International Human Rights complained that they suffered from 'improper emphasis, selective omissions or distortions',[42] while Jeri Laber of Helsinki Watch said that they offered up 'unsubstantiated information'.[43] She then pointed out several false claims. The report on Argentina stated that the government 'is believed to have provided information to family members on the deaths and, in some instances, the location of the remains of the disappeared in about 1,450 cases', when according to Laber, 'no such information had been provided'.[44] The report on Turkey referred to the new constitution as if it had already been established in practice, when in fact, said Laber, it had not.[45] And the report on Guatemala contended that since General Rios Montt had come to power, there had been a 'decrease in the level of killings', when in reality, said Laber, Amnesty International and Americas Watch had found that this was not the case.[46]

Amnesty was an early target of State Department opprobrium. When it published *Guatemala: A Government Program of Political Murder* in 1981, Latin American bureau chief Thomas Enders tried to dispute some of its facts. He argued that

> many of the incidents cannot be corroborated by other sources such as the press, the army, the police or intelligence information. In fact, the town where one incident allegedly took place (Covadonga) doesn't appear on any map of Guatemala available to the embassy.[47]

In fact, Covadonga does exist.[48]

Then, in 1982, while the Guatemalan Army was massacring entire Indian villages, the State Department circulated an embassy cable that purported to analyse human rights reports from Amnesty International, the Washington Office on Latin America, the Network in Solidarity with Guatemala and the Guatemalan Human Rights Commission. It concluded that

> a concerted disinformation campaign is being waged in the US against the Guatemalan Government by groups supporting the leftwing insurgency in Guatemala. . . . [The] Embassy believes that what is being planned, and successfully carried out, is the Communist-backed disinformation plan. . . .[49]

After meeting Guatemalan President Efrain Rios Montt in December 1982, President Reagan told the press that the Guatemalans had been getting 'a bum rap' from its critics.[50] Shortly after, Rios Montt gave his own take on the situation: 'We have no scorched-earth policy; we have a policy of scorched Communists.' The following month, the administration signalled their acquiescence to this deadly policy by lifting an embargo on military spare parts.[51]

*   *   *

If any doubts lingered about Abrams's political inclinations, they were laid to rest by comments he made on a visit to El Salvador in November 1983. There, he insinuated to the press that the left was somehow responsible for the violence of the right, when he claimed that 'many death squad members are fairly well known but there is no action taken by the far left because they like to see Salvadoran society divided'.[52] It was a craven performance, and it aroused distaste back in the United States. The NGOs were especially angered. Abrams had implicated the guerrillas in the work of the death squads – a matter of relevance to El Salvador. But he had also abandoned his role as chief American human rights advocate abroad – a matter of relevance to advocates back in Washington. The sting of betrayal was apparent in Aryeh Neier's assessment of the affair:

> One of the most distressing aspects of last week's performance in El Salavador is that one of the players was the Assistant Secretary of State for Human Rights. This office is the only one created by United States law for the specific purpose of promoting human rights internationally. First and foremost, the occupant of this office should be dedicated to using the influence of the United States to stop governments from practising political murder. Yet it is this official who visits a government that receives vast military and economic support from the United States and who takes the occasion to speak to the press in the name of the United States in an attempt to exculpate those responsible for political murders by shifting the blame.[53]

Shortly afterwards, the Watch committees and the Lawyers Committee for International Human Rights (another Ford-funded group, established 1975) published a report entitled *Failure: The Reagan Administration's Human Rights Policy in 1983*. In it they again accused Abrams of 'defending regimes that abuse human rights when such defence serves the political and geopolitical interest of the Reagan Administration'.[54] Such criticism was water off a duck's back: Abrams believed that pursuing these interests was the essence of the job. Instead of fighting turf wars, as Derian had done, or hoisting himself by his own petard, as Lefever had done, he had evolved human rights policies designed to complement the executive's wider foreign aims. As he later argued,

[Human Rights] Bureau officials viewed themselves as part of the government and part of the State Department and did not see themselves as working in opposition to it. It was important to maintain good relations with other bureaus of the department, particularly the regional bureaus, and other agencies outside the State Department so as to restore the influence of the Bureau. In this, we succeeded.[55]

Meanwhile, the bloodbath continued in El Salvador. In July 1984, the US-trained Atlactl Battalion murdered some forty people at Los Llanitos. The following month it murdered scores more near the Gualsinga River. These massacres were investigated by the Salvadoran Church, the *New York Times*, the *Boston Globe*, the *Miami Herald* and Reuters – but not by the US Embassy in San Salvador. The State Department's 1984 *Country Reports* made no mention of them, and Abrams flatly denied that they had occurred. On 13 February 1985, he crossed swords with Aryeh Neier on ABC TV's *Nightline* show:

Ted Koppel: Secretary Abrams, why was neither of those incidents reported?
Secretary Abrams: Because neither of them happened. Because it is a tactic of the guerrillas every time there is a battle and a significant number of people are killed to say that they're all victims of human rights abuses.
Aryeh Neier: . . . the *Boston Globe* and the *Miami Herald* and *The Christian Science Monitor* and Reuters and all the other reporters who went to the scene and looked at what took place, they were simply being propagandists for the guerrillas. Is that right?
Secretary Abrams: I'm telling you that there were no significant – there were no massacres in El Salvador in 1984. . . . I would have to tell you that the US Embassy is in a better position than a newspaper which has a one-man bureau to investigate what is going on in El Salvador.
Aryeh Neier: . . . When I've asked the US Embassy about this, they say they're not an investigative agency; they aren't capable of doing this; they don't do this sort of thing. Therefore, they may have more resources. But they don't do it.
Secretary Abrams: Well, I think that's false. Whenever there are accusations like this we do look at them. . . .
Ted Koppel: All right, but do you also send independent investigative teams then to check on something like a report of a massacre?
Secretary Abrams: Frequently, we do, whenever there is a –
Ted Koppel: Did you in these instances?
Secretary Abrams: My memory is that we did, but I don't want to swear to it because I'd have to go back and look at the cables. . . .[56]

If anyone was up to the job of confronting Elliott Abrams, it was Aryeh Neier. He had long been a leading light in the American Civil Liberties Union, where he stirred up hornets' nests by defending Vietnam draft-card burners and the right of American Nazis to march through Skokie, Illinois. He was also at the helm when it was revealed that former ACLU leaders had regularly passed information to FBI head Edgar Hoover from the forties to the sixties. Neier left the organisation in 1978, and joined Helsinki Watch shortly after. He is a long-time contributor to the liberal left magazine, the *Nation*, although he reportedly resigned from its editorial board in 1986 after it published a 'repulsive' piece accusing the Soviet dissident Anatoly Shcharansky of being a US spy.[57] Fences were eventually mended, though, and in 1990, he reappeared on the *Nation* masthead with a regular column, 'Watching Rights'.

Supporters praise Neier's dynamism and single-mindedness, detractors damn his 'autocratic streak'.[58] But one thing is for sure: he is no great radical. Of his early years, he recalled in 1988, 'I regarded myself as an anti-communist, but of the liberal left, very much a Norman Thomas person'. He added: 'I do not have a strong political identification now.' Interestingly, even Elliott Abrams, when asked, could not quite bring himself to accuse Neier of being a communist. Instead, he said,

> He is a strange bird politically. I don't doubt that he's anti-communist. The only thing I can figure is that he is a violent partisan who hates Ronald Reagan intently and is determined to have no enemies to his left.[59]

Officials were not so circumspect about Neier's organisation, Americas Watch, however. Abrams characterised it as 'a left-wing political group masquerading as a human rights group',[60] while staff dealing with Latin America often tried to discredit its information. A State Department rebuttal of a 1985 report about El Salvador was typical of this approach.

> The [Americas Watch] report is based primarily on pro-FMLN sources, and relies heavily on testimony from FMLN supporters from the guerrilla stronghold of Guazapa and from sympathizers and families of guerrillas in church camps in El Salvador and refugee camps in Honduras. It depends for its figures on Tutela Legal, the Catholic Legal Aid Office of the Archbishopric of San Salvador, whose methodology is questionable and whose statistics we have shown to be badly flawed and biased. The Americas Watch report accepts Tutela Legal's methodology without critical analysis. It includes errors of fact. The report is superficial, demonstrating a lack of understanding of the political environment in El Salvador and of the behaviour and customs of the Salvadoran people. To make its case, Americas Watch repeatedly dredges up incidents from the past to support the report's contention that terror continues in the present. . . . Americas Watch treads lightly on guerrilla atrocities; the 150-page report devotes only 16 pages to guerrilla human rights abuses, which are today flagrant and conspicuous in comparison with the demonstrably improved comportment of government security forces.[61]

Americas Watch refuted these charges, but the State Department persisted, working on the premise that if they threw enough mud, some of it would stick.

*   *   *

When Elliott Abrams travelled to Turkey – an American ally with an awful record of torture and murder – he went out of his way to publicly condemn the 'ill-informed and self-righteous' human rights community.[62] It was a typical display of what a colleague once described as his 'Doberman pincher school of diplomacy'.[63] Soon afterwards, in March 1985, the playwrights Harold Pinter and Arthur Miller of the writers' human rights group PEN travelled to Turkey to monitor the trial of forty-eight members of the Turkish Peace Association and express their solidarity with imprisoned writers. At the end of their trip they attended a dinner party hosted by US Ambassador Robert Strausz-Hupé, a Reagan appointee once described by Senator William Fulbright as 'the very epitome of the hard-line, no-compromise'.[64] Yet on that particular evening, it was Harold Pinter who took the hard line.

During the meal, Pinter was seated opposite Nazli Ilicak, the conservative editor of a Turkish newspaper. Arthur Miller recalled that 'the whole thing was quite formal and civil until I heard Harold growling down at the other end of the table'.[65] The growls grew louder as Ilicak baited the British playwright. 'Mr Pinter, this [torture issue] is none of your business', she declared.

> It's a Turkish problem, and it is going to be solved by Turks. Turks have to remain and face the realities of their country. You come here and listen to what the leftists tell you, and you can go home and put it all into a profitable play.

Pinter swiftly retorted: 'That is an insult and was meant as an insult, and I throw it back in your face.'

Later, Miller told journalist Lucy Komisar, Ambassador Strausz-Hupé stood up and gave a little after-dinner speech in which he thanked all his guests. Then, looking at Pinter, he said:

> This demonstrates that all viewpoints are welcome here. Here is democracy, right here, and we are proud of it. Imagine this happening in a communist country.

He harped on the same theme over coffee. 'There can be lot of opinions about anything', he remarked. 'Not if you've got an electric wire hooked to your testicles', retorted Pinter.[66] Miller recalled that they were not exactly thrown out, but that they both 'slid out at the end of the dinner'.[67]

*   *   *

Abrams delivered a speech to the Cuban-American National Foundation, an anti-Castro organisation, in Palm Beach, Florida in the mid-eighties. There, he claimed that many advocates were 'simply yesterday's peace activists in a more decorous garb', and that being the case,

> it is not surprising that their view of the world is distorted by a seemingly invincible anti-Americanism . . . and by a profound reluctance to criticize America's adversaries.[68]

This could not have been further from the truth. The human rights groups were in fact deeply patriotic, and regularly chastised the Soviet Union, Poland, Cuba and others. They embodied an important strand of American exceptionalism: namely, the belief that the United States, by virtue of its values and its power, has a unique role to play in the projection of human rights throughout the world. This sentiment was powerfully expressed by Helsinki Watch chairman Robert Bernstein at Ernest Lefever's nomination hearing:

> [W]e believe that the entire ideology of the United States depends on human rights. . . . We should be exporting our ideology. It's not obnoxious to speak about our ideas, and to tell people we think they are great and that other countries should follow them.[69]

Unlike the British-based Amnesty International or the Swiss-based International Committee of the Red Cross, the US-based groups, led by the Watch committees and the Lawyers Committee for International Human Rights, did not purport to be internationalist. They were primarily concerned with the conduct of Washington's foreign policy. As Aryeh Neier explained of Human Rights Watch:

> [A]s an American organisation, we could focus significantly on US policy, and US policy was so significant on a worldwide basis, that our impact would derive from our relationship to US policy.[70]

At the peak of the Reagan administration's power, when the President appeared to be unassailably popular and the Democratic Party appeared to be in irreversible decline, these groups kept alive the seventies' Congressional credo that the national interest was best served by disassociation from dictators. The Watch committees and the Lawyers Committee for International Human Rights often highlighted the damage being done to American prestige by its support for despots, just as Donald Fraser had done in the previous decade. 'I believe that the United States is disgracing itself in the world by its support for the government of El Salvador', Aryeh Neier testified in 1983.[71] Or, those 'in the forefront of the struggle against the apartheid system consider the United States to be their enemy', the Watch and Lawyer's committees wrote in 1984.[72] Or, 'close alliances with [Latin American] armed forces have reversed the goodwill felt toward the United States', Americas Watch wrote in the 1985.[73]

This focus on the conduct of US foreign policy was both their strength and their weakness. Unlike organisations such as Amnesty, which initially tried to build a membership though letter-writing campaigns, the American groups made little attempt to create a loyal broader-based constituency for themselves. On the one hand, this enabled them to focus on core activities, such as lobbying in Washington and collecting information abroad. On the other, the lack of a constituency also prevented them from making a decisive impact on the conduct of foreign affairs. Without the two vital elements for winning political battles – money and votes – they were unable to steer policy.[74] As a result – a senior State Department official later observed of Human Rights Watch – they lacked the clout to 'bring matters to a climax'.[75] The non-governmental organisations contributed their creative energy and investigative skills to the promotion of human rights, but governments called the shots.

* * *

In the mid-eighties, America's political spotlight shifted away from El Salvador and towards Nicaragua – another nation singled out as a Cold War battleground for the benefit of the domestic audience in the United States. The Reagan administration set about arming the anti-Sandinista contras to overthrow the Nicaraguan government, while neutralising critics at home by presenting the policy as a campaign on behalf of human rights. Once again, Elliott Abrams spear-headed this strategy, albeit from his new vantage point as head of the Latin American Bureau, where his snarling commitment to the cause earned him the sobriquet 'contra commander-in-chief'.[76] Meanwhile, Richard Schifter, an anti-communist academic, was appointed head of the Human Rights Bureau.

The administration wrung contra funds out of Congress by blackening the Sandinista's record. It claimed that the Miskito Indians were the victims of genocide, that the Nicaraguan people were captives in their own country, that Jews had been driven out by pogroms. The *Country Reports* for 1985 claimed that the International Committee of the Red Cross (ICRC) had estimated that there were 7,500 to 10,000 political prisoners in Nicaragua, when in fact it had said nothing of the sort. Other groups pointed out that those figures were preposterously high,[77] but the rebuttal made less of an impact than the original allegation. (The report also insinuated that there was something underhand about the ICRC's silence on local prison conditions, although silence is one of the organisation's operating principles.[78])

The State Department was not alone in publishing questionable information about Nicaragua. By now, the human rights field was full of NGOs, not all of them hostile to official policy. In July 1986, around the time of a crucial Congress vote to step up aid to the contras, the International League for Human Rights published the *Report on Human Rights Defenders in Nicaragua*, which strongly criticised the Sandinista government. Written by the league's programme director Nina Shea – a lapsed Catholic with an interest in the persecution of priests – it garnered sympathetic publicity in many quarters. But it drew the ire of Aryeh Neier, who stated that it was 'fundamentally wrong in conception, wrong on the law, and in many places, wrong on the facts'.[79] It also drew flak from the *Nation*, which devoted an editorial, several columns and various letters to the league's claims. The knives were out between human rights advocates.

The main charge against the league was that it had exaggerated the number of political prisoners in Nicaragua. In September 1986, Nina Shea summarised the report's findings in an article in *The New Republic*. Here, she claimed that an unnamed

> representative of an international relief agency who visits prisoners in the national penitentiaries (where prisoners are sent after they are charged) placed the number of political prisoners being held in these cells at around 3,500 – excluding 2,500 imprisoned former Somoza National Guardsmen.[80]

Shea's total of 6,000 prisoners was not as high as those earlier claimed by the State Department, but a lot higher than those actually provided by the only 'international relief agency who visits prisoners in the national penitentiaries' in Nicaragua – once again, the International Committee of the Red Cross. As a *Nation* editorial pointed out, the ICRC's June 1986 *Bulletin* said that its clientele in Nicaragua numbered '3,800 incarcerated persons', *including* National Guardsmen, contra combatants and their collaborators – more than two thousand less than the number cited by Shea.[81] The fact that she had published these figures when aid to the contras was a live issue in Congress suggested that she was pro-contra. These suspicions increased when *Nation* columnist Alexander Cockburn revealed that the league had got its information from an affiliated body, the Managua-based Permanent Commission on Human Rights, an organisation that had received money from the National Endowment for Democracy through a Washington-based contra lobbying group, Prodemca.[82]

The International League for Human Rights was one of America's oldest human rights groups. It had been established by ACLU-founder Roger Baldwin in 1942, and had been revamped in the late seventies, when it changed its name from the International League for the Rights of Man, and received a financial shot in the arm from the ever-generous Ford

Foundation. Ford kept a close eye on its activities, and, according to Alexander Cockburn, was not happy with the Nicaragua effort:

> The Ford Foundation helps support the league, and by one account it became sufficiently exercised about the obvious political chicanery in the preparation of the Nicaragua report to demand that heads roll at the league or its funding would be cut.[83]

The league's president, Jerome Shestack, vigorously refuted this claim: 'That is absolutely false, as the Ford Foundation will verify to anyone who asks.' But Cockburn stuck to his guns: 'I am confident that my information from the Ford Foundation is correct.'[84] Nina Shea, who resigned shortly after the report was published, would go on to play a leading role in evangelical campaigns against religious persecution in the nineties. But she said that many advocates stopped talking to her after this contretemps: 'I tried to interest the human rights community in the situation in Nicaragua, and that's when I got blackballed by them.'[85] Such infighting between rival groups would soon become part and parcel of the scene.

*   *   *

While Reagan's administration succeeded in casting Nicaragua as a 'totalitarian dungeon',[86] it overplayed its hand when it tried to present its support for the contras as a crusade for liberty and justice. This greatly aggravated advocates in Washington. 'Everybody in this room knows that the policies of arming the contras is not a human rights policy', testified Human Rights Watch spokeswoman Holly Burkhalter.

> I think it does a disservice to the cause of human rights to pretend that it is . . . I almost long for the days back in the 1970s where we had conservative administrations who didn't mess with this nonsense about human rights, but certainly didn't pretend for a minute that national security interests or whatever else they wanted to call them were in fact human rights policies.[87]

Tales of contra atrocities were legion. In 1985, Americas Watch reported that the biggest contra group employed 'the deliberate use of terror',[88] the Lawyers Committee for International Human Rights found them guilty of 'killings, beatings and violent harassment',[89] and the Washington Office on Latin America cited cases of murder, rape, assault and torture. When quizzed about this by a Senate committee, Secretary of State George Shultz suggested that there was something cynical about the NGOs' attempts to persuade Congress not to support the contras. 'I don't say there aren't any problems,' he said, 'but it always strikes me how when we're coming up to a vote or a decision, that all sorts of stuff starts appearing.'[90] Ronald Reagan detected more sinister motives when he claimed that 'misguided sympathizers' of the Sandinista government were 'running a sophisticated disinformation campaign of lies and distortion'.[91]

The human rights groups were fair game for red-baiters in Congress too. In May 1986, for example, Aryeh Neier was drawn into an unedifying exchange with the House Republican, John McCain (who ran against George W. Bush in 2000). McCain sarcastically congratulated Neier for the inclusion of Americas Watch in a list of Nicaragua solidarity organisations in the publication, *Big Red Diary*.

> *Mr Neier:* I am not familiar with that book. What is it?
> *Mr McCain:* It is the Australian *Big Red Diary*, organisations that are in solidarity with the Nicaraguan people.
> *Mr Neier:* That is not one of my favourite pieces of reading.
> *Mr McCain:* I am sure it is not, nor is it mine, but at least those people know whose side you are on. . . .
> *Mr Neier:* I knew you were cited in *Pravda* as a particular supporter of something. Would you concede that was a way of fairly describing you?
> *Mr McCain:* I am here to ask questions, not to answer them from you.[92]

Time was running out for Reagan's policy on Nicaragua. When the Iran-contra scandal broke in November 1986, revealing that, in defiance of Congress, the administration had sold arms to Iran, and had used the profits to illegally fund the contras, the Latin American Bureau chief – one Elliott Abrams – stood right in the firing line. When grilled by a Congressional committee about his role in the affair, he failed to divulge, for example, that he had flown to London as 'Mr Kenilworth' to solicit funds from the Sultan of Brunei. Democrat Senator Thomas Eagleton later warned him that his attempts to withhold information might lead to 'slammer time'. Abrams retorted, 'You've heard my testimony', and Eagleton cut in: 'I've heard it, and I want to puke'.[93]

But as former chair of the Joint Chiefs of Staff, Admiral William Crowe, noted of Abrams, 'This snake's hard to kill.'[94] He was given a slap on the wrist for lying to Congress about the Iran-contra issue – two years parole and 100 hours community service – but was soon pardoned by George Bush. In 1992, he wrote a book in which he confessed to silently railing against his persecutors ('You miserable, filthy bastards, you bloodsuckers!') and to giving away as little as possible to Congressional inquisitors ('Questions were weapons, and answers were shields').[95] He sat out most of the Clinton years in conservative think-tanks such as Lefever's Ethics and Public Policy Center and the Hudson Institute, still fulminating against his treatment at the hands of the 'pious clowns' of the Senate Intelligence Committee.[96] In the late nineties, he was appointed to a commission dealing with religious persecution. Then, in 2001, he was a named for a job in George W. Bush's new government. The post? Senior director of the National Security Council's Office for Democracy, Human Rights and International Operations.

*   *   *

The angry collisions between advocates and officials reflected genuine political differences, but the general trend was towards collaboration. The Reagan and Bush administrations were ideologically disposed towards using NGOs to deal with the poor and disenfranchised, and often called on their expertise. Their material was cited in government papers and their work was praised by senior officials. 'An important contribution to the *Country Reports* is made by non-governmental human rights groups', Abrams stated in early 1982.[97] 'We are particularly appreciative of . . . the role of non-governmental human rights organisations', he wrote in 1985.[98]

There is no reason to suspect that he was being disingenuous. Despite disagreements over Central America, South Africa and a few other places, the NGOs supported – and enhanced – official efforts in countries like Ethiopia, the Soviet Union, China and Poland. They had other uses too, such as getting to the foreign parts that governments could not reach. When it was inexpedient for embassy officials to travel to rebel areas, or to meet with opposition leaders, the NGOs, which did not operate under the same restraints, operated as intermediaries and information gatherers, and occasionally maintained back-channel communications. They also gave Washington greater leverage over foreign regimes at times when a façade of official silence had to be maintained. While officials kept quiet in the interests of diplomatic protocol, noisy non-governmental advocates applied the pressure.

The administration's willingness to exploit the human rights groups was dramatically highlighted during the 1990–1 Gulf crisis, when President George Bush used Amnesty International's findings to drum up domestic support for Desert Storm. He made one of his first references to Amnesty during a press conference on 9 October, where he informed journalists that the Iraqi's 'dismantling' of Kuwait was making his patience wear 'very thin'. Replying to a question he said:

> I am very much concerned, not just about the physical dismantling but of the brutality that has now been written on by Amnesty International confirming some of the tales told us by the Amir of brutality. It's just unbelievable, some of the things at least he reflected. I mean, people on a dialysis machine cut off, the machine sent to Baghdad; babies in incubators heaved out of the incubators and the incubators themselves sent to Baghdad. Now, I don't know how many of these tales can be authenticated, but I do know that when the Amir was here he was speaking from the heart. And after that came Amnesty International, who were debriefing many of the people at the border. And it's sickening.[99]

The following day, the US Congressional Human Rights Caucus convened a hearing on the occupation of Kuwait. There, a fifteen-year-old Kuwaiti girl identified only as 'Nayirah' testified that while volunteering at the al-'Addan Hospital during the first weeks of the occupation, she had seen Iraqi soldiers enter a room containing fifteen premature babies. 'They took the babies out of the incubators, took the incubators and left the babies on the cold floor to die', she said. 'It was horrifying.'[100] It later transpired that 'Nayirah' was the daughter of the Kuwaiti Ambassador to Washington, Sheikh Saud al-Nasser al-Sabah – a matter of no small import, given that the al-Sabah royal family had fled Kuwait before or during the invasion, fearing for their lives.

President Bush appeared to take this story at face value, however, and repeated it endlessly up and down the country. On 15 October, he told a Republican fund-raising lunch at Dallas, Texas, that, 'I heard horrible tales: Newborn babies thrown out of incubators and the incubators then shipped off to Baghdad.'[101] The following morning, he told a Republican fundraising breakfast in Des Moines, Iowa, that, 'At a hospital, Iraqi soldiers unplugged the oxygen to incubators supporting 22 premature babies.'[102] A week later, he told a Republican fundraising breakfast in Burlington, Vermont, that 'they had kids in incubators, and they were thrown out of the incubators so that Kuwait could be systematically dismantled.'[103] Later that day, he told a Republican campaign rally in Manchester, New Hampshire about, 'Kids in incubators thrown out so that the machinery, the incubators themselves, could be shipped to Baghdad.'[104] Five days later, he told troops at Hickam Air Force Base in Pearl Harbor, Hawaii, that 'Iraq soldiers pulled the plug on incubators supporting 22 premature babies. All 22 died.'[105] Four days later, he told a Republican campaign rally in Mashpee, Massachusetts, that 'In one hospital, they pulled 22 premature babies from their incubators, sent the machines back to Baghdad, and all those little ones died.'[106]

In December, the incubator story was given a new lease of life, when Amnesty International issued a report on occupied Kuwait that not only confirmed the original allegations, but dramatically increased the number of babies who had supposedly died. Whereas Bush had quoted the figure of twenty-two, Amnesty declared that 'over 300 premature babies were reported to have died after Iraqi soldiers removed them from incubators, which were then looted'. It quoted an unnamed Red Crescent doctor who said that 312 premature babies had been removed from incubators, and that he had personally buried 72 corpses in the al-Rigga cemetery. It also repeated the 'eyewitness' testimony of 'Nayirah' about the babies being left to die on the cold floor.[107] If the claims were true, these infant deaths would have made up a significant percentage of the estimated total death toll in Kuwait. One would have expected Amnesty to shout about it from the rooftops. Yet the organisation's account was curiously low-key. Did Amnesty have doubts about the story – and, if so, why did it lend credibility to the allegations?

George Bush made the most of the Amnesty report in his campaign to win domestic backing for the war. He referred to it in no less than six interviews in the run-up to the start of Desert Storm on 16 January 1991, and gave the impression that it was never far from his thoughts. On 17 December he told reporters that

> I read this Amnesty International report – it's not released yet, it will be in a couple of days – and I hope that everybody standing out there . . . will read that report. Because right this very minute, we're seeing a brutality in Kuwait that is unacceptable, unconscionable; and I am concerned about it.[108]

A fortnight later, Bush expanded on the theme to *Time*'s presidential profiler Hugh Sidey, who wrote:

> George Bush sits in the soft light of the Oval Office, tilted back in his chair, brow knitted, rimless glasses in his restless hands, then on his nose, then off again. He suddenly swivels, points a long forefinger at a stack of papers in the center of his neat desk. It is Amnesty International's report on Iraqi atrocities in Kuwait. He's just been asked about compromising with Saddam Hussein. 'I'm absolutely convinced you can't', he says. 'If there's a question about the moral purpose here, I really urge people to read this report. It's going to have a devastating effect. And there are comparisons between this and what happened when (Hitler's) Death's Head Regiment went into Poland.'[109]

Three days later, Bush raised the report again during a nationwide TV interview with David Frost on PBS. He said of it,

> David, it was so terrible, it's hard to describe. Just to give you a little background on this, I handed it to Barbara as we left Camp David. And she read about two pages of it and said, 'I can't read any more.'[110]

The President's high-profile endorsements should have been gratifying to Amnesty. But Bush's posturing was far too transparent. This report might have 'really made an impression' on him in the run-up to the Gulf War, but earlier reports had not had the slightest effect on him when, as CIA chief and Reagan's Vice President, he had treated Saddam as a valued ally.[111] Amnesty representatives complained that their material was being misused to serve aggressive ends. A 'Nobel Peace Prize winner should not be used as a war drum', admonished Amnesty's USA director John Healey.[112] But it was too late for such quibbling: several Senators cited the incubator story,

which Amnesty had done so much to legitimise, as one of the reasons for
their support of the Congress resolution authorising Desert Storm.

Alexander Cockburn finally blew the lid off the incubator story on
17 January 1991 with an article in the *Los Angeles Times*. He questioned
whether any Kuwait hospital would have 312 incubators, and pointed out
that the University of Southern California Medical Center had a mere 13.[113]
A fortnight later, he returned to theme in his *Nation* column, chastising
Amnesty for its role in peddling an atrocity story:

> Amnesty International was remarkably offhand in offering news of what
> would be one of the most gruesome crimes of the age. More than 300
> murdered babies and just forty-six laconic lines buried deep in its report! Is it
> likely that any hospital in Kuwait would have so many incubators?
> Columbia Presbyterian in New York, for example, has thirty-six. Is it
> plausible that doctors and nurses at al-'Addan Hospital would have stood by
> as those babies lay on the cold floor, their deaths possibly protracted over
> several hours?

Cockburn quoted Aziz Abu-Hamad, a Saudi consultant for Middle East
Watch (another Watch committee, established in 1989), who had re-
interviewed the Red Crescent doctor originally cited by Amnesty. The
doctor denied that he had used the 312 figure, and said that he was unsure
about the cause of death of the 72 babies he said he had buried. Aziz Abu-
Hamad had also interviewed other hospital personnel, including a senior
health official who had been at the al-'Addan Hospital until early October
who said that no incubators had been reported stolen. (That hospital
possessed 25 incubators after the war, the same number as before it.[114])
Cockburn asked: 'Does it matter that the Iraqis, amid their looting and
their murders, did not kill scores, if not hundreds, of babies by stealing
their incubators?' He answered: 'Of course it matters. Human rights
organisations should have higher standards than the yellow press.'[115]

There was no question that Iraqi forces had carried out atrocities during
their occupation of Kuwait, but Middle East Watch director Andrew
Whitley nonetheless suspected that some of the information doing the
rounds was exaggerated, and he described the Amnesty report as
'overdrawn'.[116] He told *Time* that the situation in Kuwait was 'bad enough
when you consider just the tragedies that can be objectively verified', and
that there was 'no need to inflate the statistics'.[117] After the end of
hostilities in late February 1991, Middle East Watch sent an investigation
team to Kuwait. Shortly afterwards, Amnesty was further discomfited when
its representatives announced that they had found no evidence that
incubators had been taken or babies killed as a result. Amnesty retracted
the story in April 1991, but the damage had been done by then.

The babies did not die for want of stolen incubators, and nor, unfortunately for Amnesty, did the story. The Bush administration – recognising that the President had partly staked his war on dead babies – continued to repeat it. When asked to respond to a 1992 Middle East Watch report indicating that the incubator story was false,[118] Human Rights Bureau head Richard Schifter trotted out the old lines, claiming that:

> in a number of hospitals, the Iraqi personnel went in and simply seized the incubators and, if there were babies in them, that was, as far as they were concerned, too bad for the babies. There is clear evidence that there were infants who died as a result of this particular act of getting the incubators disconnected.

Yet when pressed on details, Schifter's account was a good deal fuzzier and less dramatic than the story doing the rounds fifteen months earlier:

> *Mr Yatron:* How many infants died as a result of this?
> *Ambassador Schifter:* It is on that point that there may be some question, Congressman. One cannot be absolutely certain. I have asked about that and what I was told was that there was no question –
> *Mr Yatron:* Was it 20 or 100?
> *Ambassador Schifter:* What I was told was somewhere in the neighbourhood of 20 for sure. Then, with regard to others, basically the parents reported that their baby died in the hospital. It is not clear in a particular setting whether it was because the baby was in an incubator and it was disconnected or because the incubator was no longer available. That will be another possibility.[119]

Bush appeared to be unembarrassed by the subsequent revelations, and continued to tell the discredited incubator story years after the non-event. In 1997, while addressing an Air Force Association conference in Las Vegas, he recalled a conversation he had had with a bishop during the Gulf crisis. '[H]ave you read the Amnesty International report?' Bush recalls asking the bishop. 'Have you read about where they are taking the babies out of the incubators to carry off the incubator?'[120]

The incubator story was not the only thing to be overtaken by events. The Cold War philosophy that had dominated the West for half a century was shattered in a single blow by the fall of the Berlin Wall. Before long the Soviet Bloc had collapsed too. In the uncertain years that followed, new ideas were sought to fill the void left by the old ones, and once more, human rights stepped in to fill the breach.

EIGHT

With God on Their Side

When Hillary Rodham Clinton stepped on to the podium to address delegates of the 1995 UN Women's Conference in Beijing, she had already weathered a blizzard of criticism back in America. Human rights advocates protested that her presence in China conferred legitimacy on those responsible for Tiananmen Square and the oppression of Tibet. And conservatives complained that she was endorsing a conference that they said promoted radical feminism and undermined family values. (Jesse Helms, chair of the Senate's powerful Committee on Foreign Relations, got particularly hot under the collar about the NGO-organised 'Lesbian Flirtation Techniques' seminar.) The First Lady had her work cut out to placate these critics, but she managed it in audacious style – by attacking the Chinese on their home turf.

In her speech she first raised the issue of their 'one child' policy, a hobbyhorse of Republican Congressmen and Christian conservatives. 'It is a violation of *human* rights when women are denied the right to plan their own families, and that includes being forced to have abortions or being sterilized against their will', she said. Then she berated them for their organisation of the conference. 'It is indefensible that many women in nongovernmental organizations who wished to participate . . . have not been able to attend – or have been prohibited from fully taking part', she said, referring to the denial of visas to some delegates, and harassment of others. 'Let me be clear,' she continued. 'Freedom means the right of people to assemble, organize, and debate openly. It means respecting the views of those who may disagree with the views of their governments.'

The US press unsurprisingly focused on how the battling First Lady had rebuked the Beijing government. But in their rush to highlight the contrast between China and the Land of the Free, they overlooked the most important feature of her speech.

Clinton's address was not targeted, in the first instance, at the Chinese, but at the audience back home. It had been crafted, phrase by phrase, to appeal to all shades of American political opinion, from anti-abortionists and anti-gay moralists all the way through to pro-choice activists and lesbian feminists. She achieved this seemingly impossible task by fudging the controversial issues (abortion, contraception), hitting all the easy targets (wife-burning, genital mutilation, female infanticide), and dispensing platitudes that were designed to please everyone. This approach was most obvious in the middle of the speech, when she solemnly intoned,

> We need to understand that there is no formula for how women should lead their lives. That is why we must respect the choices that each woman makes for herself and her family. Every woman deserves the chance to realize her God-given potential.[1]

These anodyne sentiments were full of ingratiating intent. 'We need to understand that there is no formula for how women should lead their lives' transformed the admirable philosophy behind 'live and let live' into an inoffensive bromide to which all parties could subscribe. Likewise, 'That is why we must respect the choices that each woman makes for herself and her family' could either be interpreted as an assertion of women's independence from men, or from government, depending on one's political inclination. Some signals were coded (many supporters of women's rights persuaded themselves that Clinton had placed a stress on the word 'choices' – thus signalling a pro-choice stance on abortion). Other signals were less ambiguous. 'Every woman deserves the chance to realize her God-given potential' was a clear nod to the Bible Belt, and, incidentally, a retreat from the secularism of the Universal Declaration.

Clinton aimed to offend no one, and she succeeded brilliantly. She was never likely to displease feminists, who regarded her as one of their own, and were always willing to see what they wanted to see in her remarks, whether about domestic violence, rape or social inequality. Sure enough, on this occasion, she did not disappoint them. They pounded their desks in delight after she finished speaking, and kept cheering for twenty minutes – longer than the duration of the speech itself. But satisfying the Christian right was another matter altogether. In the event, she managed to throw enough bones to keep it happy too. As well as condemning 'forced abortion' and invoking God, she also expressed support for those fighting religious persecution and mothers campaigning for 'clean airwaves'. In addition, she managed to squeeze in no fewer than twenty-two references to the family – a deliberate sop to the enormous 'pro-family' lobby back in the United States.

Afterwards, Hillary Clinton was warmly congratulated by the delegates of a state that is virtually defined by its opposition to abortion and contraception: the Vatican. And back at home, even Senator Jesse Helms was moved to commend her 'very interesting and effective speech'.[2] But the warm glow soon wore off. In the years that followed, America's Christian conservatives would organise their own rights campaigns, and, in the process, tax the patience and ingenuity of Bill Clinton (a professed human rights president) and his administration.

*   *   *

A new campaign took root in Washington in 1995. It was the brainchild of Nina Shea of Freedom House, a long-standing campaigner on religious matters, and Michael Horowitz of the Hudson Institute, a former senior budget official under Reagan. Together, these two conservatives took up an issue that they claimed everybody else ignored: the persecution of Christians.

Nina Shea is a veteran of the human rights movement. During the eighties she worked for the International League for Human Rights, and had managed to arouse the anger of Americas Watch by writing a controversial report about repression in Nicaragua.[3] After that, she joined the Puebla Institute, a lay Catholic human rights body, initially established by contra Humberto Belli to publicise Sandinista iniquities, which focused on religious intolerance. In the late eighties and early nineties, when events in South Africa and the Soviet Bloc hogged the headlines, the institute did not make much of an impact with its campaigns on behalf of Christians. 'Puebla was one of those groups that was dying,' said Michael Horowitz, 'Nina is good, but it was going out of business.'[4] In 1995, the Puebla Institute was absorbed into Freedom House – another anti-communist organisation, once closely associated with Franklin and Eleanor Roosevelt, which, like Shea, was searching for new totalitarian dragons to slay.[5]

Michael Horowitz, her comrade-in-arms, is a New Right conservative and a self-proclaimed 'back-sliding Orthodox Jew'. He says that his interest in the plight of Christians was aroused when his Ethiopian housekeeper told him harrowing tales about the Mengistu regime (a long-standing target of conservative ire). He regards evangelical Christians as 'the Jews of the 21st century, the scapegoats of choice for many of the world's thug regimes', and says he has taken action on their behalf because 'You're only allowed to sit out one Holocaust each lifetime.'[6] He also recognised that religious persecution was just the kind of issue to force the Clinton administration on the defensive, and galvanise those Republicans who sought to inject Reagan-style crusading morality into foreign policy.

Shea and Horowitz got the bandwagon rolling by focusing on the plight of Christians in China (which Shea insisted on describing as a 'totalitarian' state).[7] In June 1996, she testified that 'For Chinese Protestant preachers, Catholic priests, and other Christian leaders toiling outside of government-controlled organizations, China is one of the world's most dangerous spiritual vineyards'.[8] Later that year, she stated that '[t]he net result of the armed forces' jackboot is that both Catholics and Protestants are saying that religious freedom has steadily eroded . . . and that 1996 was the harshest year of persecution since the Mao era'.[9] She also claimed that 'China is holding more Christian prisoners than any other country in the world', and that thousands were being '"reformed through labor" in China's vast religious gulag'.[10] If all this talk of 'totalitarians' and 'jackboots' and 'gulags' suggested repression of Hitlerite or Stalinist proportions, then so much the better.

This choice of target was a shrewd one. Shea and Horowitz were able to climb on to the shoulders of the Congressional campaign against trade with China, which focused on human rights issues such as forced labour and forced abortions. (This lobby, meanwhile, was grateful to them for giving it a new line of attack on Beijing.) But not everyone shared their assessment of the scale or intensity of religious persecution in China. William McGurn of the *Far Eastern Economic Review* argued that 'much criticism now leveled by American Christian activists seems less a snapshot of China in the late 1990s than a caricature drawn from the high days of Maoism a generation ago'.[11] Albert Pennybacker, the associate general secretary of the liberal-leaning National Council of Churches, also dismissed such claims as 'distorted' – distortions he ascribed to a 'political campaign of the ultra-rightist people in Congress'.[12]

*   *   *

The campaign found an important Congressional ally in the Republican Frank Wolf, a kindred spirit on the right. Wolf is a fervent opponent of economic relations with China, and has, at various times over the years, accused Beijing of running slave labour camps, flooding Tibet with karaoke bars, harvesting body organs from live prisoners, and peddling AK–47s to American street gangs. The most famous of his anti-Chinese denunciations took place in May 1995, when he accused them of eating aborted foetuses. While testifying before the Ways and Means Committee, he told the assembled representatives how,

> the other week, a person came in my office, just back from China, and brought in pictures which I did not want to bring because of the graphic nature. . . .

Having grabbed everybody's attention, he continued,

> . . . what they are now doing in Chinese Government hospitals is they are selling aborted fetuses, aborted babies for human consumption, to eat, to eat!

He continued,

> Now we know that they are taking human fetuses and selling them. This is parallel – strong statement coming – this is parallel to what the Nazis in Germany did.[13]

Strong stuff indeed. It fell to the State Department official at the hearing, Kent Wiedemann, to cast doubt on these charges:

These atrocious allegations that we heard of this morning from Congressman Wolf have been of great concern to us ever since they came to light from various sources. With respect to the fetuses question that turned up in a Hong Kong journal recently, we are actively investigating that, as well as the other allegations with respect to trade in human organs. Thus far, I can say that we have found no corroborating evidence for any of these allegations.[14]

The foetus-eating story advanced by Frank Wolf was pure Fu-Manchu. It began to circulate in April 1995, after the now defunct Hong Kong daily *Eastern Express* published an article claiming that the Chinese were consuming foetuses as a health food.[15] From this single, uncorroborated source, Republican representatives conjured up a full-blown atrocity. In July, Christopher Smith, the leading House anti-abortion campaigner, followed Wolf's lead. Speaking on the China Policy Act, he declared: 'Now we learn that states who supported abortion clinics sell human embryos, and there are even some credible reports that late-term unborn children are actually being consumed as a new health food.'[16] Others repeated the allegation. 'There are reports that aborted fetuses are sold and eaten', said Congresswoman Ileana Ros-Lehtinen, and 'we know that these practices violate every known standard of human rights since God made Man'.[17] Here was another version of the Kuwaiti dead babies story, dressed up in clothes tailor-made for the anti-abortion lobby.

Senator Jesse Helms demanded that the Clinton administration investigate these claims, but nothing came of it. The story was obviously false, and the foetus-eating controversy dropped out of the press as quickly as it had appeared. That was not quite the end of the matter, though. In 2000, photographs began circulating on the internet that appeared to show a man eating a large human foetus. A Malaysian magazine claimed that this fare had been served up in a Taiwanese restaurant – a claim that it retracted after a complaint from the Taipei government. It then transpired that the man in the photo was not a Taiwanese diner, but the Chinese artist Zhu Yu, who had been performing a conceptual piece entitled 'Man-eater' at a Shanghai arts festival – a case of art imitating artifice. While sceptics suspected that the 'foetus' in question was a doll's head stuck onto a duck's carcass, Zhu claimed that he had actually stolen a foetus from a medical school, cooked it, and eaten it for 'art's sake'.[18] As yet, no Congressman has swallowed the bait.

*   *   *

The anti-persecution campaign was starting to gather steam. In January 1996, Shea and Horowitz convened a conference about the persecution of Christians. This attracted a large number of evangelical leaders, including Charles 'Chuck' Colson (born-again after his Watergate infamy), and other figures who commanded large congregations from their television and radio pulpits. Soon after, the National Association of Evangelicals put out a *Statement of Conscience*, declaring that,

> religious liberty is the bedrock principle that animates our republic and defines us as a people. We must share our love of religious liberty with other peoples, who in the eyes of God are our neighbors.

It also called upon the Clinton administration to terminate 'non-humanitarian foreign assistance to governments of countries that fail to take vigorous action to end anti-Christian or other religious persecution'.[19] This proposal provided the core of subsequent initiatives, which culminated in the International Religious Freedom Act.

A shift of power within the Christian right also worked to the campaign's advantage. In spring 1997, Ralph Reed, leader of the most powerful Christian right organisation, the Christian Coalition, announced that he was stepping down and going into business as a lobbyist. Gary Bauer, of the equally conservative Family Research Council, seized on the chance to assume leadership of the movement, using the rallying cry of religious persecution. Bauer's outfit – which had built its reputation and membership on the denial of women's rights to abortion, and the denial of homosexual equality – now embraced an impeccable human rights cause: freedom of worship. The Christian Coalition and Focus on the Family soon followed suit. An idea hatched by a pair of inside-Beltway ideologues was starting to gain a wider hearing.

There were some surreal moments along the way. In 1997, when Bill Clinton was glad-handing Chinese President Jiang Zemin in the White House, a thousand or so protesters gathered for a rally across the road in Lafayette Park. Tibetan monks chanted and banged drums, students shook pebble-filled drink cans, and policemen stood around looking bored. Many of the brightest stars of the human rights firmament were also in attendance. Bianca Jagger, representing Amnesty, told Jiang: 'Stop persecuting Christians, Buddhists, and Muslims.' Kerry Kennedy Cuomo, the niece of JFK, declared, 'Ich bin ein Beijinger.' Adam Yauch of the Beastie Boys proclaimed that Tibet was 'the answer to most of the problems we are facing'. And the biggest celebrity of them all, Richard Gere, declared his faith and support for 'His Holiness' – Tibet's Dalai Lama.[20]

In the speakers' enclosure, midway through the proceedings, a buttoned-up little man with ginger eyebrows tapped Richard Gere on the shoulder. Gere swivelled round and exclaimed, 'Gary! My main man!'[21] Gary Bauer's presence on the platform alongside Bianca and Richard and Adam surprised some of the reporters covering the event, and understandably so. (What, one wonders, did Bauer, the scourge of the permissive society, make of Jagger, the former *grande dame* of that legendary New York den of iniquity, Studio 54?) But Bauer's anti-Jiang statement did not seem out of place alongside the rest of the speeches. It stressed their common cause in bellicose fashion:

> The media is obsessed with the unusual nature of this coalition. I would rather be in this coalition than the other unusual coalition: American capitalists and Chinese communists, the coalition that now includes the man from Hope, Arkansas, and the Butcher of Beijing.[22]

Once again, the cause of human rights attracted strange bedfellows.

*   *   *

Every movement needs a manifesto, and campaigners adopted Nina Shea's, *In the Lion's Den* pamphlet as their own unofficial bible. Her call to arms on behalf of Christians featured some astonishing claims. Foremost among them was the assertion that 'more Christians have died for their faith in the 20th century than in the previous 19 centuries combined'[23] – a mantra now intoned *ad nauseum* in evangelical circles. After Kenneth Roth of Human Rights Watch ridiculed the statistic ('If it were serious, she would have backed it up'[24]) Shea told *Newsweek*'s Carroll Bogert that it came from a Virginia religious group's 'Encyclopedia on Christians'. (Bogert nevertheless noted that it was the kind of assertion 'many experts greet skeptically'.[25]) *In the Lion's Den* also claimed that the 'most egregious human rights atrocities are being committed against Christians living in Communist and militant Islamic societies'.[26] This view did nothing to alleviate suspicions that the issue was being used as a stick to beat China and the Arab world.

Yet this was precisely the kind of fighting talk that endeared Shea to conservatives. The *New York Times*'s A.M. Rosenthal quoted liberally from *In the Lion's Den* in one of his many op-ed pieces on religious intolerance, and even helpfully listed the publisher's phone number.[27] Republican Congressmen who had taken up the cause were equally smitten with her. She became a regular fixture at hearings held by the House Subcommittee on Human Rights, run by the sympathetic Christopher Smith, and she generally had an easy ride. Indeed, on the rare occasions when she faced any implied criticism in Congressional forums, it was for understating her case. At one hearing, she claimed that Christian communities in the Middle East were 'vanishing before our eyes under the relentless persecution'. Yet this was not extravagant enough for Senator Sam Brownback, who egged her on:

> *Brownback:* Do I hear you correctly to state that the level of persecution of Christians is at the highest level in recorded history? Is that a correct statement?
> *Shea:* That is correct. Yes. This is the worst century of anti-Christian persecution in history.

Brownback wanted more.

> *Brownback:* Currently, in 1997, are we experiencing now in the world the highest level of Christian persecution in recorded history – period?
> *Shea:* I don't know if this year so far is higher than any other previous year. But certainly we have seen an increase in this decade in the Middle East.[28]

Brownback still was not satisfied.

> *Brownback:* So we are talking of millions in the Middle East being persecuted?
> *Shea:* We're taking about millions. . . .
> *Brownback:* Currently.
> *Shea:* Currently.
> *Brownback:* And it could be at the highest level ever.[29]

With this kind of encouragement, the campaign's prospects looked good.

The Clinton administration initially tried to appease the growing movement. In 1996, Secretary of State Warren Christopher appointed an advisory panel on religious persecution abroad and in 1997, his successor, Madeleine Albright, instructed US embassies to report on abuses. That same year, the State Department also published *US Policies in Support of Religious Freedom: Focus on Christians*, which garnered grudging praise from the right. Meanwhile, officials handled the campaign's leaders with protective gloves. Nina Shea, in particular, tended to intimidate them. Battle-hardened from years on the ideological frontline, she was tough and persistent. One described her as a 'bull-dog', while others claimed to listen to her voicemails 'in crouch mode'.[30]

Naturally, the movement was emboldened by the administration's sops. When A.M. Rosenthal called for legislation to punish nations accused of religious intolerance, Frank Wolf and another Republican, Senator Arlen Specter, heeded the call. In May 1997, they introduced the religious persecution bill, which proposed curbs on soft loans and non-humanitarian aid. Horowitz encapsulated the thinking behind it with the usual colourful soundbite:

> They're pulling fingernails out of preachers? And you want us to subsidize these guys with aid? What, are you kidding?[31]

Faced with the unwelcome prospect of a law setting out sanctions, the Clinton administration dug in its heels. But in the land of the *Mayflower* and the First Amendment, the matter had to be handled with extreme care. On one hand, it had to avoid alienating large religious communities in the United States; on the other, it had to avoid sacrificing relations with China,

Egypt and Saudi Arabia. So when officials contested the bill, they did so in vague terms arguing that it was a blunt instrument and that sanctions might hurt the very victims that they were intended to help. (They were also at pains to express their commitment to religious freedom.) The State Department's Bill Ramsay, Deputy Assistant Secretary, and David Moran of the Office of Economic Sanctions Policy, explained to one interested party, Donald Deline of Halliburton, Brown & Root, that they thoroughly disliked Wolf and Specter's bill. But, Deline reported, they were also 'constrained for obvious reasons in how active they believe they can be in opposing them'.[32]

Instead, the administration subcontracted the dirty work out to the private sector. When previously faced with tricky laws proposing human rights sanctions, it had encouraged business lobbies to share the burden of making the case against them. The National Association of Manufacturers, the Business Roundtable and the Chamber of Commerce had all campaigned in favour of unimpeded economic relations with repressive states, arguing that rights follow on the heels of commerce. (The unions retorted that workers' rights had not materialised that way in the USA.)

In April 1997 a lusty new voice joined this commercial chorus. Pursuing a calculated administration strategy, the former Carter official Anne Wexler used her Washington lobby firm, The Wexler Group, to launch the business coalition, USA*Engage. This body was specifically created to campaign against sanctions, and soon attracted a host of Fortune 500 firms, including AT&T, Boeing, Caterpillar, Coca-Cola, IBM, Motorola and Texaco. The religious persecution bill was one of its first targets.

In September 1997, Frank Kittredge, the vice president of USA*Engage, and other senior business figures, wrote to Frank Wolf to set out their objections:

> Just as missionaries cannot accomplish their goals by withdrawing from the mission field, America cannot expect to be an influence for religious freedom and human rights by removing itself from a country. . . . Our stepping out of this increasingly interconnected world and erecting sanctions will have little or no impact on those who wish to persecute others. It will, however, have a significantly negative impact on the United States.[33]

While USA*Engage was setting out its opposition to the bill, it was also working behind the scenes to build a broader coalition. According to memos leaked to the magazine *Mother Jones*, they did this on the advice of the State Department's Ramsay and Moran, who told Donald Deline that they

> believed that business would not be the best group to be out front on this issue either, but that religious leaders and religious organisations should take the lead for best results.[34]

Taking this cue, USA*Engage put out feelers to churches that, for one reason or another, might oppose the bill.[35]

As USA*Engage was well aware, the divisions between America's denominations are deep – almost as deep as the schisms between Christian liberals and the Christian right. (In 1991, Pat Robertson of the evangelical Christian Coalition described the less conservative Episcopalians, Presbyterians and Methodists as 'the spirit of the Antichrist'.[36]) And, as USA*Engage had hoped, some churches did indeed withhold endorsement of the bill. The most important of these was the USA's largest church grouping, the National Council of Churches – an umbrella organisation covering 'oldline' Protestant and Orthodox churches. This body complained that the bill highlighted the persecution of Christians at the expense of other faiths, and ignored other abuses. 'We prefer for the religious-freedom issue to be in the context of other freedom issues', said Albert Pennybacker. 'As religious people, we're concerned about the persecution of anyone for any reason.'[37] Other churches, meanwhile, opposed the bill on the grounds that it would make their missionary work harder, or that it might interfere with martyrdom pre-ordained by the Bible.

These differences set off a round of recriminations. The editors of the lay Catholic journal *Commonweal*, complained that some of the bill's rightwing supporters were only interested in scoring points:

> Some of the conservatives leading the current effort seem unable to resist the impulse to make the issue a political football in America's culture wars. They seem as interested in settling scores with the National Council of Churches and the United States Catholic Conference as in exerting effective pressure on persecuting governments.[38]

Columnist Richard John Neuhaus, of the conservative religious journal *First Things*, responded to this 'very serious charge, made only slightly less odious by the qualifying "they seem"', by remarking that,

> The NCC, following its shameful pattern during the years of the Cold War, has belittled and often denied the persecution of fellow Christians, while the record of the Catholic Conference has been, shall we say, uneven.[39]

Positions hardened and coalitions began to take shape. USA*Engage's strategy seemed to be bearing fruit. In May 1998, the *Washington Post*'s Fred Hiatt reported that he was invited by the public relations firm Fratelli to meet a delegation of foreign religious leaders opposed to the bill. This group was being chaperoned around town by the National Council of Churches. The name Fratelli rang a bell with Hiatt, who had read the leaked memos that had appeared in *Mother Jones*, and he asked who would be footing the bill for the visit.

. . . Fratelli acknowledged that it was 'on loan' to the National Council of Churches, with the bill being paid by the National Foreign Trade Council, which is more or less interchangeable with USA*Engage. And, yes, the church group was 'passing the collection plate' to USA*Engage's members, among others, to help defray the costs of the trip, the Rev. Dr. Albert M. Pennybacker acknowledged.

Pennybacker was bullish about his organisation's alliance with USA*Engage: 'It's classic Washington collaborative convergence', he said.[40] More odd bedfellows.

                              *   *   *

By now, battlelines had been drawn, and not just between churches. Congressmen who opposed to the religious persecution bill stalked the committees, spoiling for a fight. One prominent victim of an anti-bill mugging was Richard Land of the Southern Baptist Convention's Ethics and Religious Liberty Commission, who had been invited to testify in the bill's favour before the House Committee on International Relations. He used the opportunity to play to the gallery: '[M]en like my father and most of my uncles fought in the Second World War for Roosevelt's Four Freedoms, including the freedom to worship', he declared. (For the benefit of those Southern Baptists who neither remembered nor cared about Roosevelt, he added that it was the freedom 'illustrated so beautifully by Norman Rockwell with the caption, "Each according to the dictates of his conscience".'[41]) Then Land started talking foreign policy:

> I would like to see the United States of America have a policy in place that has a velvet hammer. There is velvet, but there is a hammer underneath it that says, 'If you want to do business with the United States . . . then you have to behave as part of the civilized community of nations. That means you have to abide by the UN Declaration o[f] Human Rights.'

Democrat Congressman Lee Hamilton, who opposed the bill (and would soon afterwards sponsor a USA*Engage-approved law protecting US business interests from sanctions), deftly cut Land down to size. Hamilton began by asking the Southern Baptist whether he would use his velvet hammer to cut off all relations with China:

> *Land:* Well, I certainly think that the question of most favoured nation status should be revisited. See, I am tired of contempt of the gangsters who run Red China. . . . We are a money bag democracy.
> *Hamilton:* I understand.
> *Land* (continuing): We do not care about these issues.
> *Hamilton:* I understand your rhetoric. What I am trying to –
> *Land:* It is my indignation, sir, not my rhetoric.

Hamilton: Well, I thought your rhetoric kind of reflected your indignation.
Land: Well, it is more than rhetoric, and . . . what we want from our government is more than rhetoric. We want indignation and we want indignation with teeth.
Hamilton: And that is what I am driving at.
Land: Teeth.
Hamilton: Now, we are not really giving aid to China, so I am trying to figure out what you want us to do with respect to China.

At this point, Land made a fatal tactical error, passing the initiative to Hamilton.

Land: Well sir, that is what we elect you to do, to find the most effective ways to –
Hamilton: I understand that.
Land (continuing): comply with the basic accord of the UN Declaration of Human Rights.
Hamilton: I understand that is our responsibility. I appreciate that. I am just trying to get some advice from you, but I do not have much at this point.[42]

In the showdown between human rights rhetoric and business pragmatism, business won hands down.

*   *   *

To build the campaign against persecution, Michael Horowitz used every opportunity to stir up the us-and-them sentiments of hinterland conservatives. They already instinctively blamed America's ills on the policies of Washington's 'elite' – populist shorthand for liberal, secular, Ivy League Brahmins from the East Coast. He simply focused this sentiment on a single point: the elite's alleged prejudice against Christians. It was a theme he returned to again and again.

Addressing a Senate subcommittee, he painted a sarcastic picture of the way that the mainstream media regarded the Christian community:

Are they not the ones who burned people at the stakes? Are they not the retrograde bigots? We do not like them much. They are not our kind of crowd.[43]

The elite did not understand them, he told *Christianity Today*,

Christians, went the dinner-party buzz, are the people who 'bring it on themselves', the ones 'we wouldn't want as neighbors', are 'clannish' types who never 'fit in' with 'host' cultures.[44]

The elite was also prejudiced against them, he wrote,

[We] will take on and seek to shatter the ignorant bigotry routinely practised against Evangelical Christians and Catholics at 'polite' dinner parties, 'leading' universities and establishment drawing rooms.[45]

In this way, Horowitz cultivated a persecution complex – a potentially useful complex to have at your disposal if your aim is to build support for a campaign against it.

Kenneth Roth of Human Rights Watch regarded all that with distaste. 'Under the guise of religious tolerance, Horowitz spreads divisiveness wherever he goes', he remarked.[46] Comments like this played straight into Horowitz's hands. He accused Roth's organisation of being less interested in the plight of those persecuted for their religious beliefs than in the plight of other persecuted groups. Why? Because it too was part of the elite that denigrated Christians at its dinner parties. In a 1999 interview, he elaborated on a well-worn theme:

With a staff of hundreds and a multimillion-dollar budget, Human Rights Watch publishes an annual report on human-rights violations around the world. The report's country analyses occasionally describe persecutions of religious – and occasionally of Christian – communities. When you turn to the report's last chapter, however, you see Human Rights Watch's manifest bias. That last chapter lists the organization's special, high-priority initiatives – each with dedicated, full-time staffs. There are special initiatives to protect children's rights and women's rights, to protect the rights of victims of multinational corporations and arms manufacturers, to protect the rights of prisoners, gays and lesbians, academics, and members of the press. Guess whose rights don't merit special concern? Human Rights Watch's skewed priorities – its relative indifference to the almost 200 million Christians confronting hard-core persecution – perfectly capture a twentieth-century mindset of elites toward people of faith.[47]

Nina Shea dismissed Human Rights Watch more bluntly. 'No one is paying attention to anything they say or do or write', she said,

I've got the numbers, I've got the endorsements in all the Christian communities. I've got the power. It's our side that is setting the agenda now.[48]

She was partly right. She had the numbers. Unlike the human rights groups that emerged during the seventies, the anti-persecution campaign commanded genuine grass-roots support. As Jeffrey Goldberg observed in a *New York Times Magazine* article,

There is a cosmic joke being played on American human rights activists. For years, they have been looking for ways to interest middle America in its causes, not just college activists and the cultural elite. Finally, a mass constituency seems to be coming together, but – and here's the punch line – the mass constituency consists primarily of evangelical Protestant Republicans.[49]

But were these numbers making themselves heard? The fate of the religious persecution bill suggests that the Christian human rights groups were no more able to out-gun the business lobby than the other human rights groups. In October 1998, Congress passed the International Religious Freedom Act, but only after it had been amended out of all recognition. Few who had rallied to the cause were satisfied with the new legislation. A.M. Rosenthal complained that it was 'too gentle', while Shea described it as 'inadequate'.[50] The anti-China campaign had lost its momentum too, when the Republican Congressional leadership backed China's admission to the World Trade Organisation. The Christian lobby needed a new focus.

*   *   *

Sudan is an obvious target. The National Islamic Front government under President Omar Hassan al-Bashir is waging an extremely brutal civil war against the Dinkas and other groups in the South and West of the country. Civilians in Kordofan, Darfur and Bahr al-Ghazal have, at various times, been bombed, displaced, starved and forcibly conscripted, as well as being preyed upon by government-backed militias, and caught up in rivalries between anti-government factions. This situation has, by all accounts, contributed to the persistence of intermittent hostage-taking, forced labour and even actual slavery.

Of all the horrors visited on Sudanese civilians, the Christian human rights groups have seized upon slavery and made it the focus of their campaign. The civil war is recast in simplistic, religious terms: the Islamic government is enslaving Christians. The promotional material put out by Christian Solidarity International – one of the organisations leading the charge – typifies this approach. 'The Islamic regime's holy war against Christians and animists in southern Sudan has claimed two million lives, and 200,000 people have been abducted into slavery', its website declares. It also repeats the now familiar claim that 'More Christians have been discriminated against, imprisoned, or killed for their faith in this century than at any other time.'[51]

It is not surprising that the Christian lobby concerns itself with religious persecution. But why is it so preoccupied with slavery? After all, as the NGO African Rights has pointed out with regard to Sudan, 'slavery is neither the largest cause of human suffering, nor is it integral to central government policy'.[52] But, as is usual with human rights campaigns, this one is driven by concerns that have little to do with the actual situation within the target country. Campaigners have latched on to slavery because it is an emotive issue, especially in the United States, and, even more to the point, it is an issue that resonates most powerfully among a very specific constituency – black Americans. By no coincidence, it is this very constituency that is being assiduously courted by the Christian right.

There is little love lost between black and white religious communities in the United States. The racial wounds inflicted during the civil rights era have still not heeled. But in the mid-nineties, the Christian Coalition and similar groups were searching for ways to broaden their base, and the black churches – bastions of social conservatism, too, in some cases – were a tempting target. So, they started talking up the need for 'racial reconciliation' between Christian communities. There were a few domestic initiatives, such as the coalition's donations to rebuild burned black churches. But Sudanese slavery was the potential clincher, the common ground upon which the Christian right could galvanise the faithful, both white and black.

America's relationship with Sudan was at an all-time low when the campaign got going. Washington had labelled it a terrorist state, imposed sanctions, and shut down its embassy in Khartoum. The *Country Reports* were predictably hard-hitting. The report for 1998, which included a special section on slavery and forced labour, stated that there were 'frequent and credible reports that Baggara raiders, supported by PDF [Popular Defense Forces] and regular government troops, took hundreds of women and children slaves during raids'. It added that,

> Credible reports persist of practices such as the sale and purchase of children, some in alleged slave markets. These practices all have a pronounced racial aspect, as the victims are exclusively black southerners and members of indigenous tribes of the Nuba mountains.

Even though the State Department had deliberately conjured up images of nineteenth century slave markets, Christian campaigners were not satisfied. They could hardly claim that the Clinton administration was soft on Khartoum – it had, after all, unleashed a cruise missile attack against a suspected chemical weapons site (in fact, a pharmaceutical factory) in August 1998. But as far as Nina Shea was concerned, it simply did not acknowledge the scope of the problem. She complained that the *Country Reports* were 'very distorted' on the issue:

> At one point the reports talk about 'alleged' slave markets; they also talk about forced labour, for some reason, instead of using the word 'slavery'. When it comes to children, they talk about 'hundreds' of children and women, when in fact it is tens of thousands of women and children who have been taken into slavery. This has been documented. Dan Rather did a two-part series of CBS Evening News. Christian Solidarity International and Christian

Solidarity Worldwide have bought back hundreds of slaves, thousands of slaves over the years. It is beyond dispute.[53]

In fact, the scope and nature of slavery in Sudan is hotly disputed. Not only that, but the *modus operandi* of the Christian human rights groups engaged in 'slave redemption' – buying slaves to set them free – is the source of great controversy. Their legions of critics, ranging from Unicef and Human Rights Watch to Anti-Slavery International and Save The Children, accuse them of adopting methods which perpetuate rather than eliminate the practice.

A leading advocate of the anti-slavery movement is Baroness Caroline Cox, who ran the British section of Christian Solidarity International, and then helped to form the Surrey-based breakaway, Christian Solidarity Worldwide. She is a former deputy speaker in the House of Lords and no stranger to political rough house. After receiving a peerage from Margaret Thatcher in 1982, she used her Lords seat as a platform for various conservative causes, including opposition to peace studies courses, leftwingers in education and the Campaign for Nuclear Disarmament. She has also been a member of a formidable array of right-wing groups, among them the Freedom Association, the Parental Alliance for Choice in Education, and the Committee for a Free Britain. She has been dubbed a 'Tory moral fundamentalist' and a 'Cassandra of the old Christian right'.[54] But she is very particular about her exact place in the conservative firmament. 'I am not ashamed of being to the right of centre now,' she told her biographer Andrew Boyd, 'but I don't see myself as being to the right of the Conservative Party.'[55]

In the late nineties, Cox made numerous forays to Sudan to 'redeem' slaves. Her supporters see her as a latter-day saviour, but her detractors argue that buying slaves encourages an abominable practice. Sir Robert Ffolkes, Sudan programme director of the Save The Children Fund, says that it 'condone[s] the practice of purchasing human beings', while Mike Dotteridge of Anti-Slavery International says that it allows it 'potentially to flourish'.[56] Patrick McCormick, spokesman for Unicef, makes the same point: 'We find it hard to believe that it hasn't encouraged . . . slave traders to increase their business.'[57] As Christopher Beese of Merlin, the British medical charity, says of Cox: 'She's not the most popular person in Sudan among the humanitarian aid people . . . some of them feel she is not well-enough informed.'[58] These are valid criticisms – albeit criticisms that raise important (and largely unanswered) questions about the distorting effects of *all* humanitarian efforts in Sudan.[59]

Some have also accused the Christian groups of misrepresenting the problem of slavery in Sudan. Among them is Alex de Waal, former director of African Rights, who has argued that while some small-holder slavery exists, and while the government tolerates it, the notion that Khartoum exports slaves, or runs slave markets, is unsupported by the evidence.[60] '[O]vereager or misinformed human rights advocates in Europe and the US have played upon lazy assumptions to raise public outrage', he wrote.

> Christian Solidarity International, for instance, claims that 'Government troops and Government-backed Arab militias regularly raid black African communities for slaves and other forms of booty.' The organisation repeatedly uses the term 'slave raids', implying that taking captives is the *aim* of government policy.[61]

Anti-Slavery International, meanwhile, used a 1999 report to the UN's Working Party on Slavery to challenge some of the claims being advanced about the scale of the problem. It said,

> A representative of Christian Solidarity International spoke at the beginning of this year of 'tens of thousands' of people in slavery in Sudan, and of 'concentration camps' for slaves. At Anti-Slavery International, we know of no evidence to justify an assertion that 20,000 people or more are currently held as captives and slaves in these areas of Sudan. We know that abductions have continued to be reported . . . but realise that a number as large as 20,000 would be more visible than the smaller group which we understand is actually held, of hundreds or several thousand individuals scattered around separate households.[62]

Nina Shea has little time for such quibbling. When testifying before a House subcommittee, she advanced some information of her own. In Sudan, 'a northward-bound train hauls three windowless freight cars full of children going to northern slave markets', she declared.[63] Overeager, or simply stating the facts?

In March 1996, Louis Farrakhan, leader of the Chicago-based organisation, the Nation of Islam, who had recently returned from a trip to Africa, questioned the very existence of slavery in Sudan. 'Where is the proof?' he demanded in a speech to the National Press Club.[64] A month later, two *Baltimore Sun* journalists – white correspondent Gilbert Lewthwaite and black columnist Gregory Kane – took up Farrakhan's challenge. They travelled into Sudan, accompanied by Caroline Cox, on a trip organised by Christian Solidarity International. In a rebel-controlled market at Manyiel, they paid $500 each for two boys, apparently slaves, from a man dubbed El Haj, apparently a slave trader. Lewthwaite and Kane later wrote:

> We tell El Haj we are willing to pay his asking price of five cows, or $500, for a slave. He accepts with a nod of his head. It is a negotiation of breathtaking

simplicity, struck just 50 yards from where people are buying and selling salt, dried fish and other ordinary commodities. We are not the first journalists to participate in the slave trade. Abolition-era editors raised funds to help buy freedom for slaves and to tell their stories.[65]

Some advocates questioned the nature of this transaction. An African Rights report said: 'Not only were they paying well over the odds (with all the dangers that entails); they were almost certainly paying a middleman in a hostage redemption exercise.'[66] But the *Baltimore Sun* story, and others like it, galvanised Christian communities nevertheless. Divestment campaigns sprung up in scores of churches and universities. Groups of school children started raising money to free slaves. Sudan became the destination of choice for politicians and celebrities keen to witness a 'redemption' at first hand. And, needless to say, new anti-slavery organisations proliferated.

Rivalry between these groups is fierce. Charles Jacobs, president of the American Anti-Slavery Group, publicly accused another organisation of paying too much for slaves, and for seeking publicity:

> There have been some split-off people who wanted to be in the headlines, and they left a whole lot of cash in places [in Sudan]. And, of course, that would be wrong. Christian Solidarity International only pays the customary price of $50 per head. . . .[67]

Meanwhile, the Christian Solidarity International website issues a 'caution' against apparent impostors in the crowded 'slave redemption' field. It warns: 'The similarity in their use of words such as "Christian" and "Solidarity" may lead the public to believe these groups are affiliated with CSI and/or associated with CSI's administration, goals, causes and/or trustworthy reputation, when in fact, they are not.' It continues:

> The general public should be advised that the *following groups are not affiliated with*, associated with, or working in conjunction with, CHRISTIAN SOLIDARITY INTERNATIONAL (CSI):
> 1. Christian Solidarity Worldwide (CSW), sometimes also called Christian Solidarity UK (CS-UK), or Christian Solidarity (CS);
> 2. Christian Freedom International (CFI);
> 3. Christian Solidarity Australasia (CSA):
> 4. Christian Concern International.[68]

Yet despite these schisms, Christian and conservative lobbies have begun to build a broad church opposed to slavery in Sudan. The Family Research Council, Nina Shea, Michael Horowitz, Frank Wolf and Sam Brownback are all involved. Now others have started to climb aboard the bandwagon, including the Congressional Black Caucus, the National Black Leadership Roundtable, Jesse Jackson and Al Sharpton. As intended, the campaign has begun to attract the attention of black Americans.

The breakthrough came when the liberal radio talk show host, Joe 'The Black Eagle' Madison, travelled to Sudan on a Christian Solidarity International-sponsored 'Underground Railroad' in 2000, and witnessed them 'redeeming' slaves. 'I'm an African-American, the descendant of slaves', said Madison. 'It was like I was in a time machine, watching my own ancestors in slavery. Only this is real and it's happening now.'[69] Walter Fauntroy of the National Black Leadership Roundtable, says Madison's trip has become 'the catalyst that will bring together the spiritual descendants of Frederick Douglass, Harriet Tubman, and Sojourner Truth, and the spiritual descendants of William Lloyd Garrison and John Brown in a 21st-century abolition movement.' In other words, it's the Christian right's black-and-white dream ticket – whichever way Al Sharpton and Jesse Jackson might choose to interpret it. John Eibner, the American head of Christian Solidarity International, was ecstatic: 'This is a real breakthrough for our movement, because senior black leaders are now informed and clearly committed to this issue.'[70]

On Good Friday, April 2001, Walter Fauntroy, Joe Madison and the ubiquitous Michael Horowitz were arrested for chaining themselves to the fence in front of the Sudanese Embassy in protest against slavery and anti-Christian 'genocide'. A few months later they appeared in a Washington court to answer the charge of unlawful entry. They were defended by two superstar lawyers, one black, one white: Johnnie Cochran (clients: O.J., Michael Jackson, Sean 'Puffy' Combs) and Kenneth Starr (quarry: Bill Clinton). It was, said the *Washington Post*, 'the oddest collection of bedfellows ever'.[71] Once again, human rights had proved to be a big enough bed to accommodate the full spectrum of sleeping partners.

*   *   *

While the Christian campaigners had been seeking redemption for the persecuted of China and Sudan, other human rights groups had been seeking justice for the victims of conflict in Bosnia and Rwanda. The United Nations had set up special Nuremberg-style tribunals to punish major crimes, and a new era of international justice seemed to be dawning.

NINE

Trials and Tribulations

On 7 May 1996, Dusko Tadic became the first man to stand trial in an international war crimes court since Tojo and co., nearly half a century before. The court was the UN's International Criminal Tribunal for the former Yugoslavia, convened in The Hague. The accused was not a high official – in fact he was a freelance prison guard, and held no rank whatsoever – but the charges against him were grave: the rape, torture and murder of prisoners in Serb-run prison camps in Bosnia in 1992.

It seemed like an open-and-shut case. Then, in August, a prosecution witness, Witness L (name: Dragan Opacic), took the stand. He testified that his father had been killed in the war, leaving him and the rest of his family to fend for themselves. In 1992, while still a teenager, he had tried to avoid the call-up by going to work as a guard at the Trnopolje transit camp, where he had been promised wages of DM 300 a month. He told the court that while he was working there he had seen Tadic murder and rape inmates, and that he had been compelled to do the same himself. Witness L's testimony was shocking. After describing a series of rapes in graphic detail, he then recounted how Tadic and other guards had forced him to slit the throats of two old Muslim men.

> A: [Witness L] . . . Tadic was beating that other old man and turned his head so that he could see how I was butchering that old man. I drew the knife across his head. I discarded the knife and the blood spurted on my uniform. I wanted to stand up from that old man, but they did not allow me until he expired. When he expired, they lifted me off that old man and put me on the other one. I was struggling again, fighting and crying, saying I could not do that. Zoran Karajica took the knife which I had thrown away, wiped it off the beard of that old man, the knife which was bloody. I sat down on the other [man]. Dusko Tadic put his foot on his face, on his temple, and pressed his head against the ground. . . .
>
> Q: [Prosecuting counsel, Grant Niemann] With the second old man, once Tadic had put his boot on the head of the old man, what was the next thing to happen? What happened then?
>
> A: [Witness L] Zoran Karajica gave me the knife, so as to butcher that old man too. I could not. Dusko Tadic drew out a pistol, pointed it at my head. It was a 7.62 pistol. He pointed it at my head, at my forehead, and told me that I had to do it. Bosko Dragicevic pointed the rifle at my back and then Bosko

told him not to kill me, that I would do it at least to prick the man's throat with the knife, and I could do nothing but prick that man's throat with the knife, so I stabbed this knife into his throat.
Q: *[Niemann]* You stabbed the knife rather than pricked the knife, is that right?
A: *[Witness L]* Yes.[1]

Later that day, Niemann asked Witness L to identify Dusko Tadic in the court.

A: He is sitting on the left side.
Q: Can you describe the clothes that he has on?
A: He is wearing civilian's clothes.
Q: What colour is his coat?
A: He has a blue coat, a jacket sorry. He has a shirt.
Q: Might the record reflect, your Honour?
The Presiding Judge: Yes, the record will reflect that the witness identified the accused.[2]

Witness L's evidence was especially powerful because he was a Serb testifying against a Serb, he cast himself as a tormentor as well as a victim, and he claimed to have committed and witnessed capital crimes being committed at first hand.

But Tadic's British co-counsel, Steven Kay QC, began to have his doubts about the testimony of Witness L when he first cross-examined him:

Every time I try to ask a question that would throw light upon who he [Witness L] was, I'm stopped; I try again, I'm stopped. And I'm getting the feeling that there's something behind this – that this is a completely dodgy witness. When Witness L mentioned that the fence at Trnopolje was two metres high, and I'd been there and seen that it was under a metre high, I remember turning around to the others and saying, 'I don't think he's been there.'

During a break in the case, the defence team, led by the Dutch lawyer Michail Wladimiroff, travelled back to the Trnopolje region in Bosnia to take a closer look at these allegations. There, they stumbled across Witness L's family almost by accident, when a boy rode past them on a bicycle. Kay recalled:

This boy looked exactly the same as Witness L: jet black hair, massive bushy eyebrows that looked like pieces of carpet, a thin face, sunken eyes. We thought, 'Christ!' In his statement he said that he'd been to his father's funeral, that he had no brother. We followed the boy around to the farmyard, and there we found his father – *alive*. He looked exactly like him. . . . We went to the school and found the class attendance records that indicated that on the days he said he was taking this rifle and going off to kill people, he was in class. . . . Near Trnopolje we searched for the house with the cellar where all the rapes and murders were supposed to have taken place, but there was no house like that there.[3]

The lawyers persuaded Witness L's father Janko and his brother Pero to travel to The Hague. There, they and the prosecution's chief investigator, Robert Reid, arranged a meeting between the three family members. At this encounter, Dragan Opacic at first refused to admit that he knew them. Then he relented and conceded that Janko and Pero were indeed his father and brother. He then told Reid that he 'had been set up by the "Bosnians"', who, he said, had trained him to give false evidence against Tadic. Later that afternoon, Reid told the court: 'I then asked him if he, in fact, did know Tadic?' Opacic had replied that the first time he had seen him was 'on a video' shown to him several years after he had claimed to have worked at Trnopolje.[4] The investigator continued:

I then asked him was he actually a guard at the camp and he told me that he never was. I asked him how he knew the layout of the camp and the surrounding areas so well. He stated that he used to play football with his friends . . . within the grounds of the camp. He also stated that he used to pass the camp on occasions and saw detainees within the camp. I then asked him why he had pleaded guilty to something that he had never done. He stated that he had been threatened that if he did not cooperate with the Bosnian authorities he would be executed.[5]

After reviewing Opacic's testimony, Grant Niemann announced that he was dropping the charge against Tadic relating to Trnopolje. 'Prosecution now feels that it can no longer support that witness as a witness of truth', he said, 'We invite the Chamber to disregard his evidence entirely.'[6]

This case raised obvious doubts about using anonymous witnesses, who are harder to cross-examine, and more are likely to perjure themselves. Would other undiscovered Witness Ls appear at The Hague? This turned out to be just one of many thorny legal questions raised at the latest international tribunals.

*   *   *

War crimes trials are the cutting edge of human rights crusades, and the Yugoslavia Tribunal was the first one to appear after the Cold War. It was, to all intents and purposes, the creation of the United States, which drafted its original statute, instigated a short-lived war crimes commission to test the water, and shepherded the idea through the United Nations. The Security Council finally brought it to life in May 1993. Some senior human rights figures have argued that Washington initially conceived of it as a low-cost, low-risk sop to domestic critics on Bosnia.[7] But it was much more than that. It was an opportunity to assert the authority of the self-proclaimed 'civilised nations' over pariah states, by putting their citizens in the dock. In short, it was a Nuremberg for the new post-Cold War order.

Where America led, the other Security Council members followed – albeit more reluctantly. Although all voted in favour in the court, most of the Big Five had serious doubts about the enterprise. China feared a backlash against itself and was only dissuaded from using its veto by a bribe – namely, Washington's promise to renew Beijing's most favoured nation trade status after the Tiananmen Square massacre.[8] Russia did not want to censure her allies in Belgrade. And Britain did not want it to impede the diplomatic efforts of its European mediator, David Owen. The Foreign Office thus mouthed favourable platitudes in public, while playing a spoiler role behind the scenes, insisting, for example, that it be funded out of the cash-strapped United Nation's general budget. As a consequence, the tribunal was stunted at birth for want of money. Its first annual budget was just $10.8 million, about the same as the cost of the defence alone in the trial of Oklahoma Bomber Timothy McVeigh. 'There was zero!' recalled the then court president Antonio Cassese of the early days. 'Nothing! We had four secretaries, a few computers, and the UN had rented a meeting room and three small offices. . . . The rent was paid for two weeks.'[9]

The foot-dragging did not stop there. The Big Five plus ten more sitting members of the Security Council spent over a year deliberating over whom to appoint as chief prosecutor. Tit-for-tat rejections of nominees were par for the course. The British rejected the Arab and non-aligned nations' candidate, the Egyptian Cherif Bassiouni, because they thought his commitment to arresting Serb leaders would wreck Owen's peace process. In return, the non-aligned nations refused the British candidate, John Duncan Lowe, because they thought Britain was behind Europe's inaction in Bosnia. The Russians turned down the Canadian candidate, Christopher Amerasinghe, and the American candidate, Charles Ruff, on the grounds that Nato nations' nominees were bound to be anti-Serb. And the Pakistanis rebuffed the Indian candidate, Soli Sorabjee, as a swipe against their regional rivals. In all, eight candidates were ditched. The UN Secretary General, Boutros Boutros Ghali, then appointed the Venezuelan Ramon Escovar Salom, but just as he was about to start the job, a better offer came along and he resigned. As a Security Council member's representative observed, the hunt for a prosecutor had turned into 'a ghastly nightmare'.[10]

In July 1994, the Security Council finally settled on the South African judge, Richard Goldstone – a willing candidate to whom nobody objected. Before his appointment, Goldstone had chaired a commission investigating police and military violence during South Africa's democratic transition. He enjoyed a reputation for being a tough, liberal jurist – a reputation enhanced by his unpopularity with apartheid's old guard, who had denounced his commission report as 'riddled with hearsay evidence [and] vague insinuations'.[11] Other detractors, including some on the human rights circuit, criticised him for failing to produce sufficient new evidence or convictions. They also disapprovingly noted that he was ambitious (the South African press dubbed him 'Richard-Richard' because of his apparent desire to replace Boutros Boutros Ghali).[12] These charges and more would be levelled against him again by different interlocutors during his tenure at The Hague.

By early 1995, the new organisation moved out of its tiny offices and into the old Aegon insurance building located in a dreary Hague plaza, Churchillplein (named after the one-time advocate of summary executions). Movement was still painfully slow, with no trials in progress, and only one suspect, Dusko Tadic, in the pipeline. Judges were just 'sitting around twiddling their thumbs', recalled tribunal spokesman, Jim Landale.[13] In February, frustrated court president, Antonio Cassese put out a press release demanding that the prosecution issue 'a programme of indictments' to 'effectively meet the expectations of the Security Council and of the world community at large'.[14] This was a clear signal that he saw his role as one of facilitating arraignment. The following year he urged officials to ban Serb athletes from the 1996 Atlanta Olympic Games in order to increase pressure on Belgrade to deliver up the 'war criminals' Radovan Karadzic and Ratko Mladic. The human rights lawyer, Geoffrey Robertson QC, observed that Cassese's 'presumption of their guilt, and agitation for their arrest, would have disqualified him for bias in many domestic legal systems'.[15]

*   *   *

During an early case, American defence lawyer Russell Hayman complained to judges that the prosecution would have been censured for its behaviour had the trial taken place in a Californian court. The French judge, Claude Jorda, retorted that it had never promised to abide by the rules that Hayman was used to 'in Los Angeles'.[16] Not LA Law, say supporters, but not Nuremberg law either. They argue that the Yugoslavia court – which covers war crimes, grave breaches of the Geneva Conventions, crimes against humanity and genocide – is a considerable improvement on the earlier tribunals. It has jettisoned Nuremberg's most contentious *ex post facto* charges, such as aggression, and its most doubtful procedures, such as trials *in absentia*. They also argue that unlike the vengeance dispensed at Nuremberg and Tokyo, it provides genuinely impartial justice because all members of the United Nations sit in judgement. As Antonio Cassese put it: '[F]or the first time, the community of States is rendering a justice which is not that of the victors . . . a justice animated not by a spirit of revenge but by the determination to bring the criminals to book and prevent further crimes'.[17] This is a curious argument, given that the Security Council that established the court has endorsed air-strikes against Serb forces; and that the Nato members which underwrite it have waged war on Belgrade – and won.

The tribunal is mandated to prosecute serious crimes in the Balkans, but its focus has been selective. For example, would it put Western military leaders on trial if they were accused of committing war crimes in the region? This matter came to a head in December 1999, when Canadian lawyers and Russian parliamentarians raised the issue of Nato's military actions against Serbia. The Swiss chief prosecutor, Carla del Ponte, initially responded that she would investigate anyone who violated the Geneva Conventions. Then, under pressure from Washington, she issued a sudden retraction, stating that 'Nato is not under investigation by the Office of the Prosecutor.'[18] Shortly after, Amnesty International accused Nato of illegally bombing Belgrade's TV station. Del Ponte hit back with a report explaining why she would not be pursuing the issue.[19] 'Facts and law! No political motivations! Just facts and law!' she declared.[20] But the facts and law in her report raised more questions than they answered – such as why prosecutors had indicted Milan Martic for shooting cluster-headed rockets at Zagreb in May 1995; but not Nato for dropping cluster bombs on Nis in May 1999.[21]

The Nato powers exert a disproportionate influence upon the court's business. The United States has played a vital role in its development, as senior court figures acknowledge (former court president Gabrielle Kirk McDonald described Madeleine Albright as 'the mother of the tribunal').[22] It also makes an important day-to-day contribution to its work. It regularly donates cash and equipment, such as the $2.3 million worth of computers given to the prosecution in 1994–5, and the $1.08 million pledged in 1997–8 (of which $400,000 was earmarked for 'investigations into Kosovo').[23] It also provides the court with legal expertise, and supplies the human and signals intelligence that enables the prosecution to construct its cases. The Americans and the British have recently given prosecutors greater access to satellite imagery and battle communication intercepts. In the Krstic case dealing with the Srebrenica massacre, for example, US spy planes provided photographic evidence, while the US Army and British Army provided the military intelligence analysts – Richard Butler and Richard Dannett, respectively – to interpret the evidence. The CIA reputedly maintains the encrypted telephone in the chief prosecutors' office.[24]

Yet despite this intimacy, the tribunal's relationship with the United States has not always been a happy one. Washington is not averse to calling the shots in public from time to time and embarrassing the tribunal in the process. In 1997 American officials – as opposed to court personnel – promised indicted Croats a speedy trial if they surrendered themselves. '[By] making such statements they are making us look like a politically driven tribunal that you can switch on and switch off every day, according to political circumstance', a Hague spokesman complained.[25] This is clearly a sore point. As the former chief prosecutor, Louise Arbour, has admitted, the Western powers do indeed 'slow down the flow of information or accelerate it' in line with their political aims.[26] There have been other public spats, too. In February 1998, Clinton's envoy to former Yugoslavia, Robert Gelbard, gave notice that a 'significant number of indictments will not stand up in court', and that the United States would not risk soldiers' lives arresting people with 'weak' cases against them. Arbour retorted that his assessment of the cases was speculative 'since no state, including the United States of America, has access to the evidence upon which the indictments have been confirmed'.[27] Her protests were unconvincing, though, and the tribunal quietly dropped charges against fourteen Serbs four months later.

The climax of the court's relationship with the West came during Nato's spring 1999 offensive against Serbia. A week after Nato bombs began to rain down on Belgrade, Louise Arbour softened the political terrain on behalf of the Alliance, by announcing that charges had been issued against the Serb, Zeljko Raznatovic – nicknamed 'Arkan'.[28] Her message to President Slobodan Milosevic was clear: back down over Kosovo or you will be next. As good as her word, she announced his indictment two months later. The *Washington Post* claimed that the timing of this action was dependent on America's release of material to the prosecution. But the State Department's war crimes ambassador, David Scheffer, denied this: 'the indictment was not made in the USA', he said.[29] (He did not mention that it had earlier discouraged Milosevic's arraignment when he was playing a useful role in the 1995 Dayton peace talks on Bosnia.[30] At that time, officials had argued that the arrest of alleged war criminals should not be a 'show stopper'.[31])

In April 1999, midway through the Kosovo conflict, Arbour made a whistle-stop tour of Nato capitals, collecting promises of assistance wherever she went. On 19 April in Bonn, she gratefully received from the German Defence Minister, Rudolf Scharping, aerial photographs of Kosovar villages taken by reconnaissance drones. The next day in London, the British Foreign Secretary, Robin Cook, promised her a dossier of intelligence on atrocities committed by Serbs in Kosovo. Two days later, Lionel Jospin's government in Paris said it would gather eyewitnesses, protect investigators and refugees, and pass on military information. It all added up to 'unprecedented levels of cooperation', said deputy prosecutor Graham Blewitt.[32] By contrast, when a delegation from a Paris-based Serb solidarity organisation tried to deliver a petition calling for Bill Clinton's indictment as a war criminal, they were told that the prosecutors were 'too busy' to accept it. In the end, they had to hand it in to a UN guard on the gate.[33]

Arbour's trip to London seemed to be expressly designed to highlight the tribunal's support for one side of the war. She joined Robin Cook and chief of staff General Sir Charles Guthrie at a press conference held at the Ministry of Defence, the department responsible for Britain's attacks on Serbia. At this event, Cook promised to give her 'one of the largest releases of intelligence material ever authorised by a British Government', and more to come 'as the horror unfolds'.[34] An outline of the contents of this dossier had already been conveniently released to the press, and it turned out to be a rag-bag of old newspaper stories, recycled Nato propaganda, and Whitehall fabrications. (One document proclaimed the discovery of three Serb-run rape centres at Globocica, Urosevac and an unidentified location on the Kosovar–Albanian border,[35] a claim that remains unconfirmed by credible sources to this day.) Answering a question put to her at the press conference, Louise Arbour stated that it was 'inconceivable' that the tribunal was 'servicing a political agenda'.[36] Yet her presence at this publicity stunt, designed to add to the swelling tide of atrocity stories already doing the rounds in the British media, belied her words.

A few weeks later, Nato spokesman Jamie Shea was asked by a reporter whether his organisation recognised Arbour's jurisdiction over its activities. His response was revealing:

> I believe that when Justice Arbour starts her investigation, she will because we will allow her to. It's not Milosevic that has allowed Justice Arbour her visa to go to Kosovo to carry out her investigations. If her court, as we want, is to be allowed access, it will be because of Nato. . . . Nato is the friend of the Tribunal, Nato are the people who have been detaining indicted war criminals for the Tribunal in Bosnia . . . Nato countries are those that have provided the finance to set up the Tribunal, we are amongst the majority financiers . . . we and the Tribunal are all one on this, we want to see war criminals brought to justice and I am certain that when Justice Arbour goes to Kosovo and looks at the facts she will be indicting people of Yugoslav nationality and I don't anticipate any others at this stage.[37]

In other words, he who pays the piper calls the tune.

*   *   *

The Western human rights groups operate as the court's foot soldiers, providing it with personnel, information, resources and moral support. The Boston-based Physicians for Human Rights has assisted it in the exhumation of graves and the forensic examination of corpses. The Geneva-based International Commission of Jurists has provided the judges and registry with scores of legal researchers. The European Union-funded Rehabilitation and Research Centre for Torture Victims has operated counselling services in the Victims and Witnesses Unit. The New York-based Open Society Institute, established by George Soros and led by Aryeh Neier, has donated money, subscriptions and personnel. All are committed to impartial international justice. And almost all of these organisations focus their attention on issues relating to the prosecution, rather than the defence: campaigns to speed up the arrest of suspects, the gathering and assessment of certain kinds of testimony and evidence, and the protection and counselling of the victims.

Human Rights Watch has backed the tribunal right from the start. From 1993, it mounted a campaign for war crimes trials in which it issued a steady stream of documents designed to highlight the criminality of political and military figures. In August 1993, it produced a report called *Prosecute Now!* which zeroed in on eight named individuals – five Serbs, two Croats and one Bosnian Muslim – whom they accused of crimes ranging from mass rape to genocide. (These eight men were among the first investigated by the prosecution.[38]) In February 1994, it produced a document that criticised the UN for its failure to establish an effective court, and in April 1994 they produced another focusing on ethnic cleansing in Bosnia-Herzegovina that identified six more alleged war criminals. In September 1994, Richard Goldstone met the new head of Human Rights Watch, Kenneth Roth, in New York to discuss the prosecution's access to their confidential witness testimony and other evidence. Shortly after, Human Rights Watch's Ivana Nizich began to conduct research on behalf of the tribunal.[39]

After the July 1995 Srebrenica massacre, Human Rights Watch intensified its efforts, when it drew together a coalition of twenty-seven non-governmental organisations to press for 'American leadership' to 'stop genocide' in Bosnia. This group produced a public statement demanding that the Clinton administration take 'unilateral military action', and impose sanctions to enforce cooperation with the court.[40] A steady stream of articles and letters condemning Western inaction appeared at the same time. Washington must have been grateful for the coalition's help in readying the American public for military intervention. Nato unleashed air-srikes against the Bosnian Serbs the following month.

This double act between the government and NGOs also extended to the Balkans. Washington threatened punitive bombing raids, demanded the hand-over of suspects to the Hague, and offered aid to those receptive to Nato policy. Meanwhile, the American human rights and aid agencies condemned local 'nationalist' political parties, collated evidence for the court, and distributed resources to designated communities. Insofar as these groups criticised United States' actions, it was merely for failing to pursue this strategy with sufficient vigour.

The November 1995 Dayton Agreement ended the Bosnian phase of the Balkans war, and signalled a new, and more important phase in the tribunal's history. Thereafter, the Western powers involved in Bosnia set about removing nationalist leaders, either by electoral means, or, in some cases, by threatening them with a trip to The Hague. More pliant candidates were installed in their place. In July 1996, for example, the Organization for Security and Cooperation in Europe,[41] which organised the September election in Bosnia, banned Radovan Karadzic, the elected head of the Bosnian Serbs, from standing, on the grounds that he had been indicted for (though not convicted of) war crimes.[42] Instead of complaining about this automatic presumption of Karadzic's guilt, the agencies rubber-stamped this approach by calling for the elections to be postponed until the candidates they believed to be 'war criminals' had been removed from their slates and dispatched to The Hague.[43] In June 1996, Human Rights Watch published its report, *A Failure in the Making*, which castigated the Nato powers for not arresting more suspects after Dayton.[44] Again, criticism was of the 'too little, too late' variety.

Hundreds of organisations with some kind of human rights brief – from one-person outfits to the big-name international groups – rushed into the Balkans in the wake of the Bosnia and Kosovo conflicts. Among those who joined the stampede were two organisations which are very closely linked to the United States foreign policy establishment, and which have worked alongside the prosecution to secure convictions. The American Bar Association's Central and East European Law Initiative (CEELI), which promotes the 'rule of law' in the former Eastern Bloc, devotes some of its energies towards aiding the tribunal. In 1999, for example, it created a database, partly funded by the State Department, of around 2,000 interviews with Kosovar refugees, which were passed on to The Hague and back to Foggy Bottom.[45] It has also provided funds and personnel to assist the prosecution. While independent of government, it is almost wholly reliant on funds provided by the Justice Department and the US Agency for International Development. In 1998, for instance, it received 93.9 per cent of its funds from official sources. Some might suggest that, on purely financial grounds, it was merely the Justice Department in a non-governmental guise.

In 1995, CEELI's parent body, the American Bar Association, was asked by Secretary Madeleine Albright and Human Rights Bureau chief John Shattuck to set up a non-governmental organisation devoted entirely to lobbying on behalf of the tribunal. Shortly after, CEELI and the Open Society Institute established the Coalition for International Justice, whose current advisory board includes human rights luminaries such as former prosecutor Richard Goldstone, Bianca Jagger and Aryeh Neier.[46] The coalition has fought hard for sanctions against those who have not cooperated with the tribunal. It successfully halted World Bank funding to a project in Foca in Bosnia because the local authorities had not handed over seven people accused of war crimes (or 'seven indicted war criminals', as CEELI's 1998 annual report dubbed them).[47] At the same time, it proselytises on behalf of the court through outreach projects, and through its website. Prosecutions are enthusiastically encouraged. One web-page features a rogue's gallery of the 'UN's Most Wanted'. Another, entitled 'War Criminals Watch', tracks the movements of those who have been publicly indicted ('Mladic Spotted at Belgrade Soccer Match' and 'Karadzic Reported on the Move in Eastern Bosnia').[48] It is crude stuff, but then again, it is no cruder than Washington's bounty prizes, or the tribunal's 'Wanted' posters.

*   *   *

What quality of justice is handed down in The Hague? The court draws its practices from both the Anglo-Saxon adversarial system and the Continental inquisitorial tradition. The judges run the show, presiding over cases and hearing appeals (there are no juries, because, as an annual report explains, 'This Tribunal does not need to shackle itself' with the 'ancient trial-by-jury system'.[49]) But with little precedent to guide them, the judges have had to make up the rules as they have gone along. As at Nuremberg and Tokyo, many traditional procedural safeguards have been dispensed with. There is no ban on second or third-hand 'hearsay' evidence, for example, because, it is argued, judges are better equipped than juries to weigh the merits of such testimony. The troubling upshot of this, says Michael Scharf, a former State Department official, has been that 'over ninety per cent' of the evidence cited comes from hearsay sources.[50] Furthermore, in cases involving rape and sex crimes, the prosecution is given great leeway by Rule 96(1), which states that 'no corroboration of the victim's testimony shall be required'.[51] In other words, what the accuser says, goes.

The judge-made Rule 61 has also aroused concern. The tribunal is not permitted to conduct trials *in absentia*, in recognition of the controversy created by the trial of Martin Bormann at Nuremberg. But it allows practices that amount to the same thing. Rule 61, which can be invoked if a Balkan government refuses to turn someone in to The Hague, allows prosecutors to present highlights of their case against the accused in their absence, in the hope that the bad publicity will compel the authorities to hand them over. This practice is tantamount to a mini-trial *in absentia*, but worse, because defence lawyers are banished from the courtroom (on one occasion, lawyer Igor Pantelic was instructed to hear out accusations against his client, Radovan Karadzic, from the public gallery). Such hearings have caused unease: the BBC described the hearing against Milan Martic as 'a circus', while Geoffrey Robertson QC describes the practice as 'indefensible'.[52]

In the push to condemn Balkan wrongdoers, the Office of the Prosecution wields considerable political influence. Its leader, Carla del Ponte, has the power to bring national leaders to book. In January 2001 she summoned Biljana Plavsic, the former President of the Bosnian Serb Republic, to The Hague; six months later she had also lined up Slobodan Milosevic.[53] When her predecessor Louise Arbour won a case compelling the Croatian government to hand over General Tihomir Blaskic, she recalled that people in her office 'stopped whining, saying there's no political will, no one helps us', because they suddenly released that they had 'a huge amount of power'.[54] This is reflected in the allocation of funds. The prosecution receives almost a third of the United Nation's annual sponsorship of the court ($96.4 million in total in 2001). It can also expect political and financial support from America, Britain and other Nato powers – and the moral and campaigning support of Western human rights organisations.

The defence is very much the poor relation at The Hague. In principle, the prosecution and defence should be placed on an equal footing, but this is negated, in practice, by the structure of the court, which rests on the tripod of prosecution, judges and registry. This arrangement grants the prosecution membership of a club from which the defence is expressly excluded. By the same token, prosecutors, judges and registry personnel enjoy the same privileges as UN officials, whereas defenders do not. (Lawyer Anthony D'Amato complained that while a prosecutor was allowed to take the UN flights from Belgrade to Prijedor to collect evidence against his client, he was given a small allowance and told to make his own way.[55]) And while the prosecution has been set up with a co-ordinating office and budget, the defence does not enjoy equivalent resources. It does not get much support from governments either. Steven Kay believes that some Western politicians 'have a massive problem' discussing the defence. At one meeting with European representatives, 'everyone was chewing garlic and doing the sign of the cross whenever I appeared or opened my mouth', he recalled.[56]

*   *   *

The Yugoslavia tribunal has sometimes been accused of ignoring the rights of the accused, but nothing has quite matched a controversy that has dogged its sister court, the UN's International Criminal Tribunal for Rwanda, based in Arusha, Tanzania. On 3 November 1999, it was toppled from its human rights pedestal when the appeals chamber ordered the release of genocide suspect Jean Bosco Barayagwiza on the grounds that his 'fundamental rights were repeatedly violated'.

Barayagwiza, founder of Radio Television Libre des Mille Collines, had spent eleven months in a Cameroonian jail without being charged. When he issued a writ of *habeas corpus* demanding his release, the tribunal never got around to hearing it. His first court appearance came ninety-six days after his transfer to Arusha – a clear breach of his right to be seen without delay. The appeal chamber thus ruled that the prosecutor's handling of the case was 'tantamount to negligence', and that his trial would thus be a 'travesty of justice'. It ordered that Barayagwiza be released forthwith, and all charges dropped. To emphasise the seriousness of the ruling, it was tagged 'with prejudice' in order to prevent chief prosecutor Carla del Ponte from arresting and imprisoning him again.[57] The decision was a huge blow to the prosecution.

The Rwanda tribunal was set up by the Security Council in 1994. It was given the task of bringing to justice those chiefly responsible for the massacres, but it was also intended as a tool to bring about 'national reconciliation' and the 'restoration and maintenance of peace'. It was mandated to do big things on behalf of the global community, and it wanted big fish to fry, even if it meant trampling over Rwanda in order to get its hands on them. In 1996 for example, the court overruled Kigali's request to extradite Barayagwiza, Laurent Semanza and Theoneste Bagosora from Cameroon, because it wanted to bag them for itself. As a result, the tribunal currently holds several dozen prime suspects while Rwanda has been left to deal with 120,000 of their followers – a situation that, unsurprisingly, has antagonised the government in Kigali. As Prosecutor-General Gerald Gahima points out: 'It makes it harder to forgive the ordinary people if we don't have the leaders here to be tried in Rwandan courts'.[58]

Ever since the first trials in Russia in early 1997 there has been a persistent rumble of complaint about the treatment of detainees: some have been held for inordinately long periods before trial; others have been held unlawfully. In 1998, Amnesty International issued a report that highlighted these failings. It criticised the treatment of Esdras Twagirimana, who had been arrested because of mistaken identity and unlawfully held for two months without access to a lawyer. It raised concerns about the slowness in dealing with Alfred Musema, a tea factory director, who only appeared before a court, without a lawyer, six months after he arrived at Arusha.[59] And it criticised the nine-month incarceration of Jean Kambanda, Rwanda's former prime minister, in a secret 'safe house', because it was not an officially recognised place of detention (thus removing safeguards against ill-treatment and compulsion to confess).[60] The tribunal gave these criticisms short shrift. 'It is fashionable in some quarters to denigrate and distort the efforts of the International Criminal Tribunal for Rwanda', it responded. 'To the extent that Amnesty International has joined this bandwagon, the Tribunal finds it a matter of regret.'[61]

In December 1999, the court sentenced Georges Rutaganda, a former vice-president of the Hutu *interahamwe* militia, to life imprisonment for genocide, extermination and murder. The verdict followed hot on the heels of the Barayagwiza case, and was widely viewed (and welcomed) as a corrective to that fiasco. Yet there were problems with that case too. In February 1997, his Canadian lawyer, Tiphaine Dickson, filed an 'extremely urgent' request to the tribunal to get statements from sixteen defence witnesses living in perilous conditions in Tingi-Tingi refugee camp in east Zaire (now the Democratic Republic of Congo). The court sat on this request for three weeks. Meanwhile Zairean forces under Laurent Kabila attacked the camp and all the witnesses fled, fourteen of them never to reappear. Dickson argued that the delay had violated Rutaganda's right to a fair trial because it had prevented him from establishing alibis.[62] The court expressed regret, but failed to pursue the matter.

So what has become of Jean Bosco Barayagwiza, whose release was announced so dramatically in 1999? As is the way with these things, rules were bent and deals were done. Shortly after the decision, *Internews* journalist Coll Metcalfe asked Del Ponte whether she was surprised by the decision. She replied:

> Surprise was not the word. It was really a shock. I am convinced that he is guilty. How is it possible that he is released and there is no prosecution possible?

She decided something had to be done. 'Immediately, I had a meeting with my colleagues in The Hague and asked if there was a possibility to make a request for review', she recalled. In the negotiations that ensued:

> [W]e discussed what issues we had. Did we have any chance for review? And we discussed the legal facts. We discussed that for hours and we didn't make any decision right away. In the following days we discussed it again and again and we found we had a chance.

Did this 'chance' have had anything to do with the removal of the 'with prejudice' tag preventing the re-arrest of Barayagwiza? 'I hope for this small solution', she said.

> I'd like them to just change this decision a little bit because the most important thing is that he goes before a court for judgment. If it's not before the tribunal at Arusha, then it must be a national court.[63]

As it turned out, Barayagwiza was not released from the UN prison at Arusha, and the following March, the appeals chamber further stoked the fires of legal controversy by reversing their decision. Carla Del Ponte, they said, had produced 'new facts' which persuaded them that violations of the rights of the accused had been less severe than they had originally believed.[64] Barayagwiza has been boycotting his trial, which began in October 2000, on the grounds that he will not receive a fair hearing.

*   *   *

The Hague is the booming capital of global justice, and the Yugoslavia Tribunal will soon be joined there by a new body set up to prosecute major war criminals, the UN International Criminal Court. Because this court will be brought into effect by international treaty rather than by Security Council fiat, supporters hope that it will genuinely represent the will of the entire global community. When the landslide vote for its establishment – 120 ayes, 7 noes – was announced at a diplomatic conference in Rome in 1998, most delegates sprang to their feet and cheered rapturously, a striking illustration of the high hopes invested to the enterprise. Not everyone expressed delight, though. The Americans had voted against it, and sat in grim silence amid these celebrations. Kenneth Roth of Human Rights Watch described the scene when the vote was announced:

> As cheering broke out in the UN conference room on the Viale Aventino in Rome this past July, David Scheffer, the US ambassador-at-large for war crimes issues . . . sat stone-faced, arms folded. . . . In favor of the court were most of America's closest allies, including Britain, Canada, and Germany. But the United States was isolated in opposition, along with such dictatorships and enemies of human rights as Iran, Iraq, China, Libya, Algeria, and Sudan. It was an embarrassing low point for a government that portrays itself as a champion of human rights.[65]

America's vote was an extraordinary *volte-face*, because it was a project that they themselves had initiated. Washington's support for the court dated back to the mid-nineties, when the Yugoslav and Rwanda tribunals had proved themselves to be useful safety valves for domestic demands in the United States to 'do something'. They had provided a high-profile demonstration of its commitment to bring human rights transgressors to book. Madeleine Albright, then Ambassador to the UN, gave the United Nations Secretariat the go-ahead, and an international committee was established to draw up a draft statute.

This was a model of caution. So too was the statute agreed at the Rome conference. It states that when established, the court will not try old crimes (Article 11); that all prosecutions will be vetted by a pre-trial chamber (Article 15); that the Security Council will be able to veto prosecutions

(Article 16); and that a suspect will only be pursued if domestic courts are unwilling or unable to do so (Article 17). Opponents of the court in the United States – the John Brickers *de nos jours* – have argued that it will maliciously hunt down American soldiers. But in fact, the combined effect of the aforementioned articles will ensure that any future William Calley (who was tried for the My Lai massacre) or future Henry Kissinger (who stands accused of Vietnam-era war crimes) will be safe from The Hague.

At Rome, the United States, which pushed for a weak court under Security Council control, appeared to come into conflict with Britain, which proclaimed support for a stronger institution. There was talk of a rift between the two allies, but this speculation was wide of the mark. The United States played hardball, but Britain was just as wary of a powerful court. It was only because Whitehall was confident that Washington would hold the line against such an outcome that it was able to pose as a principled supporter of international justice. This posturing, in turn, helped to create a positive image of the project, which encouraged other countries to support it, and thus neutralised potentially troublesome opponents such as Russia and China. Whether by accident or design, the Americans and the British operated a division of labour that brought about the outcome they both desired.[66]

So why did the United States delegates sulk in Rome? Their negative vote was mere brinkmanship, designed to wrest a few final concessions, and to mollify conservative critics at home. (President Clinton eventually signed the treaty, and it was submitted in dramatic, last-minute fashion on the day of the deadline.) Yet the diplomatic smoke and mirrors should not blind us to the court's real purpose. America's former war crimes supremo, David Scheffer, described it as 'the shiny new hammer' in the 'civilised world's box of foreign policy tools'.[67] The major powers have drawn up a statute that virtually guarantees that none of their citizens will ever be prosecuted. This will leave it free to carry out its intended function: meting out punishment to alleged transgressors from the war-ravaged and judicially-challenged pariah states. When it comes to global justice, it is always better to give than to receive.

Conclusion

In 1945, the Egyptian government warned its delegation to the San Francisco conference that the application of the principle of human rights 'may lead to dangerous evils', namely, the 'unjustified interference of foreign powers'.[1] More than half a century later, many Egyptians still see it as a stalking horse. When, in 1992, Human Rights Watch released a report recommending sanctions against the Cairo government to compel it to stop using torture, the proposal was dismissed as a typical example of Western hypocrisy. 'Such a demand was not acceptable to the Egyptian public', wrote Bahey el Din Hassan, director of the Cairo Institute for Human Rights Studies, because it 'perceived that the same criterion was not applied to Israel, which has a notorious record of torture and arbitrary detention in the occupied territories'.[2]

Egyptians have given other Western initiatives equally short shrift. When the USA's Commission on International Religious Freedom (a body created by the 1998 International Religious Freedom Act[3]) announced that it intended to visit the country in 2001 to investigate the plight of Coptic Christians, it was not welcomed. Prominent among critics of the trip was the Coptic community itself, which swiftly denounced external meddling in its affairs. According to the newspaper *Al-Ahram*, the head of the Coptic Orthodox Church, Pope Shenouda, stated that 'It complicates the situation to have a foreign intruder in such a sensitive issue'. Meanwhile, Mounir Fakhri Abdel-Nour, a prominent Christian member of the opposition Wafd Party, led protests in Parliament against the visit, arguing that, 'This is no goodwill tour or peace mission; it is outright foreign intervention in our internal affairs.'[4]

They were particularly unenthusiastic about the commission's leader, who was none other than Elliott Abrams, the American rightwinger who had spent the early eighties playing down human rights abuses, and the late nineties talking up religious persecution. To add insult to injury, he is also a fervent supporter of Israel, which he considers to be 'the only true democracy in a region where thuggery reigns' – a sentiment that does not endear him to the Arab world.[5] The Cairo press took the opportunity to remind their readers of the more unsavoury moments in his career, especially his part in the Iran-contra scandal. It also speculated, with some justification, that the new Bush administration was using the investigation to keep President Hosni Mubarak in line over the Palestinian question and sanctions on Iraq. Abrams, who was once accused of conducting 'Doberman pincher' diplomacy, denounced such 'misinformation' with characteristic disdain.[6]

On arrival in Cairo, the commission was granted an audience with President Mubarak, Pope Shenouda and the Muslim leader, the Sheikh of al-Azhar. This diplomatic courtesy was more or less obligatory, given that the US provides the country with around $2 billion in aid every year. But when it hosted a welcome gala for politicians, clerics and advocates, the turnout was disappointing, to say the least. Press estimates of the number of Egyptian guests in attendance ranged from zero to two ('with one of the two reported guests subsequently denying her presence', according to a later account).[7] Prominent among the absentees were the local human rights groups, who issued a joint statement explaining their refusal to meet the commission. The United States, they said, operated 'double standards' by 'devoting attention to religious freedoms in the Middle East while supporting shameful violations of the rights of the Palestinian people'.[8] By contrast, the Egyptians have been scrupulously even-handed towards the Americans – repudiating Elliott Abrams and Human Rights Watch with equal vigour.

*   *   *

The Egyptians are by no means the only people to denounce such campaigns. Sri Lankans, Bosnians, Chileans, Nigerians and many others have at various times described them as arrogant, intrusive and even imperialist. Does this criticism have any impact? Yes and no. Human rights activists are extremely sensitive to such censure, especially when it emanates from the intended beneficiaries of their work. Western leaders, on the other hand, often appear to be indifferent to the opinions of those on the receiving end of their policies. This is not because they are unusually callous or deaf to reason, but because their political priorities lie closer to home.

Politicians instinctively understand the importance of having a positive national self image and a sense of shared purpose. This has been the driving force behind human rights initiatives ever since America shaped the postwar order at San Francisco. This impulse was clearly articulated by the House Democrat, Dante Fascell, in 1981, during the early days of the Reagan administration, when he delivered a rousing call for a strong moral component in US foreign policy.

> I believe that nations act in accordance with their self-images. And the way in which we behave internationally has a very real effect not only on how we are perceived, but on how we *are*. We have seen too many examples in recent

history of how easy it is in times of national crisis for a country to be drawn into courses of action in foreign affairs that have lost sight of human values and ended disastrously for itself and its allies. The human rights policy, in that sense, operates as a compass to ensure we stay on course. So I think it can be seen that our human rights policy is not just for others. It's for us too.[9]

*   *   *

The self-preoccupation of the most powerful states explains the fickleness of their human rights campaigns. Victims of repression abroad are the pretext for intervention, rather than the reason for it. They thus become expendable once they have served their purpose. The list of such forgotten victims is a long one. Russian Jews, Nicaraguan Indians, Iranian Baha'is, Ethiopian farmers, Polish trades unionists, Tibetan nuns, Argentine radicals, Soviet camp inmates, Kosovar rape-victims, Chinese dissidents, Iraqi Kurds and Tutsi refugees are just a few of the groups that have had their fifteen minutes of fame. Presidents and Prime Ministers, fund-raisers and relief agencies, foreign correspondents and war photographers, pop stars and catwalk models, have all beaten a path to their door. Then, when the spotlight moved on somewhere else, they were plunged back into obscurity once again. Little attention is paid to their subsequent plight.

A case in point is the Carter administration's apparent lack of interest in the effects of its actions abroad. Although officials often proclaimed their commitment to human rights, and repeatedly polled *Americans* about their opinions on the issue, they maintained a deafening silence about the effects of their policies in the Eastern Bloc and Latin America. This was partly because there was not much to write home about (the *Country Reports* indicate that the situation stayed the same or got worse in most targeted nations). But it also highlighted an unpalatable truth: the administration was conducting a 'foreign' policy whose impact on foreigners was largely incidental.

It fell to a handful of academics to conduct a proper post-mortem on the consequences of Carter's actions overseas. Studies carried out in the eighties were generally tentative or negative in their conclusions. A 1981 Congressional Research Service report, written by Stanley Heginbotham, observed that despite some marginal improvements in a few countries, the record abroad in the late seventies was 'hardly encouraging'.[10] A 1989 study by David Forsythe suggested that while sanctions may have ameliorated abuses over time, they usually provoked a demonstrable 'negative reaction' when first imposed.[11] And in 1987, David Carleton and Michael Stohl concluded that in the years 1976 to 1983, there was at best, 'no statistical relationship' between US aid and human rights, and at worst, 'there [was] a significant negative relationship; that is, the more abusive a regime, the more aid received'.[12]

It would be easy to put this self-serving behaviour down to some kind of government conspiracy – a school of thought summed up by Barry Levinson's 1997 film *Wag the Dog*, in which shadowy fixers divert public attention from a White House sex scandal with a bogus made-for-TV war. This satire struck a chord with those who had grown cynical about the way that Bill Clinton and other Western leaders appeared to pick and choose (not to mention exaggerate or invent) their causes to suit their own requirements. But while one should not underestimate a propensity to conspire, the human rights impulse cannot simply be dismissed as a con trick. Something more complex and less calculated is going on. Heads of government believe that their role is to promote virtue within the limits imposed by political practicalities. So when they spout homilies about dignity and justice, it is rarely an entirely empty gesture. As Fascell said, 'our human rights policy is not just for others. It's for us too.'

*   *   *

The essence of this modern political phenomenon is perfectly captured by a story straight from the heart of middle America. In 1998, Barbara Vogel's fourth-grade class at the Highline elementary school in Aurora, Colorado, started to raise money to free slaves in Sudan. It all began after they had completed their history unit on American slavery. 'I had taught my children that . . . chattel slavery was a thing of the past', she recalled. But then she read an article about Sudanese slaves in the *Rocky Mountain News*, and realised that 'I had taught them wrong'. When she read the piece to her pupils they were moved to tears, and were inspired to raise $1,000 by collecting pennies in a jar. Later, a feature on the CBS *Evening News* and an article in *Time* brought fame and more money. Thus began the American children's campaign, STOP – Slavery That Oppresses People. Barbara Vogel said: 'We call ourselves abolitionists, after great Americans like Harriet Tubman and Frederick Douglass.'[13]

In 2000, Jesse Helms invited Barbara Vogel and her class to address the Senate Committee on Foreign Relations. The hearing was very different from the usual parade of bureaucrats, academics and lawyers. The children delivered speeches, and the adults were not ashamed to cry.

> *Ms Vogel:* Can I still teach them that our government stands for fight and for freedom? Can I still teach them that our country stands for principles more than practicality?
> *The Chairman:* There is some Kleenex for you.
> *Ms Vogel:* Thank you. I promised I was not going to do this. Can I still tell them that we are the home of the brave?[14]

Vogel described to the Senators a trip she had made to Sudan, where she had seen for herself some 4,300 women and children who had 'just been redeemed from slavery by the brave rescuers at Christian Solidarity International'. Her account gives a revealing insight into the Western humanitarian mentality.

> It was in Sudan that I realized that I was not the rescuer. I was there as a representative of a nation that needs its own rescuing. The enslavement of black women and children in Sudan is not merely a tragic by-product of some distant conflict. It is a direct challenge to our Nation. Will we squander our freedom for frivolous pursuits? . . . Or will we triumph over America's own terrible legacy of slavery by extending emancipation to millions who remain in bondage? . . . It may sound odd, but I believe the enslaved women and children of Sudan can be the key to our hope and our own redemption.[15]

Vogel found salvation among the dispossessed of Sudan, and in the process, she stumbled upon the fundamental appeal of all human rights campaigns: they hold out to the benefactors the promise of redemption. Small wonder, then, that governments are so keen to champion the cause of the persecuted. When they side with the angels, they acquire a moral authority. They stand for more than a tax cut or a soundbite: they stand for a united society, and for a whole way of life.

*　　*　　*

The American poet Archibald MacLeish, who occupied various government positions during the forties, and who attended the consultants' meeting at the San Francisco conference, once said:

> There are those who will say that the liberation of humanity, the freedom of man and mind, is nothing but a dream. They are right. It is. It's the American dream.[16]

Today human rights are no longer just the stuff of dreams; they have become the *lingua franca* of modern political discourse. They allow politicians to occupy the moral high ground by day and sleep the sleep of the just by night. In the aftermath of September 11, no one can be sure exactly what the immediate future holds. (At the time of writing, anti-terrorism is the immediate response.) But one thing can be stated with confidence. Nothing else offers the positive moral appeal of human rights. In the absence of a more powerful alternative, the idea looks set to occupy a prominent place on the West's agenda for some time to come.

Notes

Notes on Sources

AMAE: Archives du Ministère des Affaires Etrangères, Paris.
FRUS: Foreign Relations of the United States, US State Department.
NARA: National Archives and Records Administration, College Park, Maryland.
PRO: Public Record Office, Kew, Surrey.

Introduction

1. Elaine Pagels, 'Human Rights: Legitimizing a Recent Concept,' *Annals of the American Academy of Political and Social Science*, Vol. 442, March 1979, 58.
2. *Human Rights and US Foreign Policy*, Department of State Office of Public Communication, No. 8959, December 1978, 1.
3. Hillary Rodham Clinton, Human Rights Day address, 10.12.97. www.usis.usemb.se/hrday/index.html
4. Elaine Pagels, 'Human Rights: Legitimizing a Recent Concept', *Annals of the American Academy of Political and Social Science*, Vol. 442, March 1979, 58.
5. Harlan Cleveland statement, *Reconciling Human Rights and US Security Interests in Asia*, House Committee on Foreign Affairs, Subcommittees on Asian and Pacific Affairs, and Human Rights and International Organizations, 15.12.82, 490–1 (original emphasis).
6. Issiah Berlin, *Four Essays on Liberty*, 129.
7. Lynn Hunt, *The French Revolution and Human Rights*, 10.
8. *Ibid.*, 4 (original emphasis).
9. www.yale.edu/lawweb/avalon/rightsof.htm
10. Article One's egalitarian spirit was undermined by a qualifying clause: 'Social distinctions may be founded only upon the general good.'
11. H.G. Wells, *The New World Order*, 141.
12. *Ibid.*, 143.
13. Jan Hermann Burgers, 'The Road to San Francisco: The Revival of the Human Rights Idea in the Twentieth Century', *Human Rights Quarterly*, No. 14, November 1992, 471–4.
14. Annual Message to Congress, 6.1.41. www.presidency.ucsb.edu/docs/pppus/rooseveltfd/1941/3.htm
Winston Churchill later teased Roosevelt about 'freedom from want'. 'I suppose,' he inquired, 'it means privation and not desire.' (Jim Bishop, *FDR's Last Year*, 416.)
15. John MacGregor Burns, *Roosevelt: The Soldier of Freedom*, 387 (emphasis added).
16. John Morton Blum, *V Was for Victory*, 29.
17. Townsend Hoopes and Douglas Brinkley, *FDR and the Creation of the UN*, 207.
18. *Ibid.*, 46. Roosevelt was so pleased with 'United Nations' that he burst into the room of his White House visitor, Winston Churchill, while the Prime Minister was in the bath, to get his immediate approval.

19. William L. O'Neill, *A Democracy at War*, 195.
20. Roosevelt said of the UN General Assembly: 'It is not really of any great importance. It is an investigatory body only.' (Robert A. Divine, *Second Chance*, 276.)
21. NARA, RG 59, Notter files, Records of the US Delegation to the UN Conference on International Organization, 1944–5, Box 215: 'Article 9', 3.9.43.
22. NARA, RG 59, Notter files, Records of the Advisory Committee on Postwar Foreign Policy, 1942–5, Box 75: 'Bill of Rights', 31.7.42.
23. NARA, RG 59, Notter files, Records of the Advisory Committee on Postwar Foreign Policy, 1942–5, Box 75: 'Bill of Rights', 26.10.42.
24. NARA, RG 59, Notter files, Records of the Advisory Committee on Postwar Foreign Policy, 1942–5, Box 75: 'Bill of Rights', 11.11.42.
25. NARA, RG 59, Notter files, Policy Summaries, 1943–4, Box 156: 'International Law', 2.6.43.
26. Ronald Steel: 'Motherhood, Apple Pie and Human Rights', *New Republic*, 4.6.77, 14.

Chapter One

1. Clark M. Eichelberger, *UN: The First Twenty Years*, 69.
2. Accounts differ over when the meeting with Virginia Gildersleeve took place, and over how many consultants were involved. Some participants say it took place on 1 May, but Joseph Proskauer says that it took place on the morning of 2 May. This seems to be borne out by the minutes, which record Proskauer publicly referring to a meeting with Gildersleeve 'this morning'. (*A Segment of My Times*, 221; NARA, RG 59, 500.CC, 1945–9, Box 1999: 'Meeting of Consultants', 2.5.45.)
3. O. Frederick Nolde, *Free and Equal*, 21–2.
4. *Ibid.*, 22. This was not an accurate portrayal of Stettinius's comments. The verbatim transcript, which Nolde possessed, shows that Stettinius said the opposite: 'Dr Bowman and I both, who represented you at Dumbarton Oaks, fought through that hot summer, as hard as we have fought on anything for expansion of the language to promote praise for the rights and fundamental freedoms. There are the very words with which we started. Fundamentally to me, that is one of the corner stones of this entire undertaking and *I have full confidence that we are going to win out on that issue.*' (Emphasis added.) (NARA, RG 59, 500.CC, 1945–49, Box 1999: 'Meeting of Consultants', 2.5.45.)
5. O. Frederick Nolde, *Free and Equal*, 23.
6. Joseph M. Proskauer, *A Segment of My Times*, 225. Proskauer's account of his speech was embellished. What he actually said was: 'We know there is a chance you won't succeed – that it may cause opposition, but I am here to tell you, sir, that if you *try* and fail, you have still succeeded, because you will have satisfied the public opinion of America.' (Original emphasis.) Murray's speech was rearranged. What he actually said was: 'I wish to express to the Secretary my own appreciation and the appreciation of my organization for the splendid interest you are manifesting in the promotion of these ideas. The name of the CIO was omitted in the course of the Judge's talk. . . . I should like the meeting to know, and especially the Secretary, that our organization subscribes wholesomely and wholeheartedly to this proposal. . . .' There is no evidence that Proskauer challenged anyone to register their dissent, or that Stettinius exclaimed that he had no idea of the depth of the feeling on the subject. (NARA, RG 59, 500.CC, 1945–9, Box 1999: 'Meeting of Consultants', 2.5.45.)
7. Walter Kotschnig quoted in Dorothy B. Robins, *Experiment in Democracy*, 132.

8. 'Report to the President on the Results of the San Francisco Conference by the Chairman of the United States Delegation, The Secretary of State', 26.6.45.

9. See, among others, John P. Humphrey, *Human Rights and the United Nations*; Dorothy B. Robins, *Experiment in Democracy*; Margaret E. Keck and Kathryn Sikkink, *Activists beyond Borders*; Felice Gaer, 'Reality Check: Human Rights Organisations Confront Governments at the United Nations', *Third World Quarterly*, 16(3), September 1995. Only Cathal Nolan, *Principled Diplomacy*, has challenged this version of events.

10. NARA, RG 59, 500.CC, 1945–9, Box 1999: 'Meeting of Consultants', 2.5.45.

11. NARA, RG 59, Records of the US Delegation to the UN Conference of International Organization, 1944–5, Box 208: 'Promotion of Respect for Human Rights and Fundamental Freedoms' 7.4.45. (Annotated 'To SF Conf'.) The idea of establishing an international commission on human rights was first floated in 1942, when it was included in a list of proposals for the enforcement of a bill of rights. (NARA, RG 59, Notter files, Records of the Advisory Committee on Postwar Foreign Policy, 1942–5, Box 75: 'Bill of Rights: International Implementation', 4.11.42.)

12. This set of proposals, drafted by McDiarmid on 7 April 1945 and reiterated by Stettinius on 15 May, was inserted into the UN Charter, signed on 26 June 1945. The fact that the proposals advanced by Nolde, Proskauer and others on 2 May were almost identical to McDiarmid's suggests that they had been advised by State Department officials, or consultants closely involved with the State Department's postwar planning, about what would be acceptable.

13. NARA, RG 59, Notter files, US Delegation to the UN Conference, 1944–5, Box 208: 'Promotion of Respect for Human Rights and Fundamental Freedoms', 7.4.45. (Annotated: 'To SF Conf'.)

14. O. Frederick Nolde, *Free and Equal*, 22.

15. Shirley Hazzard, *Defeat of an Ideal*, 6.

16. The OSS design team leader, Oliver Lundquist, came up with the logo featuring the map of the world, the olive leaves, and the background of soothing blue – a colour dubbed 'Stettinius' blue, after the Secretary of State. In his original design, intended solely for use on conference security passes, Lundquist had lopped Argentina off the map as his personal revenge for that nation's dalliance with the Nazis. (Nicholas J. Cull, 'Selling Peace: The Origins, Promotion and Fate of the Anglo-American New Order During the Second World War', *Diplomacy and Statecraft*, 7(1), March 1996, 22–3.)

17. Stephen Schlesinger writes: 'The 645 pages of intercepted diplomatic messages emerged from a clandestine army intelligence operation working out of the War Department under the umbrella of Communications Intelligence or "Comint". Later nicknamed "Ultra" after the British decoding project, the unit gave America access to the wartime embassy cable traffic of its allies (except Britain and the Soviet Union), neutral nations and belligerents. The "Magic" summaries produced by Ultra reveal that: Washington knew in advance the negotiating positions of almost all the 50 of so countries that assembled in San Francisco.' ('FDR's Five Policemen: Creating the United Nations', *World Policy Journal*, 11(3), Fall 1994, 88–9.)

18. Thomas M. Campbell and George C. Herring, *The Diaries of Edward R. Stettinius Jr*, 397.

19. PRO, FO 371/50714, US Delegation press statement, 'Statement by the Honorable Edward R. Stettinius Jr', 15.5.45.

20. PRO, FO 371/50723, UK Delegation press release, 'Remarks of G. Myrddin Evans', 11.6.45.

21. www.un.org/aboutun/charter/index.html

22. PRO, FO 371/50730, Smuts quoted in United Nations Information Organisation, 'United Nations Conference on International Organisation', July 1945, 6.
23. NARA, RG 59, 500.CC, 1945–9, Box 2000: 'Public Liaison Meeting', 8.5.45.
24. NARA, RG 59, 500.CC, 1945–9, Box 1998: Tuck (Cairo) to Secretary of State, 24.4.45.
25. www.un.org/aboutun/charter/index.html
26. PRO, FO 371/50714, US Delegation press statement, 'Statement by the Honorable Edward R. Stettinius Jr', 15.5.45.
27. PRO, CAB 121/162, UK Delegation (San Francisco) to FO, 19.5.45.
28. PRO, FO 371/50716, Hadow, 17.5.45. Alger Hiss, later famously accused of being a Soviet spy, was the State Department official responsible for organising the San Francisco conference.
29. PRO, FO 371/50731, Holliday report, undated, *c.* late June to early July 1945, 9.
30. *Ibid.*, 10.
31. *Ibid.*, 13.
32. PRO, FO 371/50731, Halifax (Washington) to Eden, 6.7.45.
33. PRO, FO 371/50731, Jebb, 31.7.45.
34. Carol Anderson, 'Symposium: African Americans and US Foreign Relations', *Diplomatic History*, 20(4), Fall 1996, 535.
35. Joseph P. Lash, *Eleanor: The Years Alone*, 55.
36. NARA, RG 59, Sandifer files, Box 8: 'Commission on Human Rights', *c.* 25.5.46.
37. *Ibid.*
38. Roosevelt's name was not the only one put forward for the job of American representative. In March 1946, Professor Theodore Smith wrote to Dean Rusk to nominate his father-in-law, Joseph Proskauer for the job. (NARA, RG 59, 501.BD Human Rights, Box 2186: Smith to Rusk, 20.3.46.)
39. NARA, RG 59, Sandifer files, Box 8: Human Rights Working Group, 30.9.46.
40. PRO, FO 371/57317, Draft 'Commission on Human Rights', undated, *c.* March 1946.
41. PRO, FO 371/59740, 'Human Rights Commission', date-stamped 11.9.46.
42. PRO, FO 371/67487, FO to UK Permanent Representative at UN (New York), 7.3.47.
43. PRO, FO 371/59740, 'Human Rights Commission', date-stamped 11.9.46.
44. PRO, FO 371/59741, Mason, 30.9.46.
45. PRO, FO 371/57941, Jowitt to McNeil, 28.10.46.
46. PRO, FO 371/59740, Noel-Baker, 7.9.46.
47. NARA, RG 59, Sandifer files, Box 8: 'Possible nominees for the Drafting Committee on International Bill of Rights', undated, *c.* 1946 to early 1947.
48. PRO, FO 371/59740, Beckett, 10.8.46.
49. Johannes Morsink, *The Universal Declaration of Human Rights*, 118.
50. Joseph P. Lash, *Eleanor: The Years Alone*, 70.
51. Johannes Morsink, *The Universal Declaration of Human Rights*, 119.
52. *Ibid.*, 284–7.
53. www.un.org/Overview/rights.html
54. NARA, RG 59, Sandifer files, Box 8: Sandifer to Simsarian and Hendrick, 27.7.48.
55. NARA, RG 59, Records of the Bureau of International Organisation Affairs and its Predecessors, Position papers 1945–74, Box 27: 'Working Relationship in Commission', undated, *c.* summer 1948.
56. NARA, RG 353, Records of the Subcommittee on Human Rights and the Status of Women, 1947–9, Box 110: 'Right to Resist Oppression', 16.5.47 (emphasis added).
57. PRO, FO 371/72809, Draft 'Report on the Third Session of the Human Rights Commission', undated, *c.* June 1948.

58. NARA, RG 59, 501.BD Human Rights, Box 2189: Caffery (Paris) to Secretary of State, 30.9.48.
59. PRO, FO 371/72809, Draft 'Report on the Third Session of the Human Rights Commission', undated, *c.* June 1948. Occasionally colleagues unfairly underestimated Cassin. After a tête-a-tête with some French lawyers of his acquaintance, the Foreign Office official Eric Beckett related their view that 'when you come to the bottom of it, Professor Cassin did not really know a great deal about the subject' of human rights. (PRO, FO 371/72810, Beckett, 6.8.48.) Yet, for what it is worth, Cassin's contribution to the declaration was overstated in one crucial respect: his designation as 'father' of the declaration was based on the erroneous assumption that he wrote the first draft – an impression that Cassin himself failed to correct. (Marc Agi's biography, *René Cassin*, is subtitled: *Père de la Déclaration universelle des droits de l'homme*.) As Johannes Morsink indicates in his book, *The Universal Declaration of Human Rights*, the first draft was in fact written by John Humphrey, the head of the Secretariat's Human Rights Division (Morsink, 29).
60. PRO, FO 371/67608, UK Delegation to UN (New York) to FO, 18.11.47.
61. NARA, RG 59, Sandifer files, Box 13: De Palma to Popper, 30.12.47.
62. NARA, RG 59, 501.BD Human Rights, Box 2187: Memorandum of Stinebower/Alexander conversation, 14.1.47.
63. John Humphrey wrote that Roosevelt was 'received everywhere she goes in Europe with greater respect and enthusiasm than any head of state would be.' (A.J. Hobbins (ed.), *On the Edge of Greatness*, 85.)
64. A. Glenn Mower Jr, *The United States, the United Nations and Human Rights*, 39.
65. *Ibid.*, 44.
66. Joseph P. Lash, *Eleanor: The Years Alone*, 63.
67. A. Glenn Mower Jr, *The United States, the United Nations and Human Rights*, 43.
68. E.J. Kahn Jr, 'The Years Alone – I', *New Yorker*, 12.6.48, 36.
69. PRO, FO 371/67610, UK Delegation to UN (Geneva) to FO, 16.12.47.
70. E.J. Kahn Jr, 'The Years Alone – I', *New Yorker*, 12.6.48, 33.
71. PRO, FO 371/72806, Wilson to Heppel, 7.5.48.
72. NARA, RG 59, 501.BD Human Rights, Box 2187: Memorandum of Conversation, 13.2.47. Geoffrey Wilson at first advised Charles Dukes, and then took over the job after Dukes's death in 1948.
73. NARA, RG 59, Sandifer files, Box 8: Sandifer to Simsarian and Hendrick, 27.7.48.
74. *Ibid.*
75. Tom J. Farer, 'The United Nations and Human Rights: More Than a Whimper Less Than a Roar', *Human Rights Quarterly*, No. 9, 1987, 555.
76. John Humphrey, *Human Rights and the United Nations*, 28.
77. NAACP leader Walter White, quoted in Mary L. Dudziak, 'Desegregation as a Cold War Imperative', *Stanford Law Review*, 41(1), November 1988, 95. The NAACP petition was submitted to the UN in October 1947.
78. Carol Anderson, 'Symposium: African Americans and US Foreign Relations', *Diplomatic History*, 20(4), Fall 1996, 558.
79. Mary L. Dudziak, 'Desegregation as a Cold War Imperative', *Stanford Law Review*, 41(1), November 1988, 95–6. Eleanor Roosevelt's role in suppressing the NAACP petition was soon forgotten. In 1977, Allard Lowenstein, an American envoy to the UN, claimed that, 'In 1947, when Mrs Eleanor Roosevelt – who was in so many ways the seminal figure in insisting that the United States become involved in human rights – was chairwoman of the UN Human Rights Commission, there was a petition from the National Association for the Advancement of Colored People about racial discrimination in the United States. The Soviet Union at the time insisted that the

Commission should investigate the United States. Mrs Roosevelt very clearly stated that any petition properly presented on the issue of human rights was the legitimate concern of the Human Rights Commission. This was 1947!' (*Digest of United States Practice in International Law*, 1977, 170.)

80. NARA, RG 59, Bureau of International Organization Affairs and its Predecessors, Position papers 1945–74, Box 27: 'Discrimination against Negroes in the United States', 30.8.48.

81. Carol Anderson, 'Symposium: African Americans and US Foreign Relations', *Diplomatic History*, 20(4), Fall 1996, 562.

82. Edmund Penning-Rowsell, 'Second Class Citizens', *New Statesman and Nation*, 3.4.48.

83. Gabrielle Kirk McDonald, 'The Universal Declaration of Human Rights: The International and the American Dream', in Barend van der Heijden and Bahia Tahzib-Lie (eds), *Reflections on the Universal Declaration of Human Rights*, 182.

84. PRO, FO 371/72812, UK Delegation to UN (Paris) to FO, 15.11.48.

85. Joseph Wronka, *Human Rights and Social Policy in the 21st Century*, 99.

86. NARA, RG 59, 501.BD Human Rights, Box 2189: G. Petrov, 'The Unbecoming Role of Eleanor Roosevelt', *Literaturnaya Gazeta*, 23.10.48 (translated by US Embassy and sent to Washington 5.11.48).

87. A.J. Hobbins (ed.), *On the Edge of Greatness*, 63.

88. See for example, Cassin setting out this aim. (AMAE, Nations Unies et Organisations Internationales, Secrétariat des Conférences, Vol. 382: Cassin to Affaires Etrangères, 10.6.48.)

89. NARA, RG 353, Records of the Subcommittee on Human Rights and the Status of Women, 1947–9, Box 109: 'Report of Commission of Human Rights', 19.2.47.

90. NARA, RG 353, Records of the Subcommittee on Human Rights and the Status of Women, 1947–9, Box 111: 'Report on Second Session, Commission on Human Rights', 7.1.48.

91. NARA, RG 353, Records of the Subcommittee on Human Rights and the Status of Women, 1947–9, Box 112: 'Declaration of Human Rights', 29.6.48.

92. L.K. Hyde, *The United States and the United Nations*, 166.

93. Minutes of the Fourth Meeting of the United States Delegation to the General Assembly, Paris, 24.9.48; *FRUS*, Vol. 1, 1948, 291.

94. Minutes of the Fifth Meeting of the United States Delegation to the General Assembly, Paris, 25.9.48; *FRUS*, Vol. 1, 1948, 292.

95. NARA, RG 59, Sandifer files, Box 8: Simsarian report, 'Three Regional Meetings of the American Bar Association on Human Rights', 22.3.49.

Chapter Two

1. PRO, LO 2/43, 'Statement of Policy', undated, *c.* 23.10.45.

2. Letters, *The Times*, 31.10.45.

3. Letters, *The Times*, 2.11.45.

4. Letter from Raymond Jennings, Philip J. Sykes, Hector Hillaby, Michael Albery, Oliver Smith, W.S. Wigglesworth, *The Times*, 5.11.45.

5. Arieh J. Kochavi, *Prelude to Nuremberg*, 86.

6. Henry L. Stimson took on the trial's critics in 1947, when he argued that 'The whole moral position of the victorious Powers must collapse if their judgments could be enforced only by Nazi methods.' ('The Nuremberg Trial: Landmark in Law', *Foreign Affairs*, January 1947, 25(2), 179.)

7. Frank M. Buscher, *The US War Crimes Trial Program in Germany*, 16.
8. Arieh J. Kochavi, *Prelude to Nuremberg*, 205.
9. Bradley F. Smith, *The Road to Nuremberg*, 51.
10. Robert E. Conot, *Justice at Nuremberg*, 11.
11. See Gary Jonathan Bass, *Stay the Hand of Vengeance*, 173.
12. Bradley F. Smith, *The Road to Nuremberg*, 132.
13. Sheldon Glueck, professor of criminal law at Harvard University, wrote: 'The more I read [the Kellogg-Briand Pact] in the light of recent history, the more it seems to laugh in my face as a piece of ghoulish and dishonest international law mumbo-jumbo.' (NARA, RG 238, US Counsel for the Prosecution, London, Correspondence, 1945–6: Glueck to Chanler, 17.5.4 5.)
14. NARA, RG 238, US Counsel for the Prosecution, Washington, Correspondence 1945–6, Box 7: Taylor, 'An Approach to the Preparation of the Prosecution of Axis Criminality', 2.6.45. Sidney Alderman, a leading American prosecutor, commended the report as 'very thoughtful and excellent'. He added: 'I find myself in practically 100% agreement with Colonel Taylor's views.' (NARA, RG 238, US Counsel for the Prosecution, Washington, Correspondence 1945–6, Box 7: Alderman to Jackson, 5.6.45.)
15. See Bradley F. Smith, *The Road to Nuremberg*, 53.
16. See, for example, the comment by Richard Goldstone, the former chief prosecutor of the UN tribunal on former Yugoslavia: 'It's well known that the Allied leaders, particularly Stalin and Churchill, were quite keen on simply lining the Nazi leaders up against a wall and summarily executing them.' (*Accounting for Atrocities* conference, Bard College, 5–6 October 1998. www.bard.edu/hrp/atrocities/index.htm) This may have been true for Churchill, but it was not for Stalin, a leader already well-versed in wringing advantage from political trials. The Allies were unsure of the Soviet position on the Nazi leaders until October 1944, when, during a meeting in Moscow, Stalin made it clear that he objected to Churchill's proposal for summary executions, and indicated that he wanted them put in the dock.
17. On 9 November 1943, Churchill wrote a note proposing that, 'Once identified, the said officer will have the outlaw or outlaws shot to death within six hours and without reference to higher authority.' (Arieh J. Kochavi, *Prelude to Nuremberg*, 74.)
18. After Napoleon Bonaparte was defeated at Waterloo in 1815, the victorious powers – Britain, Russia and Austria – made the joint decision to exile him to St Helena for life without trial.
19. PRO, LCO 53/78, 'Draft Cabinet paper: Treatment of War Criminals', from about June 1942.
20. See Geoffrey Best, *Nuremberg and After*, 4–5.
21. Francis Biddle, *In Brief Authority*, 419.
22. NARA, RG 238, US Counsel for the Prosecution, Washington, Correspondence 1945–6, Box 7: US Political Advisor (Berlin) to Secretary of State, 19.8.45.
23. PRO, FO 371/51003, Ivor Pink, 'Some impressions of the Nuremberg Trial', undated, *c.* November 1945.
24. The American and British teams fielded three one-time Attorney Generals: US Supreme Court Justice Robert Jackson, who had previously served under FDR as both Attorney General and Solicitor General; Hartley Shawcross, the serving British Attorney General, and David Maxwell-Fyfe, the previous incumbent. The American team also included Francis Shea, a former assistant Attorney General, and General William Donovan, head of the Office of Strategic Services – forerunner of the CIA.
25. www.yale.edu/lawweb/avalon/imt/proc/imtconst.htm
    The charge of conspiracy – a draconian catch-all concept found only in Anglo-Saxon

law – provoked considerable criticism in legal circles.

26. AMAE, Nations Unies et Organisations Internationales, Secrétariat des Conférences (Crimes de Guerre: Nuremberg), Box 90: Affaires Étrangères to diplomatic missions, 8.12.46.
27. *Proceedings*, 2/101. www.yale.edu/lawweb/avalon/imt/proc/11-21-45.htm
28. www.yale.edu/lawweb/avalon/imt/proc/imtconst.htm
29. David J. Scheffer, 'International Judicial Intervention', *Foreign Policy*, No. 102, Spring 1996, 36.
30. Michael Biddiss et al., *The Nuremberg Trial and the Third Reich*, 96.
31. NARA, RG 238, US Counsel for the Prosecution, Washington, Documents 1945–6, Box 19: Jackson (Nuremberg) to War Department, 1.11.45.
32. Robert E. Conot, *Justice at Nuremberg*, 68.
33. *Ibid.*
34. *Ibid.*
35. NARA, RG 238, US Counsel for the Prosecution, Washington, Documents 1945–6, Box 19: Jackson (Nuremberg) to War Department, 1.11.45.
36. NARA, RG 238, US Counsel for the Prosecution, Wheeler Correspondence, Box 1: 'Assistance to Mr Justice Jackson in Preparation of Case', undated, *c.* July–August (with hand-written annotation: 'From State Dept').
37. NARA, RG 238, US Counsel for the Prosecution, Washington, Correspondence 1945–6, Box 7: Taylor, 'An Approach to the Preparation of the Prosecution of Axis Criminality', 2.6.45 (original emphasis).
38. *Proceedings*, 8/547. www.yale.edu/lawweb/avalon/imt/proc/03-05-46.htm
39. *Proceedings*, 17/378. www.yale.edu/lawweb/avalon/imt/proc/07-02-46.htm
40. *Proceedings*, 17/380. www.yale.edu/lawweb/avalon/imt/proc/07-02-46.htm
41. Rebecca West, *A Train of Powder*, 52.
42. *Ibid.*, 53.
43. Orme Sargent quoted in Patrick Salmon, 'Crimes Against Peace: The Case of the Invasion of Norway at the Nuremberg Trials', in Richard Langhorne (ed.), *Diplomacy and Intelligence During the Second World War*, 264.
44. PRO, CAB 21/2290, Attlee, 29.3.46.
45. See PRO, WO 311/39, Dean (Nuremberg) to FO, 17.5.46.
46. PRO, WO 311/39, Dean (Nuremberg) to FO, 13.3.46.
47. *Proceedings*, 8/594. www.yale.edu/lawweb/avalon/imt/proc/03-06-46.htm
48. PRO, LCO 2/2994, Liddell Hart to Jowitt, 3.11.48.
49. Roman Rudenko acquired further notoriety in the West when, in 1960, he prosecuted American U2 spy plane pilot Gary Powers.
50. PRO, FO 371/51003, Ivor Pink, 'Some impressions of the Nuremberg Trial', undated, *c.* November 1945.
51. Barton J. Bernstein, 'The Atomic Bombings Reconsidered', *Foreign Affairs*, 74(1), January–February 1995, 146.
52. Telford Taylor, *Nuremberg and Vietnam*, 143.
53. PRO, LCO 2/2994, Liddell Hart to Jowitt, 3.11.48. Liddell Hart is here referring to the proposed trial of four German generals, discussed later.
54. *Proceedings*, 13/521. www.yale.edu/lawweb/avalon/imt/proc/05-14-46.htm
55. Robert E. Conot, *Justice at Nuremberg*, 334.
56. Telford Taylor, *The Anatomy of the Nuremberg Trials*, 187.
57. *Proceedings*, 11/415. www.yale.edu/lawweb/avalon/imt/proc/04-15-46.htm
58. *Proceedings*, 11/400–1. www.yale.edu/lawweb/avalon/imt/proc/04-15-46.htm
59. Robert E. Conot, *Justice at Nuremberg*, 376.
60. Rebecca West, *A Train of Powder*, 3.

61. H. Montgomery Hyde, *Norman Birkett*, 518.
62. *Ibid.*, 520.
63. PRO, FO 371/57422, Beckett, 19.1.46.
64. Ismay, *The Memoirs of General the Lord Ismay*, 157.
65. AMAE, Nations Unies et Organisations Internationales, Secrétariat des Conférences (Crimes de Guerre: Nuremberg), Box 90: Grousse (Havana) to Affaires Etrangères, 15.10.46.
66. Maffey (Eire) to Dominions Office, 12.10.46.
67. AMAE, Nations Unies et Organisations Internationales, Secrétariat des Conférences (Crimes de Guerre: Nuremberg), Box 90: L'Ambassadeur de France (Colombie) to Affaires Etrangères, 22.10.46.
68. Churchill quoted by Jörg Friedrich, *Accounting for Atrocities* conference, Bard College, 5–6 October 1998. www.bard.edu/hrp/atrocities/index.htm
69. *Hansard*, Commons, Vol. 456, 15.9.48, Col. 85.
70. *Hansard*, Commons, Vol. 457, 28.10.48, Cols 256–7
71. PRO, LCO 2/2994, Robertson (Berlin) to Foreign Secretary, 7.8.48.
72. Letters, *Daily Telegraph*, 25.8.48.
73. Letters, *Daily Telegraph*, 26.8.48.
74. *Hansard*, Commons, Vol. 457, 26.10.48, Col. 67.
75. PRO, LCO 2/2994, Gollancz to Attlee, 27.6.49.
76. Foreword by Maurice Hankey, in Reginald Thomas Paget, *Manstein*, xi.
77. James J. Weingartner, *Crossroads of Death*, 221.
78. The Senate's rejection of the 1948 Genocide Convention showed the shallowness of the United States' commitment to the Nuremberg legacy. Denouncing the Nazis for their 'crimes against humanity' was acceptable, but signing up to the binding treaty prohibiting genocide was not. Thus a familiar double standard was established, under which it was right to punish foreigners for their sins, but wrong to punish Americans for the same crimes. Washington eventually got around to signing the Genocide Convention four decades later, in 1986, but only after gutting it of any obligations to themselves.
79. British cabinet minutes refer, for example, to 'special misgivings' about this action. (PRO, PREM 8/1570, CM 51, 8.2.51.)
80. Tom Bower, *Blind Eye to Murder*, 424.
81. Peter Maguire, *Accounting for Atrocities* conference, Bard College, 5–6 October 1998. www.bard.edu/hrp/atrocities/index.htm
82. Frank M. Buscher, *The US War Crimes Program in Germany*, 91.
83. Peter Maguire, *Accounting for Atrocities* conference, Bard College, 5–6 October 1998. www.bard.edu/hrp/atrocities/index.htm
84. Henry Rousso (trans., Arthur Goldhammer), *The Vichy Syndrome*, 56.
85. PRO, FO 371/103666, Kirkpatrick (Wahnerheide) to FO, 6.7.53.
86. Photograph accompanying article by Chapman Pincher, 'War Crimes Book Banned', *Daily Express*, 11.8.45.
87. When reporting on the controversy over *The Scourge of the Swastika*, most British newspapers described Nazi horrors at length without specifically mentioning the persecution of the Jews.
88. Lord Russell of Liverpool, *The Scourge of the Swastika*, 52–3.
89. PRO, T 215/266, Bridges to Winnifrith, 6.8.54.
90. 'Book on German War Crimes', *Manchester Guardian*, 12.8.54.
91. Lord Russell, 'This Is Why I Chose Freedom', *Daily Express*, 12.8.54. The wrapper showed a huge pair of jackboots casting a long shadow over huddled prisoners; the photographs showed concentration camp inmates.

92. Lord Russell, 'This Is Why I Chose Freedom', *Daily Express*, 12.8.54 (original emphasis).
93. Simonds letter to Russell quoted in 'Opinion', *Daily Express*, 16.8.54.
94. PRO, T 215/266, Fraser to Platt, 16.8.54.
95. 'Opinion', *Daily Express*, 11.8.54; Peter Fryer, 'They Cannot Gag Him', *Daily Worker*, 12.8.54; A.J. Cummings, 'This Impudent Censorship', *News Chronicle*, 12.8.54.
96. 'Our London Correspondence', *Manchester Guardian*, 12.8.54.
97. Otto John returned to West Germany in 1955 and was sentenced to four years in jail, all the while protesting that he had been abducted and forced to cooperate with the East German security forces.
98. 'Forget the German War Crimes!' *Tribune*, 13.8.54.
99. Lord Russell, 'This Is Why I Chose Freedom', *Daily Express*, 12.8.54.
100. Peter Maguire, *Accounting for Atrocities* conference, Bard College, 5–6 October 1998. www.bard.edu/hrp/atrocities/index.htm
101. NARA, RG 238, US Counsel for the Prosecution, Washington, Correspondence 1945–6, Box 7: Taylor, 'An Approach to the Preparation of the Prosecution of Axis Criminality', 2.6.45.

Chapter Three

1. PRO, FO 371/66554, Ogden (Shanghai) to UK Ambassador (Nanking), 25.6.47.
2. PRO, FO 371/66554, Garner, 31.7.47.
3. The eleven nations represented at the Tokyo Tribunal were the Big Five – the USA, the Soviet Union, China, Britain and France – plus Australia, Canada, India, the Netherlands, New Zealand and the Philippines.
4. John Stanton, 'Reluctant Vengeance: Canada at the Tokyo War Crimes Tribunal', *Journal of American and Canadian Studies*, No. 17. infowww.cc.sophia.ac.jp/amecana/E2/Journal.htm
5. Barton J. Bernstein, 'The Atomic Bombings Reconsidered', *Foreign Affairs*, 74(1), January/February 1995, 140.
6. *Ibid.*, 141.
7. B.V.A. Röling and Antonio Cassese, *The Tokyo Trial and Beyond*, 87.
8. 'War Crimes: Road Show', *Time*, 20.5.46.
9. John L. Ginn, *Sugamo Prison, Tokyo*, 39.
10. In autumn 1945, the Canadians asked the Americans if they would try Japanese accused of committing atrocities against Canadians, in US-convened courts in Asia. The Americans agreed only on condition that the Canadians contributed a judge and prosecutor to the Tokyo Tribunal. (John Stanton, 'Reluctant Vengeance: Canada at the Tokyo War Crimes Tribunal', *Journal of American and Canadian Studies*, No. 17. infowww.cc.sophia.ac.jp/amecana/E2/Journal.htm)
11. PRO, LCO 2/2983, Government of India External Affairs Department to UK Ambassador (Washington), 28.1.46.
12. *Proceedings*, 196–7. See transcripts at NARA, LSE, and in R.J. Pritchard and S.M. Zaide (eds), *The Tokyo War Crimes Trial, Index and Guide*.
13. *Ibid.*, 235.
14. *Ibid.*, 235–6.
15. *Ibid.*, 98.
16. The New Zealand judge Northcroft commented that there were 'two of the Judges with whom I cannot converse without interpreters', one of whom was Zaryanov. It is not clear who the other non-English speaking judge was, although Röling suggests that

it may have been the French judge, Henri Bernard. (PRO, LCO 2/2992, Northcroft (Tokyo) to Chief Justice (Wellington), 18.3.47; John W. Dower, *Embracing Defeat*, 465.)

17. Richard H. Minear, *Victors' Justice*, 82.
18. *Proceedings*, 238.
19. 'Opening Statement of the Prosecution'.
20. PRO, FO 371/66552, Beckett, 5.5.47 (original emphasis).
21. PRO, FO 371/69831, 'Enclosure No. 3', 2.1.48.
22. PRO, FO 371/69831, Gascoigne (Tokyo) to Foreign Secretary, 14.2.48.
23. *Proceedings*, 20,478.
24. *Ibid.*, 20,479.
25. *Ibid.*, 20,480.
26. *Ibid.*, 20,481.
27. *Ibid.*, 20,481; 20,482.
28. 'Counsel Rebuked at Tokyo Trial', *The Times*, 23.4.47.
29. AMAE, Nations Unies et Organisations Internationales, Secrétariat des Conférences (Crimes de Guerre: Extrême-Orient), Box 103: Oneto (Tokyo) to Affaires Etrangères, 14.6.47.
30. PRO, FO 371/66553,Gascoigne (Tokyo) to Foreign Secretary, 16.6.47.
31. PRO, FO 371/66554, Gascoigne (Tokyo) to Foreign Secretary, 10.7.47.
32. T.S. Rama Rao, 'The Dissenting Judgment of Mr Justice Pal at the Tokyo Trial', *The Indian Year Book of International Affairs*, 2, 1953, 286.
33. Radhabinod Pal, *International Military Tribunal for the Far East*, 114.
34. Solis Horowitz, 'The TokyoTrial', *International Conciliation*, No. 465, November 1950, 512.
35. C. Hosoya et al (eds), *The Tokyo War Crimes Tribunal*, 192.
36. Richard J. Aldrich, *Intelligence and the War Against Japan*, 345.
37. *Ibid.*, 347.
38. The Acting Political Advisor in Japan (Atcheson) to Truman, 4.1.46; *FRUS*, Vol. 8, 1946, 90. Had the Americans sought guidance from Nuremberg, they would have noted that Robert Jackson had denounced as a relic of 'the divine right of kings' the idea that heads of state should be immune from prosecution. Jackson also declared, 'We stand on the principle of responsible government declared some three centuries ago to King James by Lord Chief Justice Coke, who proclaimed that even a King is still "under God and the law".' (PRO, FO 115/4187, 'Report by Robert Jackson to the President', 7.6.45.)
39. Philip R. Piccigallo, *The Japanese on Trial*, 16.
40. Roger Buckley, 'Britain and the Emperor: The Foreign Office and Constitutional Reform in Japan, 1945–46', *Modern Asian Studies*, 12(4), October 1978, 562.
41. Letters, *Far Eastern Economic Review*, 6.7.89.
42. AMAE, Nations Unies et Organisations Internationales, Secrétariat des Conférences (Crimes de Guerre: Extrême-Orient), Box 103: Oneto (Tokyo) to Broustra, 9.12.48.
43. PRO, FO 371/69831, Gascoigne (Tokyo) to Foreign Secretary, 25.1.48.
44. PRO, LCO 2/2992, Comyns Carr (Tokyo) to Attorney (Shawcross), 2.1.48.
45. 'Tokio Sentences', *Manchester Guardian*, 13.11.48.
46. PRO, FO 371/69831, Scott, 'The International Military Tribunal of the Far East', 6.7.48.
47. Philip R. Piccigallo, *The Japanese on Trial*, 16.
48. PRO, LCO 2/2992, Northcroft (Tokyo) to Chief Justice (Wellington), 18.3.47.
49. PRO, FO 371/66552, Dening to Sargent, 30.4.47.
50. PRO, LCO 2/2992, Patrick (Tokyo) to Normand, undated, *c.* late 1946 to early 1947.

51. PRO, LCO 2/2992, Patrick (Tokyo) to Cooper (Edinburgh), 29.3.47.
52. PRO, LCO 2/2992, Northcroft (Tokyo) to Chief Justice (Wellington), 18.3.47.
53. PRO, LCO 2/2992, Gascoigne (Tokyo) to FO, 9.10.47.
54. PRO, FO 371/66551, Gascoigne (Tokyo) to FO, 26.1.47. The British envoy to Japan, Alvary Gascoigne also reported that 'The General [MacArthur] knew Keenan had during the Spring been drinking too much and arrangements had been made to have him watched.'
55. PRO, FO 371/66551, Comyns Carr (Tokyo) to Attorney (Shawcross), 17.12.46.
56. PRO, LCO 2/2992, Comyns Carr (Tokyo) to Reed (Law Officers Department), 21.10.47.
57. PRO, FO 371/66551, Gascoigne (Tokyo) to FO, 26.1.47. Gascoigne sent another telegram the same day reporting that MacArthur had derided Comyns Carr as 'a man who is trying to get an international reputation, which he has not got up to the present'. (PRO, FO 371/66551, Gascoigne (Tokyo) to FO, 26.1.47.)
58. PRO, LCO 2/2992, Shawcross to Lord Chancellor, 23.1.48.
59. PRO, FO 371/69831, Gascoigne (Tokyo) to Foreign Secretary, 25.1.48.
60. *Ibid.*
61. PRO, LCO 2/2992, Comyns Carr (Tokyo) to Attorney (Shawcross), 2.1.48.
62. PRO, FO 371/69831, Gascoigne (Tokyo) to Foreign Secretary, 25.1.48.
63. PRO, LCO 2/2992, Comyns Carr (Tokyo) to Attorney (Shawcross), 2.1.48.
64. MacArthur quoted in PRO, LCO 2/2992, Gascoigne (Tokyo) to FO, 14.5.47.
65. John Stanton, 'Reluctant Vengeance: Canada at the Tokyo War Crimes Tribunal', *The Journal of American and Canadian Studies*, No. 17.
infowww.cc.sophia.ac.jp/amecana/E2/Journal.htm
In letters written in spring 1947 to Louis St Laurent, the Canadian Secretary of State for External Affairs, McDougall wrote: 'I am convinced that the accused have not had and cannot have a fair trial.' He advanced the view that the United States government 'either did not take the constitution of the Court seriously', or that incompetents had been appointed in Tokyo due to the 'repercussions in Washington political and judicial circles from Nuremberg'.
66. www.yale.edu/lawweb/avalon/imtfech.htm
67. PRO, LCO 2/2992, Northcroft (Tokyo) to Chief Justice (Wellington), 28.3.47.
68. 'Incident at Tokyo War Trial', *The Times*, 6.3.47.
69. Radhabinod Pal, *International Military Tribunal for the Far East*, 172. See also, John W. Dower, *Embracing Defeat*, 466–7.
70. PRO, LCO 2/2992, Northcroft (Tokyo) to Chief Justice (Wellington), 28.3.47.
71. AMAE, Nations Unies et Organisations Internationales, Secrétariat des Conférences (Crimes de Guerre: Extrême-Orient), Box 100: Oneto (Tokyo) to Affaires Etrangères, 30.5.47.
72. AMAE, Nations Unies et Organisations Internationales, Secrétariat des Conférences (Crimes de Guerre: Extrême-Orient), Box 100: Oneto (Tokyo) to Broustra, 9.12.48.
73. Frank White, 'How Trial Judges Voted', *Nippon Times*, 10.12.48. It is possible that Bernard Röling was responsible for the leak, given his later critical comments about the voting on the sentences, and particularly the vote on Hirota.
74. PRO, FO 371/69834, Chancery (Tokyo) to FO, 13.12.48.
75. 'USA and Others *v.* Araki and Others: Separate Opinion of the President', 1.11.48, 18.
76. PRO, FO 371/69833, Scott, 15.11.48.
77. William J. Sebald with Russell Brines, *With MacArthur in Japan*, 164.
78. Radhabinod Pal, *International Military Tribunal for the Far East*, 621.
79. *Ibid.*, 30.
80. *Ibid.*, 17.

81. John W. Dower, *Embracing Defeat*, 632.
82. Richard J. Aldrich, *Intelligence and the War Against Japan*, 137.
83. B.V.A. Röling and Antonio Cassese, *The Tokyo Trial and Beyond*, 28
84. PRO, DO 35/2938, Gascoigne (Tokyo) to Dening, 25.11.48.
85. PRO, FO 371/69834, Ledwidge, 17.12.48.
86. AMAE, Nations Unies et Organisations Internationales, Secrétariat des Conférences (Crimes de Guerre: Extrême-Orient), Box 103: Bernard, 'Statement' (in English), 22.11.48.
87. PRO, FO 371/69834, Scott, 23.12.48.
88. PRO, FO 262/2091, Ellingworth, 2.7.53.
89. PRO, FO 262/2092, Halford (Tokyo) 3.9.53.
90. PRO, FO 262/2092, Dening (Tokyo), 3.9.53. The British and the other Allied powers did made concessions on the war criminals issue, however, and all the surviving defendants were freed by 1956.
91. David McCullough, *Truman*, 475. See also, Philippe Nobile, 'Were They War Criminals?' *Independent on Sunday*, 14.2.99.
92. Margaret Truman, *Harry S. Truman*, 555.
93. *Ibid.*, 556.

Chapter Four

1. Christopher Mayhew and Lyn Smith (eds), *A War of Words*, 135–6.
2. PRO, FO 371/72798, Gore-Booth to Salt (UK Delegation to UN, New York), 28.1.48.
3. PRO, FO 371/72799, Gore-Booth, 24.1.48.
4. PRO, FO 371/72799, 'Draft anti-Soviet speech', undated, *c*. January 1948.
5. PRO, FO 371/72799, Morgan (Labour) to Gore-Booth, 26.1.48.
6. PRO, FO 371/72799, 'Note for Draft Speech by the United Kingdom Delegate', undated, *c*. January 1948. The eight colonies mentioned as using compulsory labour were the Gold Coast, Kenya, Nigeria, North Borneo, Nyasaland, Sierra Leone, Tanganyika Territory and Uganda.
7. PRO, FO 371/72811, UK Delegation to UN (Paris) to Foreign Office, 15.10.48.
8. Christopher Mayhew, *Time to Explain*, 111.
9. A.J. Hobbins (ed.), *On the Edge of Greatness*, 60.
10. PRO, FO 371/72811, UK Delegation to UN (Paris) to Foreign Office, 15.10.48.
11. PRO, FO 371/72811, UK Delegation to UN (Paris) to Foreign Office, 17.10.48.
12. NARA, RG 59, Records of the Assistant Secretaries of State for United Nations Affairs, 1945–54, Box 3: 'Presentation of Materials', UNA to Under Secretary, 21.5.52.
13. NARA, RG 59, Bureau of International Organization Affairs and its Predecessors, Position papers 1945–74, Box 28: 'Evidence of Existence of Forced Labour', 2.9.53.
14. NARA, RG 59, Bureau of International Organization Affairs and its Predecessors, Position papers 1945–74, Box 28: 'Evidence of Existence of Forced Labour', 9.9.53.
15. *Ibid.*
16. NARA, RG 59, Records of Assistant Secretaries of State for United Nations Affairs, 1945–54, Box 5: 'Propaganda in the United Nations', undated, *c*. 1954. This report was probably produced within the State Department.
17. James Frederick Green, *The United Nations and Human Rights*, 135.
18. PRO, FO 371/72811, UK Delegation to UN (Paris) to Foreign Office, 17.10.48.
19. Caroline Pruden, *Conditional Partners*, 71.
20. *Ibid.*, 75.

21. *Ibid.*, 77.
22. Eleanor Roosevelt's friend and biographer Joseph Lash dubbed her a 'Reluctant Cold-Warrior', but James Green, who worked with her at the UN, said that she was only 'reluctant' insofar as she preferred harmony to enmity. (See Lash chapter entitled 'Reluctant Cold-Warrior' in *Eleanor: The Years Alone*, 82–107; M. Glen Johnson, 'The Contributions of Eleanor and Franklin Roosevelt to the Development of International Protection from Human Rights', *Human Rights Quarterly*, No. 9, 1987, 39.) Interestingly, both liberals and conservatives highlight Roosevelt's contribution to human rights rather than her participation in the Cold War, albeit for different reasons.
23. NARA, RG 59, Sandifer files, Box 8: Marshall to Rusk, 18.8.48. (Some words are partly obscured on the carbon copy in the files.)
24. NARA, RG 59, 501.BD Human Rights, Box 2189: Caffery (Paris) to Secretary of State, 1.9.48.
25. NARA, RG 59, 501.BD Human Rights, Box 2189: Tyler (Paris) to State Department, 29.9.48.
26. 'The Struggle for Human Rights', *Department of State Bulletin*, 19(484), 10.10.48, 458 and 460. (The *Bulletin* changed the title of the speech.)
27. Irene Reiterman Sandifer, *Mrs Roosevelt as We Knew Her*, 68.
28. NARA, RG 59, 501.BD Human Rights, Box 2189: Translation by US Embassy, Moscow, dispatched to Washington 5.11.48.
29. A.J. Hobbins (ed.), *On the Edge of Greatness*, 177.
30. John Humphrey, *Human Rights and the United Nations*, 105. When Roosevelt first heard that the Soviets had walked out of the UN in protest at its refusal to recognise Communist China, she wrote a sympathetic note to the Assistant Secretary of State for UN Affairs, John Hickerson, saying: 'I do appreciate how beastly the USSR is to work with.' (NARA, RG 59, Records of the Assistant Secretaries of State for United Nations Affairs, 1945–54, Box 3: Roosevelt to Hickerson, 23.2.50.)
31. A.J. Hobbins (ed.), *On the Edge of Greatness*, 249.
32. NARA, RG 353, Records of the Subcommittee on Human Rights and the Status of Women, 1947–9, Box 111: Lovett to Roosevelt, undated, *c.* late November to early December 1947.
33. NARA, RG 59, 501.BD Human Rights, Box 2188: Lovett to Roosevelt, 2.5.48.
34. The Soviets had no intention of submitting to human rights scrutiny, and did not support the Convention. A telegram from the US delegation in Geneva to Washington noted: 'USSR attitude. Disclosed private talks wants no convention.' (NARA, RG 59, BD.501 Human Rights, Box 2188: Troutman to Rusk and Gross, 7.12.47.)
35. PRO, FO 371/72799, Hebblethwaite, 16.2.48.
36. PRO, FO 371/72810, Rundall to Kirkpatrick, 3.9.48.
37. PRO, FO 371/72806, Wilson to Heppel, 7.5.48.
38. NARA, RG 59, 501.BD Human Rights, Box 2188: Austin to Sandifer and Gross, 14.5.48.
39. PRO, FO 371/72810, Chancery (Washington) to FO, 23.8.48.
40. UN, E/CN.4/95, 'Commission on Human Rights Drafting Committee, Second Session', 21.5.48, 20.
41. *Ibid.*, 22.
42. NARA, RG 59, Sandifer files, Box 8: Cates to Sandifer, 16.8.50.
43. Duane Tananbaum, *The Bricker Amendment Controversy*, 19. These loopholes remain in the UN's human rights covenants, which was eventually adopted by the General Assembly in December 1966. Governments are allowed to suspend or circumvent freedoms on the grounds of national security, territorial integrity, public policy, public

morality, the protection of rights and the reputation of others. Derogation is also permitted during public emergencies.

44. See Mary L Dudziak, 'Desegregation as a Cold War Imperative', *Stanford Law Review*, 41(1), November 1988.
45. In 1948, George F. Kennan, head of the Policy Planning Staff, and a prominent advocate of a 'realist' foreign policy, wrote a memo raising doubts about the Universal Declaration: 'I wish to say that the Staff has great misgivings as to the wisdom of the Executive branch negotiating declarations of this nature setting forth ideals and principles which we are not today able to observe in our own country, which we cannot be sure of being able to observe in the future, and which are in any case of dubious universal validity. It seems to us that this invites charges of hypocrisy against us in the future and reduces, rather than enhances, the respect throughout the world for UN pronouncements.' (NARA, RG 59, Sandifer files, Box 8: Kennan to Under Secretary, 8.7.48.)
46. NARA, RG 59, Sandifer files, Box 8: Sandifer to Roosevelt, 4.4.51.
47. NARA, RG 59, Sandifer files, Box 8: Green (Geneva) to Sandifer, 21.5.53.
48. AMAE, Nations Unies et Organisations Internationales, Secrétariat des Conférences, Box 382: Cassin (Geneva) to Affaires Etrangères, 10.4.53.
49. NARA, RG 59, Records of the Assistant Secretaries of State for United Nations Affairs, 1945–54, Box 3: 'US Position in UN on Self-Determination Question', 25.2.52.
50. AMAE, Nations Unies et Organisations Internationales, Secrétariat des Conférences, Box 382: Cassin, 'Commission des Droits de l'Homme', 1.7.52.
51. NARA, RG 59, Sandifer files, Box 8: Green (Geneva) to Sandifer, 21.5.53.
52. NARA, RG 59, Sandifer files, Box 8: Memorandum, 'Developments in the Human Rights Commission on Self-Determination', 16.4.52.
53. 'Political Ohio', *Life*, 12.6.44.
54. John Gunther, *Inside USA*, 436.
55. Eric F. Goldman, *Rendezvous with Destiny*, 300.
56. The *Life* article listed Bricker's policies: 'He has put himself flatly on record for 1) a militarily strong US which will help maintain order in the world after the war; 2) retention of some of the US military bases built in foreign countries; 3) a permanent organisation for world peace in which the US 'must do her full share'; and 4) a return to the international gold standard. He has gone on record against 1) an international police force, and 2) any foreign military alliance.' ('Political Ohio', *Life*, 12.6.44.)
57. Duane Tananbaum, *The Bricker Amendment Controversy*, 56.
58. *Ibid.*, 151.
59. Natalie Hevener Kaufman and David Whiteman, 'Opposition to Human Rights treaties in the United States Senate: The Legacy of the Bricker Amendment', *Human Rights Quarterly*, No. 10, 1988, 309.
60. Frank Holman, American Bar Association president, quoted in Duane Tananbaum, *The Bricker Amendment Controversy*, 84 (original emphasis).
61. PRO, FO 371/107126, Makins, 'Weekly Summary' (Washington), to FO, 11.4.53.
62. Duane Tananbaum, *The Bricker Amendment Controversy*, 102.
63. Cathal Nolan, *Principled Diplomacy*, 223–4 (original emphasis).
64. See Natalie Hevener Kaufman, *Human Rights Treaties and the Senate*, 105.
65. Memorandum by the Assistant Secretary of State for UN Affairs to the Secretary of State, 9.2.53, *FRUS*, Vol. 3, 1952–4, 1,543.
66. *Ibid.*, 1,544.
67. Statement made by the United States representative before the Commission on Human Rights, Geneva, 8.4.53, *FRUS*, Vol. 3, 1952–4, 1,572.
68. James Frederick Green, *The United Nations and Human Rights*, 65.

69. PRO, FO 371/107126, Hoare (Geneva) to FO, 8.4.53.
70. PRO, FO 371/107126, Pell (Geneva) to FO, 13.4.53.
71. NARA, RG 59, Sandifer files, Box 8: Green (Geneva) to Sandifer, 22.4.53.
72. Maurice Cranston, *Human Rights To-Day*, 44.
73. Duane Tananbaum, *The Bricker Amendment Controversy*, 179–80.
74. 'Vote, Vote Vote', *Time*, 8.3.54.

Chapter Five

1. Roderick Barclay, *Ernest Bevin and the Foreign Office*, 67.
2. 'Strasbourg Folly', *Daily Express*, 27.10.53.
3. 'And For Hypocrisy Beat This', *Daily Worker*, 27.10.53.
4. Whitehall hoped that five omissions from their list of colonies – Aden Protectorate (too 'primitive'), Hong Kong (too important), Southern Rhodesia (too tricky), Brunei (Sultan not consulted in time), and the New Hebrides (a condominium with non-ratifying France) – would be overlooked.
5. The exceptions to this were the four Articles which were mandatory in all circumstances: Articles 2 (the death penalty), 3 (torture, inhuman or degrading treatment or punishment), 4(1) (slavery or servitude) and 7 (retroactive criminal liability and punishment).
6. *Gangrene*, introduced by Peter Benenson, 33.
7. PRO, FO 371/123915.
8. PRO, FO 371/123915, Governor (Cyprus) to CO, 28.7.56.
9. *Ibid.*
10. PRO, FO 371/123926, Terrill: 'Corporal Punishment in Cyprus' (addendum) undated, *c.* September 1956.
11. PRO, FO 371/123915, draft letter from FO to War Office Under-Secretary of State, 27.8.56.
12. PRO, FO 371/123922, Hildyard (Madrid) to FO, 1.9.56.
13. PRO, FO 371/123922, Home Office: 'Corporal Punishment: Summary of Information Obtained from Overseas', undated, *c.* 1954.
14. *Ibid.*, and reports in the same file. In Whitehall, whipping still had some staunch defenders, including the member of the Colonial Office's Social Services Department who argued that it was 'a mild and humane treatment' which had a 'wholly salutary' effect on the adolescents of Cyprus. (PRO, FO 371/123926, Terrill: 'Corporal Punishment in Cyprus', undated, *c.* September 1956.) But a letter from a Foreign Office to the Home Office indicates that there was general unease about this method of punishment: 'this subject . . . is controversial', it said. (PRO, FO 371/123915, draft letter from FO to Home Office Under-Secretary of State, 27.8.56.)
15. PRO, FO 371/123887, Palamas to Hammarskjold, 26.4.56, plus enclosures.
16. PRO, FO 371/123887, Cox, 11.5.56.
17. In the records relating to the court martial, Linzee's first name is given as both 'Robert' and 'Robin'.
18. PRO, WO 71/1231, O'Driscoll's statement, 29.1.56; PRO, WO 71/1231, Deputy Judge Advocate General to General Officer Commanding (Cyprus), 20.4.56.
19. PRO, WO 71/1231, Linzee's statement, 28.1.56; PRO, WO 71/1231, Deputy Judge Advocate General to General Officer Commanding (Cyprus), 20.4.56.
20. PRO, WO 71/1231, Baker: 'Statement of mitigation', 1.4.56.
21. PRO, WO 71/1231, Deputy Judge Advocate General to General Officer Commanding (Cyprus), 20.4.56.

22. PRO, WO 71/1231, Gentle to the Court Martial Appeal Court, 24.9.56.
23. *Ibid.*
24. PRO, WO 71/1231, Deputy Judge Advocate General to General Officer Commanding (Cyprus), 20.4.56.
25. PRO, WO 71/1231, 'Exhibit J1' and 'Exhibit N1', 14.1.56.
26. PRO, WO 71/1231, Deputy Judge Advocate General to General Officer Commanding (Cyprus), 20.4.56.
27. PRO, WO 71/1231, 'Exhibit J1', 14.1.56. Constantinou's statement was translated as the following: 'During the period of my detention with the Army and the Police I was treated with all respect, kindness and carefulness. What is said about my having been maltreated is baseless. I simply spoke in the way I did because I was afraid of my future security. This statement is made voluntarily and not after pressure. (Sgd) Christos Nicolau.'
28. PRO, WO 71/1231, Deputy Judge Advocate General to General Officer Commanding (Cyprus), 20.4.56.
29. *Ibid.*
30. PRO, FO 371/136395, Southern Department to Chancery (Athens), 14.2.58.
31. PRO, FO 371/136395, Gosling to McPetrie, 28.1.58.
32. PRO, FO 371/136400, Highham (CO) to Sinclair (Nicosia), 8.4.58.
33. PRO, FO 371/136399, Goodall, 4.3.58.
34. PRO, FO 371/123908, 'Information about members of the European Commission of Human Rights', undated, *c.* July 1956. The Foreign Office was not sure which way Ireland's James Crosbie, the Netherlands' L.J.C. Beaufort, Luxembourg's Paul Faber, and Belgium's Genevieve Jansen-Pevtschin would swing in a vote.
35. PRO, FO 371/136395, Williams (Limassol) to Administrative Secretary, 14.1.58.
36. PRO, FO 371/136395, Goodall, 28.1.58. Another official minuted: 'If we should want later to denigrate the Sub-Commission and its eventual Report, this incident will come in useful.' (PRO, FO 371/136395, Addis, 29.1.58.)
37. PRO, FO 371/136395, Foot (Cyprus) to CO, 21.1.58.
38. PRO, FO 371/131022, Thomson, 24.10.57.
39. PRO, FO 371/131022, Cambridge, 31.10.57.
40. PRO, CO 936/531, Buist, 7.10.58.
41. PRO, CO 936/531, Steel, 28.4.59.
42. PRO, CO 936/531, Burr, 11.7.58.
43. *Hansard*, Commons, Vol. 607, 16.6.59, Col. 270.
44. *Gangrene*, introduced by Peter Benenson, 20.
45. *Ibid.*, 9–10.
46. Peter Benenson, 'The Forgotten Prisoners', *Observer*, 28.5.61.
47. PRO, FO 371/167032, 'Record of Discussion' of 31.5.62 meeting; PRO, FO 371/167032, 'Deputation on the European Convention', Thomas to Foreign Secretary, 25.6.62.
48. PRO, FO 371/167032, 'Record of Discussion' of 31.5.62 meeting.
49. PRO, FO 371/67032, 'Deputation on the European Convention', Thomas to Foreign Secretary, 25.6.62.
50. International Secretariat Report, June 1964 to May 1965, 3.
51. PRO, LCO 2/8097, Intel, 'Amnesty International', 9.5.67. This information appears in a 1967 Foreign Office circular that recaps the 1963 decision to provide Amnesty with 'discreet support' (emphasis added).
52. Amnesty International Annual Report, June 1963 to May 1964, 4. The following year's International Secretariat Report, June 1964 to May 1965, notes that in 1963–4, Amnesty's income was 'a little over £4,000', 12.
53. Amnesty International Annual Report, June 1963 to May 1964, 5.

54. *Ibid.*, 3.

55. *Ibid.*, 11.

56. PRO, CO 1048/570, Benenson to Lansdowne, 26.9.63.

57. *Ibid.*

58. Jonathan Power, *Amnesty International*, 14.

59. Amnesty members may have consoled themselves with the knowledge that the organisation monitored gaol conditions and torture on behalf of all detainees, although it did not campaign for the release of those not deemed to be 'prisoners of conscience'.

60. PRO, CO 1048/570, Basutoland, Bechuanaland and Swaziland High Commissioner to CO, 22.11.63.

61. PRO, CO 1048/570, *Now in the Future is it Peace or War?* and 'Annex', November 1963.

62. PRO, CO 1048/570, Cunningham memorandum, undated, *c.* 1965.

63. PRO, CO 1048/570, 'Notes by Commissioner of Police' (Bechuanaland), undated, *c.* 1965.

64. PRO, CO 1048/570, 'Confidential note on Commander Cunningham', South African Department, 5.1.65.

65. PRO, CO 1048/570, Basutoland Resident Commissioner to CO, 2.3.65.

66. PRO, CO 1048/570, 'Confidential note on Commander Cunningham', South African Department, 5.1.65.

67. PRO, CO 1048/570, Norman-Walker (Bechuanaland) to Campbell, 3.9.65 (original emphasis).

68. PRO, FO 371/174252, FO to Port-au-Prince, 18.12.64.

69. Even the United States was discomfited by Duvalier's brutality, and, in 1963, had decided against providing a major aid programme on those grounds. (Lars Schoultz, *Human Rights and United States Policy toward Latin America*, 189.)

70. PRO, FO 371/174252, FO to Port-au-Prince, 18.12.64.

71. PRO, FO 371/174252, Padley to Benenson, 18.12.64.

72. PRO, FO 371/179555, Elgar (Haiti) to Harding, 20.1.65.

73. PRO, FO 371/179555, Taylor (UK Delegation to UN, New York) to Powell-Jones, 15.1.65.

74. PRO, FO 371/179555, Elgar (Haiti) to Harding, 20.1.65.

75. Henry Kamm, 'Reign of Terror Reported in Haiti', *New York Times*, 22.1.65.

76. PRO, FO 371/179555, Elgar (Haiti) to Harding, 27.1.65.

77. Egon Larsen, *A Flame in Barbed Wire*, 27.

78. PRO, FO 371/179555, Benenson to Elgar (Haiti), 24.1.65.

79. PRO, DEFE 24/252, Rastgeldi, 'Aden Report', undated, *c.* Autumn 1966, 6.

80. *Ibid.*, 7.

81. PRO, DEFE 24/252, Turnbull: 'Note on the Security Situation in Aden in December 1965' 25.1.67.

82. PRO, PREM 13/1294, Turnbull (Aden) to FO, 25.9.66.

83. PRO, DEFE 24/252, Turnbull (Aden) to FO, 24.1.67.

84. PRO, DEFE 24/252, Report: Haider Abdullah Hussein Audhali, (Case number 223), undated, *c.* late 1966.

85. PRO, DEFE 24/252, Report: Ahmad Muhammad Haidan, (Case number 237), March 1967.

86. PRO, DEFE 24/252, Report: Nasser Ahmad Bin Uthaiman Ba Bakri, (Case number 240), March 1967.

87. PRO, DEFE 24/252, Report: Salih Salim Bin Uthaiman Ba Bakri, (Case number 239), March 1967; PRO, DEFE 24/252, Report: Muhammad al Abudi Ahmad, (Case number 230), March 1967.

88. PRO, DEFE 24/252, Report: Abdul Alim Ali Muhammad Baidara, (Case number 217), undated, *c.* late 1966.
89. PRO, DEFE 24/252, Report: Muhammad Ali Abdullah, (Case number 232), March 1967.
90. PRO, DEFE 24/252, Report: Muhammad Said Farah, (Case number 211). This prisoner made no complaint, but his injuries were investigated at the instigation of the Red Cross investigator.
91. PRO, DEFE 24/252, Report: Said Ali Hassan, (Case number 246), March 1967.
92. PRO, PREM 13/1294, Palliser to Nairne, 21.11.66.
93. 'Aden: Rastgeldi Report Vindicated', *Amnesty International Bulletin*, No. 18, February 1967.
94. PRO, PREM 13/1294, Franck to Wilson, 18.10.66.
95. PRO, PREM 13/1294, Enclosure, Franck to Wilson, 18.10.66.
96. PRO, PREM 13/1294, 'Allegations of Torture in Aden', Brown to Wilson, 31.10.66.
97. Amnesty International circular, 'Aden', October 1966.
98. Jonathan Power, *Amnesty International*, 15–16.
99. PRO, PREM 13/1294, Lord Chancellor to Prime Minster, 4.11.66.
100. *Hansard*, Commons, Vol. 738, 19.12.66, Col. 1,007.
101. Peter Benenson, 'Report on Aden 1963–1966', 11.11.66, 11.
102. Amnesty International circular: 'Aden', October 1966.
103. Howard B. Tolley Jr, *The International Commission of Jurists*, 30–1.
104. Frances Stonor Saunders, *The Cultural Cold War*, 354.
105. Howard B. Tolley, *The International Commission of Jurists*, 34–5. Interestingly, two directors of the American Fund for Free Jurists Inc were also directors of the American Civil Liberties Union. (Tolley, 51.)
106. Sol Stern, 'NSA: A Short Account of International Student Politics and the Cold War', *Ramparts*, March 1967.
107. Duff Hart-Davis, 'Strange Secrets of the Amnesty Row', *Sunday Telegraph*, 5.3.67.
108. Official correspondence indicates that Amnesty did, indeed, remit large sums of sterling to Rhodesia – some £22,700 between June 1966 and January 1968 – to relieve hardship among detainees and their dependants. (PRO, FCO 36/100, Glover to Clinton-Thomas, 2.2.68.) This was a far cry from the organisation's modest total yearly income of £4,000, declared for the year 1963–4.
109. Duff Hart-Davis, 'Strange Secrets of the Amnesty Row', *Sunday Telegraph*, 5.3.67.
110. Bernard Hall, 'Student in "Amnesty" Cash Rumpus Sticks to Her Guns', *Daily Express*, 6.3.67.
111. Duff Hart-Davis, 'Strange Secrets of the Amnesty Row', *Sunday Telegraph*, 5.3.67; Phillip Knightley and Hugo Young, 'Secret State Aid to Amnesty', *Sunday Times*, 5.3.67.
112. Jonathan Power, *Amnesty International*, 17.
113. PRO, LCO2/8097, Benenson to Gardiner, 6.1.67.
114. Charles Forte, *Forte*, 130.
115. PRO, LCO2/8097, Benenson to Gardiner, 6.1.67. Elsewhere in the letter, Benenson aired suspicions that the money may have come from the intelligence services rather than from Charles Forte. 'If in fact Mr Forte has been a complete facade in this operation, which I hope is not the case, then I am prepared to consider repaying the same sum to HM Government. . . . But I am not prepared ever again to meet little men in the bar of the Charing Cross Hotel or to have any dealings whatsoever with persons whose identity cannot be properly verified and whose authority does not spring from Parliament.'
116. A Foreign Office minute indicates that soon after setting up the Human Rights Advisory Service, Benenson approached the Information Research Department

regarding its proposed activities, which would, an official noted, 'embrace the UN as well as Council of Europe'. (PRO, FO 371/190600, Coles, 16.4.66.) The Human Rights Advisory Service was reportedly referred to in the 'Harry' letter of 2.2.66: 'Harry has developed a sudden enthusiasm for litigation. What with North Hull and the Vicar [Rhodesia's Chief Justice, Gerald Beadle] . . . Harry wants a fair buzz of legal activity'. (Phillip Knightley and Hugo Young, 'Secret State Aid to Amnesty', *Sunday Times*, 5.3.67.)

117. PRO, LCO 2/8097, Benenson to Gardiner, 6.1.67.
118. *Ibid.*
119. PRO, FCO 36/100, S. Grant to G.C. Grant, 7.3.67.
120. PRO, LCO 2/8097, Benenson to Gardiner, 6.1.67. See also, a report on Benenson's meeting with the Attorney General and the Solicitor General at the Garrick Club on 7 January 1967, during which he claimed that five Colonial Secretaries had been removed from office because they had complained about the situation in Aden. (PRO, LCO 2/8097.)
121. PRO, LCO 2/8097, Benenson to Gardiner, 6.1.67.
122. In 1966, a member of the British Embassy at Stockholm reminded the Foreign Office that 'the Swedish government were contributing to various organisations including Amnesty International'. Citing press reports, he continued: 'the Swedish section of Amnesty International had asked the Prime Minister if the sum of 1 million kr. (over £700,000) could be allocated to Amnesty International in this year's budget (no such allocation has been made but there will no doubt be some contribution again, through SIDA, the Swedish International Development Agency.' (PRO, FO 371/185900, Lambert (Stockholm) to Mandel, 24.1.66.)
123. Peter Burns, 'Elsinor: Mandate for Change', *Air* (Amnesty International Review), No. 19, May 1967.
124. PRO, LCO 2/8097, Intel, 'Amnesty International', 9.5.67.
125. PRO, FO 371/137789, untitled enclosure on NCCL, *c*. 1957–8.
126. PRO, FCO 36/436, Thomson/Ennals meeting, 13.12.68.
127. In the FCO discussions that followed, S.J.L. Wright minuted: 'Mr Ennals appears to have been misinformed in believing that HMG did supply money to Amnesty for work in Rhodesia, as there is no evidence for it at all. The inquiry held by [the academic] Mr [Peter] Calvocoressi at Amnesty's instigation declared the accusations to be baseless, as they seem to have sprung entirely from paranoiac developments in the mind of Mr Peter Benenson, the founding chairman of Amnesty'. In the same sequence of minutes, M.S. Baker-Bates added, 'We have not given funds to Amnesty in the past'. (PRO, FCO 36/436, 12.1.69.)
128. PRO, FCO 36/436, Thomson/Ennals meeting, 15.1.69.
129. Egon Larsen, *A Flame in Barbed Wire*, 126.

Chapter Six

1. Roberta Cohen, 'Human Rights Decision-Making in the Executive Branch: Some Proposals for a Coordinated Strategy', in Donald P. Kommers and Gilburt D. Loescher (eds), *Human Rights and American Foreign Policy*, 219.
2. Donald M. Fraser, 'Freedom and Foreign Policy', *Foreign Policy*, No. 26, Spring 1977, 142.
3. These campaigners were not responding to domestic pressure from the electorate, however. Donald Fraser indicated that there was 'very little' interest in human rights, and 'no demand' for his campaign among his liberal Minnesota constituents. (Kathryn

Sikkink, 'The Power of Principled Ideas: Human Rights Policies in the United States and Western Europe', in Judith Goldstein and Robert O. Keohane, *Ideas and Foreign Policy*, 161.)

4. Section 32 of the Foreign Assistance Act of 1973; Section 402 of the Trade Act of 1974 (approved January 1975); Section 310 of the International Development and Food Assistance Act of 1975, amending Section 116 of the Foreign Assistance Act.

5. Lars Schoultz, *Human Rights and United States Policy toward Latin America*, 197.

6. Roberta Cohen, 'Human Rights Decision-Making in the Executive Branch: Some Proposals for a Coordinated Strategy', in Donald P. Kommers and Gilburt D. Loescher (eds), *Human Rights and American Foreign Policy*, 220.

7. Lars Schoultz, *Human Rights and United States Policy Toward Latin America*, 125.

8. Roberta Cohen, 'Human Rights Decision-Making in the Executive Branch: Some Proposals for a Coordinated Strategy', in Donald P. Kommers and Gilburt D. Loescher (eds), *Human Rights and American Foreign Policy*, 221.

9. J. Owen Zurhellen Jr, former Deputy Assistant Secretary for East Asian and Pacific Affairs, quoted in Lars Schoultz, *Human Rights and United States Policy toward Latin America*, 6.

10. Laurie S. Wiseberg and Harry M. Scoble, 'Monitoring Human Rights Violations: The Role of Non-Governmental Organizations', in Donald P. Kommers and Gilburt D. Loescher (eds), *Human Rights and American Foreign Policy*, 200.

11. Arthur Schlesinger Jr, 'Human Rights and the American Tradition', *Foreign Affairs*, America in the World, 1978, 512.

12. 'A Harsh Warning on Human Rights', *Time*, 21.6.76.

13. 'Jimmy's Big Breakthrough', *Time*, 5.5.76.

14. Arthur Schlesinger Jr, 'Human Rights and the American Tradition', *Foreign Affairs*, America in the World, 1978, 513.

15. Daniel P. Moynihan, 'The Politics of Human Rights', *Commentary*, August 1977, 22.

16. *Ibid.*, 19.

17. Elizabeth Drew, 'Human Rights', *New Yorker*, 18.7.77, 36.

18. 'The Battle, Blow by Blow', *Time*, 18.10.76.

19. 'The Blooper Heard Round the World', *Time*, 18.10.76.

20. Elizabeth Drew, 'Human Rights', *New Yorker*, 18.7.77, 37.

21. Inaugural address, 20.1.77. www.presidency.ucsb.edu/docs/inaugurals/carter.htm

22. *Digest of United States Practice in International Law*, 1977, 196.

23. 'Carter and the Russians: Semi-Tough', *Time*, 21.2.77.

24. Henry A. Kissinger, 'Morality and Power', Ernest W. Lefever (ed.), *Morality and Foreign Policy*, 60.

25. Ronald Steel, 'Motherhood, Apple Pie and Human Rights', *New Republic*, 4.6.77, 14.

26. Elizabeth Drew, 'Human Rights', *New Yorker*, 18.7.77, 41.

27. Inaugural Address, 20.1.77. www.presidency.ucsb.edu/docs/inaugurals/carter.htm

28. John Dumbrell, *The Carter Presidency*, 118.

29. Support for human rights advocacy tends to be broad but shallow. For example, a survey conducted by the Chicago Council on Foreign Relations in 1978 showed that 67 per cent of those polled favoured human rights promotion, but only 1 per cent placed human rights among their top two or three global issues. (John Dumbrell, *The Carter Presidency*, 185.)

30. See Robert L. Borosage, 'Domestic Consequences of United States Human Rights Policies', in Natalie Hevener Kaufman (ed.), *The Dynamics of Human Rights in US Foreign Policy*, 54.

31. Elizabeth Drew, 'Human Rights', *New Yorker*, 18.7.77, 36.

32. *Ibid.*, 54.

33. *Human Rights and US Foreign Policy*, House Committee on Foreign Affairs, Subcommittee on International Organizations, 10.5.79, 114.
34. Arthur Schlesinger Jr, 'Human Rights and the American Tradition', *Foreign Affairs*, America in the World, 1978, 514.
35. R.J. Vincent, 'Human Rights in Foreign Policy', in Dilys M. Hill (ed.), *Human Rights and Foreign Policy*, 58.
36. *Ibid.*, 56.
37. According to Lyndon Johnson, this maxim was part of a poem written by Katie Louchheim, who later served as a State Department official. (Remarks at the Social Security Administration Headquarters in Baltimore, 12.10.66. www.presidency.ucsb.edu/docs/pppus/johnsonlb/1966/509.htm
38. R.J. Vincent, 'Human Rights in Foreign Policy', in Dilys M. Hill (ed.), *Human Rights and Foreign Policy*, 58.
39. Roberta Cohen, 'Human Rights Decision-Making in the Executive Branch: Some Proposals for a Coordinated Strategy', in Donald P. Kommers and Gilburt D. Loescher (eds), *Human Rights and American Foreign Policy*, 231.
40. Elizabeth Drew, 'Human Rights', *New Yorker*, 18.7.77, 54.
41. Roberta Cohen, 'Human Rights Decision-Making in the Executive Branch: Some Proposals for a Coordinated Strategy', in Donald P. Kommers and Gilburt D. Loescher (eds), *Human Rights and American Foreign Policy*, 232.
42. Roger W. Fontaine, 'The End of A Beautiful Relationship', *Foreign Policy*, No. 28, Fall 1977, 166.
43. Sandy Vogelgesang, *American Dream, Global Nightmare*, 150.
44. Laurie S. Wiseberg and Harry M. Scoble, 'Monitoring Human Rights Violations: The Role of Non-Governmental Organizations', in Donald P. Kommers and Gilburt D. Loescher (eds), *Human Rights and American Foreign Policy*, 200.
45. Chauncey Alexander, Council on Hemispheric Affairs, *Human Rights and the Phenomenon of Disappearances*, House Committee on Foreign Affairs, Subcommittee on International Organisations, 18.10.79, 386.
46. Stephen B. Cohen, 'Conditioning US Security Assistance on Human Rights Practices', *American Journal of International Law*, 76(2), April 1982, 249.
47. *Human Rights in Asia: Communist Countries*, House Committee on Foreign Affairs, Subcommittees on Asian and Pacific Affairs, and International Organizations, 1.10.80, 52.
48. Donald Spencer, *The Carter Implosion*, 75.
49. Iain Guest, *Behind the Disappearances*, 247.
50. Lars Schoultz, *Human Rights and United States Policy toward Latin America*, 331.
51. A. Glenn Mower Jr, *Human Rights and American Foreign Policy*, 68.
52. Stephen B. Cohen, 'Conditioning US Security Assistance on Human Rights Practices', *American Journal of International Law*, 76(2), April 1982, 259.
53. John Dumbrell, *The Carter Presidency*, 152.
54. *Human Rights and United States Foreign Policy: A Review of the Administration's Record*, House Committee on International Relations, Subcommittee on International Organizations, 25.10.77, 30.
55. Sandy Vogelgesang, *American Dream, Global Nightmare*, 174.
56. Joshua Muravchik, *The Uncertain Crusade*, 37–8.
57. Congressional Research Service, *Human Rights and US Foreign Assistance*, November 1979, 80.
58. Stephen B. Cohen, 'Conditioning US Security Assistance on Human Rights Practices', *American Journal of International Law*, 76(2), April 1982, 260.
59. Iain Guest, *Behind the Disappearances*, 167.

60. Allen 'Tex' Harris, *Inside A US Embassy: How the Foreign Service Works for America*. www.afsa.org/inside/chapter3.pdf
61. *Fiscal Year 1980 International Security Assistance Authorization*, Senate Committee on Foreign Relations, 28.2.79, 77.
62. Joshua Muravchik, *The Uncertain Crusade*, 18.
63. Richard E. Feinberg, *The Intemperate Zone*, 253.
64. The accuracy and quality of these reports was variable. Jo Marie Griesgraber, the deputy director of the Washington Office on Latin America, noted in 1979 that the Guatemala report was 'a whitewash', and that in other places such as in Colombia, 'the Embassies regard the human rights reports as a useless bother'. (*Human Rights and US Foreign Policy*, House Committee on Foreign Affairs, Subcommittee on International Organizations, 21.6.79, Appendix, 387.)
65. *Human Rights and US Foreign Policy*, House Committee on Foreign Affairs, Subcommittee on International Organizations, 10.5.79, 47.
66. Charles Gati, *US Policy toward Eastern Europe*, House Committee on International Relations, Subcommittee on Europe and the Middle East, 12.9.78, 118.
67. State Department, *Human Rights and US Foreign Policy*, No. 8959, December 1978, 12.
68. *Reconciling Human Rights and US Security Interests in Asia*, House Committee on Foreign Affairs, Subcommittees on Asian and Pacific Affairs, and Human Rights and International Organizations, 10.8.82, 4.
69. Joshua Muravchik, *The Uncertain Crusade*, 139.
70. Barbara Crossette, 'Hatreds, Human Rights, and the News: What We Ignore', *SAIS Review*, 13(1), Winter–Spring 1993, 10.
71. Lars Schoultz, *Human Rights and United States Policy toward Latin America*, 205.
72. Quoted by Richard Lillich, *Human Rights and US Foreign Policy*, House Committee on Foreign Affairs, Subcommittee on International Organizations, 10.5.79, 81.
73. Elizabeth Drew, 'Human Rights', *New Yorker*, 18.7.77, 46.
74. Arthur Schlesinger Jr, 'Human Rights and the American Tradition', *Foreign Affairs*, America in the World, 1978, 515.
75. Sandra Vogelgesang, 'What Price Principle? US Policy on Human Rights', *Foreign Affairs*, 56(4), July 1978, 827.
76. Repeated by Representative Henry Hyde, *Reconciling Human Rights and US Security Interests in Asia*, House Committee on Foreign Affairs, Subcommittees on Asian and Pacific Affairs, and Human Rights and International Organizations, 9.12.82, 456.
77. Roberta Cohen, 'Human Rights Decision-Making in the Executive Branch: Some Proposals for a Coordinated Strategy', in Donald P. Kommers and Gilburt D. Loescher (eds), *Human Rights and American Foreign Policy*, 224.
78. *Human Rights and US Foreign Policy*, House Committee on Foreign Affairs, Subcommittee on International Organizations, 21.6.79, 155.
79. Stephen B. Cohen, 'Conditioning US Security Assistance on Human Rights Practices', *American Journal of International Law*, 76(2), April 1982, 264.
80. David P. Forsythe, *Human Rights and United States Foreign Policy*, 53.
81. *Ibid.*, 57.
82. *Ibid.*, 61.
83. *US Policy toward South Africa*, House Committee on Foreign Affairs, Subcommittees on International Economic Policy and Trade, Africa, and International Organizations, 13.5.80, 337–8.
84. State Department, 'US Commitment to Human Rights', Policy paper, No. 198, 13.6.80, 4.

85. *Implementation of Congressionally Mandated Human Rights Provisions* (Vol. 1), House Committee of Foreign Affairs, Subcommittee on Human Rights and International Organizations, 30.7.81, 48 (original emphasis).
86. Richard Holbrooke statement, *Reconciling Human Rights and US Security Interests in Asia*, House Committee on Foreign Affairs, Subcommittees on Asian and Pacific Affairs, and Human Rights and International Organizations, 10.8.82, 9.
87. *Ibid.*, 13.
88. *Reconciling Human Rights and US Security Interests in Asia*, House Committee on Foreign Affairs, Subcommittees on Asian and Pacific Affairs, and Human Rights and International Organizations, 15.12.82, 480.
89. *Ibid.*, 516.

Chapter Seven

1. First inaugural address, 20.1.81.
   www.presidency.ucsb.edu/docs/inaugurals/reagan1.htm
2. Ernest Lefever, C-Span, *Booknotes*, 22.3.98.
   www.booknotes.org/transcripts/50455.htm
3. *Nomination of Ernest W. Lefever*, Senate Committee on Foreign Relations, 18.5.81, 76.
4. *Ibid.*, 478–80.
5. *Ibid.*, 507.
6. *Ibid.*, 100.
7. *Ibid.*, 512.
8. *Ibid.* 78.
9. Iain Guest, *Behind the Disappearances*, 285.
10. Ernest Lefever, C-SPAN, *Booknotes*, 22.3.98.
    www.booknotes.org/transcripts/50455.htm
11. Joshua Muravchik, *The Uncertain Crusade*, xviii.
12. Dave Luebke cartoon (1980), David P. Forsythe, *Human Rights and World Politics*, 114.
13. David Heaps, *Human Rights and United States Foreign Policy*, 37.
14. Charles Maechling Jr, 'Human Rights Dehumanized', *Foreign Policy*, No. 52, Fall 1983, 121.
15. David Heaps, *Human Rights and United States Foreign Policy*, 37.
16. See Chapter 6.
17. William Safire, 'Human Rights Victory', *New York Times*, 4.11.81.
18. David Heaps, *Human Rights and United States Foreign Policy*, 37.
19. Elliott Abrams, United States Institute of Peace, *US Human Rights Policy*, 16.6.99.
    www.usip.org/oc/sr/sr990616/sr990616.html
20. Tamar Jacoby, 'The Reagan Turnaround on Human Rights', *Foreign Affairs*, 64(5), Summer 1986, 1,072.
21. *Nomination of Elliott Abrams*, Senate Committee on Foreign Relations, 17.11.81, 15.
22. *Ibid.*, 4.
23. William M. LeoGrande, *Our Own Backyard*, 443.
24. State Department, *Country Reports on Human Rights Practices for 1981*, February 1982.
25. For a description of this process, see David Reiff, 'El Gulag', *New Republic*, 28.7.86.
26. The détente-era Conference on Security and Cooperation in Europe, created in July 1973, was given a statutory basis by the Helsinki Final Act of 1 August 1975. It

committed the signatories – the North American and West European nations; and the
Soviet Union and the East European nations respectively – to continuing negotiations on
security, trade and human rights. America ensured that the earliest conferences, held in
Belgrade (1977–8) and Madrid (1980–3), focused on Soviet Bloc human rights abuses.

27. This section on Helsinki Watch draws heavily on William Korey, *NGOs and the Universal Declaration of Human Rights*. At Belgrade, one of those who criticised Goldberg's pursuit of human rights was his deputy, Albert 'Bud' Sherer, who wrote: 'Goldberg's one thought was to protect Carter's credibility on human rights. As he self-righteously hammered away at the cause of Soviet dissidents, reaping encomiums from émigré groups and the president, he progressively alienated friend and foe alike at the conference.' ('Goldberg's Variations', *Foreign Policy*, No. 39, Summer 1980, 156–7.)

28. William Korey, *NGOs and the Universal Declaration of Human Rights*, 238.

29. *Ibid.*, 342. The Ford Foundation played a crucial part in the development of the human rights movement in the seventies and eighties. A graph based on *The Foundation Grants Index* shows that Ford provided the lion's share of US foundation grants for international human rights work in the years 1977 to 1991, especially in the first five years. (Kathryn Sikkink, 'Human Rights, Principled Issue-Networks, and Sovereignty in Latin America', *International Organization*, 47(3), Summer 1993, 421.) In particular, Ford was responsible for financially kick-starting many new human rights NGOs in the late seventies, including Helsinki Watch and the other Watch committees, the Lawyers Committee for International Human Rights, and the International Human Rights Law Group. It also revived older groups such as the International League for Human Rights.

30. William Korey, *NGOs and the Universal Declaration of Human Rights*, 238.

31. *Ibid.*, 238–9.

32. *Ibid.*, 239.

33. Max M. Kampelman, *Entering New Worlds*, 231.

34. Aryeh Neier statement, *Implementation of Congressionally Mandated Human Right Provisions* (Vol. 1), House Committee on Foreign Affairs, Subcommittee on Human Rights and International Organizations, 17.9.81, 173.

35. Morton M. Kondracke, 'Broken Watch', *New Republic*, 22.8.88, 9.

36. Mark Danner, 'The Truth of El Mozote', *New Yorker*, 6.12.93, 116.

37. *Ibid.*, 102 and 116.

38. Embassy cable submitted to the hearing, *Certification Concerning Military Aid to El Salvador*, Senate Committee on Foreign Relations, 8.2.82, 21.

39. *Review of the State Department Country Reports on Human Rights Practices for 1981*, House Committee on Foreign Affairs, Subcommittee on Human Rights and International Organizations, 28.4.82, 23.

40. Mark Danner, 'The Truth of El Mozote', *New Yorker*, 6.12.93, 118.

41. *Ibid.*

42. *Review of US Human Rights Policy*, House Committee on Foreign Affairs, Subcommittee on Human Rights and International Organisations, 28.6.83, 55.

43. *Ibid.*, 69.

44. *Ibid.*

45. *Ibid.*, 70.

46. *Ibid.*

47. Jonathan Power, *Like Water on Stone*, 64.

48. Amnesty's Guatemala researcher recalled the 'marvellous occasion' when she triumphantly pointed out Covadonga on a map while briefing Organization of American States delegates. (*Ibid.*)

49. Quoted in Holly Burkhalter statement, *US Human Rights Policy*, House Committee on Foreign Affairs, Subcommittee on Human Rights and International Organisations, 19.2.86, 29.

50. Ronald Reagan, 'Question-and-Answer Session With Reporters on the President's Trip to Latin America', 4.12.82.
www.reagan.utexas.edu/resource/speeches/1982/120482g.htm

51. Cynthia Brown (ed.), *With Friends like These*, 199.

52. Quoted in Aryeh Neier statement, *Political Killings by Governments of Their Citizens*, House Committee on Foreign Relations, Subcommittee on Human Rights and International Organizations, 16.11.83, 154.

53. *Ibid.*, 155–6.

54. Americas Watch, Helsinki Watch, Lawyers Committee on International Human Rights, *Failure: The Reagan Administration's Human Rights Policy in 1983*, January 1984, 19.

55. Elliott Abrams, United States Institute of Peace, *US Human Rights Policy*, 16.6.99.
www.usip.org/oc/sr/sr990616/sr990616.html
Caleb Rossiter observed in 1984 that the Human Rights Bureau had been 'relegated to a low, uncontroversial status'. He continued: 'Operating more as a public relations bureau for anti-Communism, the Bureau rarely threatens the interests and domain of the geographic bureaus or the security agencies, and so no longer engenders the conflicts it did under Derian.' (A. Glenn Mower Jr, *Human Rights and American Foreign Policy*, 76.) In 1985 Abrams was transferred from the Human Rights Bureau to the Latin American Bureau – a transition that would have been inconceivable for his predecessor.

56. Americas Watch, *Managing the Facts: How the Administration Deals with Reports of Human Rights Abuses in El Salvador*, December 1985, 12.

57. Morton M. Kondracke, 'Broken Watch', *New Republic*, 22.8.88, 9. This piece was presumably Alexander Cockburn's 'Beat the Devil' column of 1 March 1986, subheaded 'Was Shcharansky a Spy?' Neier's name disappeared from the *Nation*'s masthead in May 1986.

58. Samuel Walker, *In Defence of American Liberties*, 317.

59. Morton M. Kondracke, 'Broken Watch', *New Republic*, 22.8.88, 9.

60. *Ibid.*

61. State Department, 'Analysis of Americas Watch September 1985 Report on El Salvador', appendix, *The Air War and Political Developments in El Salvador*, House Committee on Foreign Affairs, Subcommittee on Western Hemisphere Affairs, 14.5.86, 161.

62. Tamar Jacoby, 'The Reagan Turnaround on Human Rights', *Foreign Affairs*, 64(5), Summer 1986, 1,081.

63. Frank McNeil quoted in William M. LeoGrande, *Our Own Backyard*, 444.

64. David Jones, 'Profile of a Senior Statesman', *State Magazine*, June 1999.
www.state.gov/www/publications/statemag/statemag_jun99/feature2.html

65. Michael Billington, *The Life and Work of Harold Pinter*, 298.

66. Lucy Komisar, 'Harold Pinter: Salted by Jewish Concerns', *Forward*, 13.7.01.
www.forward.com/issues/2001/01.07.13/arts1.html

67. Michael Billington, *The Life and Work of Harold Pinter*, 298.

68. Quoted in Kai Bird and Max Holland, 'Dispatches', *Nation*, 6.10.84.

69. *Nomination of Ernest W. Lefever*, Senate Committee on Foreign Relations, 18.5.81, 291.

70. William Korey, *NGOs and the Universal Declaration of Human Rights*, 344.

71. *Human Rights in El Salvador*, House Committee on Foreign Affairs, Subcommittees on Human Rights and International Organizations, and Western Hemisphere Affairs, 26.7.83, 29.

72. Helsinki Watch, Americas Watch and the Lawyers Committee on International Human Rights, *Failure: The Reagan Administration's Human Rights Policy in 1983*, January 1984, 62.
73. Cynthia Brown (ed.), *With Friends like These*, 42.
74. See David P. Forsythe, *Human Rights and World Politics*, 153.
75. William Korey, *NGOs and the Universal Declaration of Human Rights*, 362.
76. William M. LeoGrande, *Our Own Backyard*, 444.
77. The Watch Committees and Lawyers Committee for Human Rights, *Critique: Review of the Department of State's Country Reports on Human Rights Practices for 1985*, May 1986, 72.
78. *Ibid.*, 4.
79. Morton M. Kondracke, 'Broken Watch', *New Republic*, 22.8.88, 9.
80. Nina H. Shea, 'Human Rights in Nicaragua', *New Republic*, 1.9.86, 21.
81. 'Correction Please', *Nation*, 6.9.86.
82. Letters, *Nation*, 31.1.87. A League publication refers to the Permanent Commission on Human Rights as an 'affiliate'. (*Human Rights Bulletin*, Fall 1986, 1.)
83. Alexander Cockburn, 'Beat the Devil', *Nation*, 6.12.86.
84. Letters, *Nation*, 31.1.87.
85. Jeffrey Goldberg, 'Washington Discovers Christian Persecution', *New York Times Magazine*, 21.12.97.
86. Ronald Reagan, 'Remarks to an Outreach Working Group on United States Policy in Central America', 18.7.84.
www.reagan.utexas.edu/resource/speeches/1984/71884d.htm
87. *Status of US Human Rights Policy, 1987*, House Committee on Foreign Affairs, Subcommittee on Human Rights and International Organizations, 19.2.87, 144.
88. 'Putting the Squeeze on Congress', *Time*, 18.3.85.
89. William M. LeoGrande, *Our Own Backyard*, 414.
90. 'Putting the Squeeze on Congress', *Time*, 18.3.85.
91. William M. LeoGrande, *Our Own Backyard*, 415.
92. *The Air War and Political Developments in El Salvador*, House Committee on Foreign Affairs, Subcommittee on Western Hemisphere Affairs, 14.5.86, 153.
93. David Corn, 'Elliott Abrams: It's Back!' *Nation*, 2.7.01.
94. *Ibid.*
95. Joseph Finder, 'Righteous Indignation', *New York Times*, 15.11.92.
96. Terry J. Allen, 'Public Serpent', *In These Times*, 6.8.01.
97. Abrams statement submitted to *Review of State Department Country Reports on Human Rights Practices for 1981*, House Committee on Human Rights, Subcommittee on Human Rights and International Organizations, 28.4.82, 10.
98. *Country Reports on Human Rights Practices for 1984*, February 1985, 3.
99. The President's News Conference, 9.10.90.
www.presidency.ucsb.edu/docs/pppus/bushghw/1990/100901.html
100. Middle East Watch, *Kuwait's 'Stolen' Incubators: The Widespread Repercussions of a Murky Incident*, 6.2.92, 82.
101. Remarks at a Fundraising Luncheon for Gubernatorial Candidate Clayton Williams in Dallas, Texas, 15.10.90.
www.presidency.ucsb.edu/docs/pppus/bushghw/1990/101503.html
102. Remarks at a Republican Fundraising Breakfast in Des Moines, Iowa, 16.10.90.
www.presidency.ucsb.edu/docs/pppus/bushghw/1990/101600.html
103. Remarks at a Republican Fundraising Breakfast in Burlington, Vermont, 23.10.90.
www.presidency.ucsb.edu/docs/pppus/bushghw/1990/102300.html
104. Remarks at a Republican Campaign Rally in Manchester, New Hampshire, 23.10.90.

www.presidency.ucsb.edu/docs/pppus/bushghw/1990/102301.html
105. Remarks to Officers and Troops at Hickam Air Force Base in Pearl Harbor, Hawaii, 28.10.90.
www.presidency.ucsb.edu/docs/pppus/bushghw/1990/102800.html
106. Remarks at a Republican Campaign Rally in Mashpee, Massachusetts, 1.11.90.
www.presidency.ucsb.edu/docs/pppus/bushghw/1990/110101.html
107. Amnesty International, *Iraq/Occupied Kuwait: Human Rights Violations since August 2, 1990*, December 1990, 57.
108. Remarks and a Question-and-Answer Session with Reporters following Discussions with Allies on the Persian Gulf Crisis, 17.12.90.
www.presidency.ucsb.edu/docs/pppus/bushghw/1990/121701.html
109. Hugh Sidey, 'The Presidency – History Lessons', *Time*, 31.12.90.
110. David Corn, 'Beltway Bandits', *Nation*, 21.1.91.
111. Michael Kramer, 'Counting Up the Atrocities', *Time*, 31.12.90.
112. *Human Rights Abuses in Kuwait and Iraq*, House Committee on Foreign Affairs, 8.1.91, 3.
113. Naseer Aruri, 'Human Rights and the Gulf Crisis: The Verbal Strategy of George Bush' in Phyllis Bennis and Michel Moushabeck (eds), *Beyond the Storm*, 316.
114. Middle East Watch, *Kuwait's 'Stolen' Incubators: The Widespread Repercussions of a Murky Incident*, 6.2.92, 90.
115. Alexander Cockburn, 'Beat the Devil', *Nation*, 4.2.91.
116. Naseer Aruri, 'Human Rights and the Gulf Crisis: The Verbal Strategy of George Bush' in Phyllis Bennis and Michel Moushabeck (eds), *Beyond the Storm*, 316.
117. Michael Kramer, 'Counting up the Atrocities', *Time*, 31.12.90.
118. Middle East Watch, *Kuwait's 'Stolen' Incubators: The Widespread Repercussions of a Murky Incident*, 6.2.92.
119. *Oversight of the State Department's Country Reports on Human Rights Practices for 1991 and US Human Rights Policy*, House Committee on Foreign Affairs, Subcommittee on Human Rights and International Organizations, 4.3.92, 51.
120. Air Force Association, 'Air Force Fifty: Two Day International Airpower Symposium', Las Vegas, 23–24 April 1997. www.afa.org/library/reports/bush.html

Chapter Eight

1. Hillary Rodham Clinton, 'Women's Rights are Human Rights', 5.9.95. (Original emphasis). douglass.speech.nwu.edu/clin_a64.htm
2. *United Nations World Conferences*, Senate Committee on Foreign Relations, 4.6.96, 28.
3. See Chapter 7.
4. Michael Horowitz quoted in Jeffrey Goldberg, 'Washington Discovers Christian Persecution', *New York Times Magazine*, 21.12.97.
5. Freedom House thus was founded in 1941 as part of Franklin Roosevelt's campaign to neutralise the isolationists and to draw America into the Second World War. The President urged the leaders of two organisations – Fight for Freedom and the Committee to Defend America by Aiding the Allies – to unite and fight for 'citizen support for his troubled efforts to bring America into effective opposition to Nazism and Fascism'. Freedom House began life fighting for America's entry into a war behind the banner of freedom and democracy. Later, under the honorary chairmanship of Eleanor Roosevelt, Freedom House devoted itself to fighting another war – the Cold War. (See William Korey, *NGOs and The Universal Declaration of Human Rights*, 444.)

6. Paul Blustein, 'A Jew Battles Persecution of Christians', *Washington Post*, 9.10.97; Jeffrey Goldberg, 'Washington Discovers Christian Persecution', *New York Times Magazine*, 21.12.97.
7. *Consequences of MFN Renewal for China*, Senate Committee on Foreign Relations, 6.6.96, 50.
8. *Ibid.*, 51.
9. *Was There a Tiananmen Massacre? The Visit of General Chi*, House Committee on International Relations, Subcommittee on International Operations and Human Rights, 18.12.96, 20.
10. *Consequences of MFN Renewal for China*, Senate Committee on Foreign Relations, 6.6.96, 51; *Was There a Tiananmen Massacre? The Visit of General Chi*, House Committee on International Relations, Subcommittee on International Operations and Human Rights, 18.12.96, 20.
11. William McGurn, 'The Chinese Chance', *Slate*, 24.9.97. slate.msn.com/?id=2465
12. Joseph Albright, 'China's Stand on Religion Earns Qualified Praise', *The Atlanta Journal and Constitution*, 15.10.98.
13. *US-China Trade Relations and Renewal of China's Most-Favoured-Nation Status*, House Committee on Ways and Means, Subcommittee on Trade, 23.5.95, 14.
14. *Ibid.*, 60.
15. See 'Miss Poppy Dixon', 'Eating Fetuses', *Adult Christianity*, October 2000. www.jesus21.com/poppydixon/sex/chinese_eating_fetuses.html
16. *China Policy Act of 1995, Congressional Record*, House, 20.7.95.
17. *Ibid.*
18. 'Baby-Eating Photos are Part of Chinese Artist's Performance', *Taipei Times*, 23.3.01.
19. National Association of Evangelicals, *Statement of Conscience concerning Worldwide Religious Persecution*, 23.1.96.
20. Mindy Belz, 'Yankee Go Home?' *World*, 8.11.97.
21. Terry Mattingly, 'Spring-cleaning at the Religious Desk', *Gospel Communications Network*, 22.4.98. www.gospelcom.net/tmattingly/col.04.22.98.html
22. Mindy Belz, 'Yankee Go Home?' *World*, 8.11.97.
23. Nina Shea, *In the Lion's Den*, cover.
24. Jacob Heilbrunn, 'Christian Rights', *New Republic*, 7.7.97, 24.
25. Carroll Bogert 'Facing the Lions', *Newsweek*, 25.8.97.
26. William Korey, *NGOs and the Universal Declaration*, 456.
27. *Ibid.*, 459.
28. *Religious Persecution in the Middle East; Faces of the Persecuted*, Senate Committee on Foreign Relations, Subcommittee on Near Eastern and South Asian Affairs, 1.5.97, 34.
29. *Ibid.*, 35.
30. Carroll Bogert 'Facing the Lions', *Newsweek*, 25.8.97.
31. Paul Blustein, 'A Jew Battles Persecution of Christians', *Washington Post*, 9.10.97.
32. Document reproduced at www.motherjones.com/mother_jones//MJ98/silverstein2.html
33. Jacob Heilbrunn, 'The Sanctions Sellout', *New Republic*, 25.5.98.
34. Document reproduced at www.motherjones.com/mother_jones//MJ98/silverstein2.html See also, Ken Silverstein, 'So You Want to Trade with a Dictator', *Mother Jones*, 28.4.98. www.motherjones.com/mother_jones/MJ98/silverstein.html
35. According to one August 1997 memo, representatives of the aircraft giant Boeing were to contact the Reverend Billy Graham, who ran missions in China, and Marjorie Chorlins of Motorola was to contact Drew Christiansen of the US Catholic Conference. www.motherjones.com/mother_jones/MJ98/silverstein3.html
36. 'Guerillas and Bodybags and Sharks . . . Oh, My!' *Americans United*, 12.12.01. www.au.org/press/pr121201.htm

37. Kenneth Jost, 'Anti-Christian Persecution Pervades in Much of World', *Congressional Quarterly*, 13.12.97.
38. Quoted in Richard John Neuhaus 'The Public Square', *First Things*, November 1997. www.firstthings.com/ftissues/ft9711/public.html
39. *Ibid.*
40. Fred Hiatt, 'So Religions Can Be Free', *Washington Post*, 10.5.98.
41. *Freedom from Religious Persecution Act of 1997* (Pt 2), House Committee on International Relations, 10.9.97, 23.
42. *Ibid.*, 31.
43. *Religious Persecution in the Middle East; Faces of the Persecuted*, Senate Committee on Foreign Relations, Subcommittee on Near Eastern and South Asian Affairs, 10.6.97, 49.
44. Michael Cromartie, 'The Jew Who Is Saving Christians', *Christianity Today*, 1.3.99.
45. Fred Hiatt, 'So Religions Can Be Free', *Washington Post*, 10.5.98.
46. Paul Blustein, 'A Jew Battles Persecution of Christians', *Washington Post*, 9.10.97.
47. Michael Cromartie, 'The Jew Who Is Saving Christians', *Christianity Today*, 1.3.99.
48. Jeffrey Goldberg, 'Washington Discovers Christian Persecution', *New York Times Magazine*, 21.12.97.
49. *Ibid.*
50. Franklin Foer, 'Cross-Purposes', *Slate*, 24.9.97. slate.msn.com/default.aspx?id=2464
51. www.csi-int.ch/ www.csi-int.ch/csi/csi-about.htm
52. African Rights, *Food and Power in Sudan*, 342.
53. *Country Reports on Human Rights Practices for 1998*, House Committee on International Relations, Subcommittee on International Operations and Human Rights, 26.2.99, 52.
54. Andrew Boyd, *Baroness Cox*, 400.
55. *Ibid.*, 401.
56. Paul Egglestone, 'Tory Peer Ignores Critics and Bullets in Sudan', *Sunday Telegraph*, 28.1.01.
57. Mike Williams, 'Sudan Haunted by Slavery', BBC Online Network, 15.8.99. news.bbc.co.uk/hi/english/world/africa/newsid_421000/421086.stm
58. Andrew Boyd, *Baroness Cox*, 324.
59. See African Rights, *Food and Power in Sudan*, for a summary of the humanitarian agencies' failure to assess the effects of their own Sudan programmes.
60. Alex de Waal, 'Sudan: Social Engineering, Slavery and War', *Covert Action Quarterly*, Spring 1997, 63.
61. *Ibid.* (Original emphasis).
62. Anti-Slavery International report to ECOSOC's Working Group on Slavery, 'Effective Measures to Free Sudanese Held Captive and Forced to Work', 23 June–2 July 1999. www.antislavery.org/archive/submission/submission1999-06Sudanese.htm
63. *Country Reports on Human Rights Practices for 1998*, House Committee on International Relations, Subcommittee on International Operations and Human Rights, 26.2.99, 52.
64. Michael S. Serrill, 'Slaves: On Sale Now', *Time*, 1.7.96.
65. Gilbert A. Lewthwaite and Gregory Kane: 'Witness To Slavery', *Baltimore Sun*, 18.6.96.
66. African Rights, *Food and Power in Sudan*, 342.
67. *Crimes against Humanity in Sudan*, House Committee on International Relations, Subcommittees on International Operations and Human Rights, and Africa, 27.5.99, 42.
68. www.csi-int.ch/csi/csi-about.htm (Original emphasis.)

69. Gail Russell Chaddock, 'Slavery in Sudan Becomes a "Cause" in US', *Christian Science Monitor*, 5.10.00.
70. *Ibid.*
71. Al Kamen, 'Sudan Protest Makes Odd Bedfellows', *Washington Post*, 30.4.01.

Chapter Nine

1. Tadic *Proceedings*, 5,285–6, www.un.org/icty/ind-e.htm
2. Tadic *Proceedings*, 5,305.
3. Steven Kay interview, 17.12.99.
4. Tadic *Proceedings*, 7,764. An investigation by the Office of the Prosecutor later revealed that Dragan Opacic's story about the Bosnian authorities compelling him to give false testimony was also false. (IWPR *Tribunal Update*, No. 6, 2–4 Dec 1996.)
5. Tadic *Proccedings*, 7,765.
6. *Ibid.*, 7,758.
7. According to the senior UN official Sadruddin Aga Khan, the tribunal was seen as 'a convenient way to quiet human rights activists and other supporters of the Bosnians . . . [and as] a bargaining chip to win Serbian and Croatian agreement to a peace settlement.' (Roger S. Clark and Madeleine Sann (eds), *The Prosecution of International Crimes*, 159.)
8. Aryeh Neier, *War Crimes*, 131.
9. Michael P. Scharf, *Balkan Justice*, 66.
10. *Ibid.*, 78.
11. Doug Cassel, *Worldview Commentary*, No. 6, 'Yugoslavia: Will War Criminals Be Prosecuted?' 13.7.94.
    www.law1.nwu.edu/depts/clinic/ihr/hrcomments/1994/july13-94.html
12. *Ibid.*
13. Steve Crawshaw, 'Justice in Our Time?' *Independent on Sunday*, 8.4.01.
14. ICTY press release CC/PIO/003-E, 1.2.95.
15. Geoffrey Robertson, *Crimes Against Humanity*, 279.
16. Kitty Felde, '"LA Law" at a War Tribunal: Clash of Legal Systems, Styles', *Christian Science Monitor*, 3.7.97.
17. Virginia Morris and Michael P. Scharf, *An Insider's Guide to the International Criminal Tribunal for the Former Yugoslavia*, 333. The US official David Scheffer went even further when he suggested that 'victims' justice' had replaced victors' justice. ('International Judicial Intervention', *Foreign Policy*, No. 102, Spring 1996, 36.)
18. Press statement by Carla del Ponte, PR/ P.I.S./ 459-e, 30.12.99.
19. 'Final Report to the Prosecutor by the Committee Established to Review the NATO Bombing Campaign Against the Federal Republic of Yugoslavia'.
    www.un.org/icty/pressreal/nato061300.htm
20. IWPR *Tribunal Update*, No. 180, 12–18 June 2000.
21. 'Final Report to the Prosecutor by the Committee Established to Review the NATO Bombing Campaign Against the Federal Republic of Yugoslavia'.
    www.un.org/icty/pressreal/nato061300.htm
22. William Korey, *NGOs and the Universal Declaration of Human Rights*, 204; Remarks by Judge Gabrielle Kirk McDonald at the United States Supreme Court, Washington, DC, 5.4.99. www.un.org/icty/pressreal/SPE990405.htm
23. ICTY *Bulletin*, No. 2, 22.1.96. www.un.org/icty/BL/02bdg95e.htm
    ICTY 1998 Annual Report, UN A/53/219-S/1998/737, 10.8.98.
    www.un.org/icty/rapportan/rapport5-e.htm

The tribunal's donations table gives a revealing snapshot of the court's sources of support. Of the total $30.1 million cash donated by 2000, 87.3 per cent came from Western sources (the American government and US foundations accounted for 42 per cent of the total, followed by Britain – 10 per cent; and the Netherlands – 8 per cent). Malaysia, Pakistan and Saudi Arabia donated the remaining 12.6 per cent, presumably as a gesture of support to Bosnian Muslims. Other non-Western countries donated just 0.05 per cent of the total. Even taking into account differences in wealth, and the fact that nations indirectly support the court through their United Nations dues, it is obvious that the West is the Tribunal's most enthusiastic backer, while the non-Western world is notably cool. (ICTY 2000 Annual Report, UN A/55/273-S/2000/777, 7.8.00, 38.)

24. Gary Jonathan Bass, *Stay the Hand of Vengeance*, 261.
25. IWPR *Tribunal Update*, No. 46, 29 September–3 October 1997.
26. Arbour interview, 27.4.99, cited at
    listserv.buffalo.edu/cgi-bin/wa?A2=ind9904&L=justwatch-l&D=1&O=D&F=&S=&
    P=153881
27. IWPR *Tribunal Update*, No. 65, 23–28 February 1998.
28. ICTY press release, CC/PIU/391-E, 31.3.99.
29. Michael Ignatieff, *Virtual War*, 124.
30. The Americans have a big say over who gets arrested, and when they are arrested. Scott Peterson in *Christian Science Monitor* reported that before the November 1996 Presidential elections, Clinton's officials were keen to avoid any misadventures in Bosnia that might overshadow their Dayton success – in particular, the risk of a botched arrest of Radovan Karadzic. They were apparently 'visibly dismayed' in June that year, when Antonio Cassese demanded Karadzic's immediate apprehension. ('The Karadzic Capture That Almost Was', *Christian Science Monitor*, 27.4.01.)
31. Michael P. Scharf, *Balkan Justice*, 87.
32. IWPR *Tribunal Update*, No. 122, 19–24 April 1999.
33. IWPR *Tribunal Update*, No. 124, 3–8 May 1999.
34. MoD briefing, 20.4.99. www.kosovo.mod.uk/brief200499.htm
35. Rachel Sylvester and John Davison, 'Serbs Use "Slave Labour" to Hide Mass Slaughter', *Independent on Sunday*, 18.4.99.
36. MoD briefing, 20.4.99. www.kosovo.mod.uk/brief200499.htm
37. Nato press conference, 16.5.99. www.nato.int/kosovo/press/p990516b.htm
38. William Korey, *NGOs and the Universal Declaration of Human Rights*, 324.
39. *Ibid.*, 326.
40. *Ibid.*, 327–8.
41. The OSCE, formally founded in January 1995, was the institutional successor of the Conference on Security and Cooperation in Europe.
42. David Chandler, Bosnia: *Faking Democracy after Dayton*, 102.
43. *Ibid.*, 101.
44. At this stage, the American officials had other things on their minds – namely, Clinton's re-election campaign in November 1996. For this reason they put pressure on the OSCE to ensure the elections went ahead in Bosnia in accordance with Dayton, but held off arresting people lest something went wrong. (Scott Peterson, 'The Karadzic Capture That Almost Was', *Christian Science Monitor*, 27.4.01.)
45. See 'NATO's Mistakes/Kosovo Data', *Common Ground Radio*, 11.4.00,
    commongroundradio.org/transcpt/00/0015.html
    listserv.buffalo.edu/cgi-bin/wa?A2=ind0004&L=justwatch-l&D=1&O=D&F=&S=&
    P=17195
46. www.cij.org
47. CEELI Annual Report 1998, Pt. 1, 8. www.abanet.org/ceeli/update/98AnnPart1.pdf

48. www.cij.org
49. ICTY 1994 Annual Report. www.un.org/icty/rapportan/first-94.htm
50. Michael Scharf, *Accounting for Atrocities* conference, Bard College, 5–6 October 1998. www.bard.edu/hrp/atrocities/index.htm
51. Rules of procedure and evidence. www.un.org/icty/basic/rpe/IT32_rev19.htm#Rule 96
52. BBC comment on Martic hearing, cited in Cedric Thornberry, 'Saving the War Crimes Tribunal', *Foreign Policy*, No. 104, Fall 1996, 83; and Geoffrey Robertson, *Crimes Against Humanity*, 283.
53. Mirko Klarin's 'Tribunal Update' report about Plavsic's arrest gives a tantalising insight into the behind-the-scenes collaboration between the tribunal and its Western backers. Tribunal officials said that Plasvic had surrendered after she received a 'signal' that an indictment and arrest warrant had been issued against her – a signal which, according to 'unofficial but reliable sources', emanated from 'United States diplomatic circles in Bosnia'. Subsequently, American and British diplomats, as well as the Tribunal's Office of the Prosecution, communicated with Plavsic and her defence counsel. (IWPR *Tribunal Update*, No. 204a, 8–13 January 2001.)
54. Michael Ignatieff, *Virtual War*, 127.
55. See D'Amato's comments at:
    listserv.acsu.buffalo.edu/cgi-bin/wa?A2=ind0007&L=twatch-l&P=R36644
56. Steven Kay, American Bar Association annual meeting, London, 19.7.00.
57. Appeals chamber decision, 'Jean-Bosco Barayagwiza v. The Prosecuton', 3.11.99.
58. Philip Gourevitch, *We Wish to Inform You That Tomorrow We Will Be Killed With Our Families*, 253.
59. Amnesty International, 'United Nations (UN) International Criminal Tribunal for Rwanda: Trials and Tribulations', April 1998.
60. Canadian defence lawyer John Philpot claims, in addition, that Kambanda was 'arrested by force and transferred from Kenya to Arusha . . . without any extradition proceedings'. listserv.acsu.buffalo.edu/cgi-bin/wa?A2=ind9805&L=twatch-l&P=R4879
61. *Ubutabera*, No. 36, May 1998.
62. *Ubutabera*, No. 59, 29.3.99.
63. J. Coll Metcalfe, 'An Interview with United Nations' Chief War Crimes Prosecutor, Carla del Ponte', *Internews*, 9.12.99.
64. 'Barayagwiza Again Demands His Release', *Hirondelle*, 1.8.00.
65. Kenneth Roth, 'The Court the US Doesn't Want', *New York Review of Books*, 19.11.98.
66. During the Rome conference, America sought to weaken the powers of the prosecutor and to strengthen the influence of the Security Council, while Britain sought to restrict the circumstances under which states could trigger a prosecution. Between them, they covered all the bases. As the conference progressed, the British delegates were accused of watering down the court's statute, and acting as a 'stalking horse' for the United States. (*On the Record*, ICC, Pt 2, 30.6.98. www.advocacynet.org/news_118.html)
67. David J. Scheffer, 'International Judicial Intervention', *Foreign Policy*, No. 102, Spring 1996, 51.

Conclusion

1. NARA, RG 59, 500.CC, 1945–9, Box 1998: Tuck (Cairo) to Secretary of State, 24.4.45 (see also, Chapter 1).
2. Bahey el Din Hassan, 'The Credibility Crisis of International Human Rights in the Arab World', *Human Rights Dialogue*, 2(1), Winter 2000, 9.

3. See Chapter 8.
4. Omayma Abdel-Latif, 'US Commission Faces Closed Doors', *Al-Ahram* Weekly Online, 22–28 March 2001. www.ahram.org.eg/weekly/2001/526/eg1.htm
5. *Ibid.*
6. State Department official Frank McNeil quoted in William M. LeoGrande, *Our Own Backyard*, 444; Omayma Abdel-Latif, 'US Commission Faces Closed Doors', *Al-Ahram* Weekly Online, 22–28 March 2001.
www.ahram.org.eg/weekly/2001/526/eg1.htm
7. Vickie Langohr, 'Frosty Reception for US Religious Freedom Commission in Egypt', *Middle East Report*, 29.3.01. www.merip.org/pins/pin53.html
8. *Ibid.*
9. *Implementation of Congressionally Mandated Human Rights Provisions* (Vol. 1), House Committee on Foreign Affairs, Subcommittee on Human Rights and International Organizations, 30.7.81, 40. (original emphasis).
10. *Fiscal Year 1980 International Security Assistance Authorization*, Senate Committee on Foreign Relations, 28.2.79, 75.
11. David P. Forsythe, 'US Economic Assistance and Human Rights: Why the Emperor has (Almost) No Clothes', in Forsythe (ed.), *Human Rights and Development*, 181.
12. David Carleton and Michael Stohl, 'The Role of Human Rights in US Foreign Assistance Policy: A Critique and Reappraisal', *American Journal of Political Science*, 31(4), November 1987, 1,002–3. In contrast to the other studies cited, David L. Cingranelli and Thomas E. Pasquarello produced moderately positive results, but their methodology was later challenged by Carleton and Stohl. (Cingranelli and Pasquarello, 'Human Rights Practices and the Distribution of US Foreign Aid to Latin American Countries', *American Journal of Political Science*, No. 29, August 1985.
13. *Slavery throughout the World*, Senate Committee on Foreign Relations, 28.9.00, 9.
14. *Ibid.*, 12.
15. *Ibid.*, 13.
16. Archibald MacLeish quoted by President Carter (State Department, *Continuing the CSCE Process*, Policy paper, No. 204, 29.7.80).

Bibliography

Aldrich, R.J., *Intelligence and the War against Japan: Britain, America and the Politics of Secret Service*, Cambridge, 2000.

Barclay, R., *Ernest Bevin and the Foreign Office, 1932–1969*, London, 1975.

Bass, G.J., *Stay the Hand of Vengeance: The Politics of War Crimes Tribunals*, Princeton, New Jersey, 2000.

Benenson, P., *Gangrene*, Intro., London, 1959.

Bennis, P. and Moushabeck, M. (eds), *Beyond the Storm: A Gulf Crisis Reader*, Edinburgh, 1992.

Berlin, I., *Four Essays on Liberty*, Oxford, 1979.

Best, G., *Nuremberg and After: The Continuing History of War Crimes and Crimes against Humanity*, Reading, 1984.

Biddiss, M., Balfour, T., Laschet, M., McInnes, J., *The Nuremberg Trial and the Third Reich*, Harlow, Essex, 1992.

Biddle, F., *In Brief Authority*, Garden City, New York, 1962.

Billington, M., *The Life and Work of Harold Pinter*, London, 1996.

Bishop, J., *FDR's Last Year: April 1944–April 1945*, New York, 1974.

Blum, J.M., *V Was for Victory: Politics and American Culture during World War II*, New York, 1976.

Bower, T., *Blind Eye to Murder: Britain, America and the Purging of Nazi Germany*, London, 1997.

Boyd, A., *Baroness Cox: A Voice for the Voiceless*, Oxford, 1998.

Brown, C. (ed.), *With Friends like These: The Americas Watch Report on Human Rights and US Policy in Latin America*, New York, 1985.

Burns, J.M., *Roosevelt: The Soldier of Freedom, 1940–1945*, London, 1971.

Buscher, F.M., *The US War Crimes Trial Program in Germany, 1946–1955*, New York, 1989.

Campbell, T.M., and Herring, G.C, *The Diaries of Edward R Stettinius Jr, 1943–1946*, New York, 1975.

Chandler, D. *Bosnia: Faking Democracy after Dayton*, London, 2000.

Clark, R.S., and Sann, M. (eds), *The Prosecution of International Crimes: A Critical Study of the International Tribunal for the Former Yugoslavia*, New Brunswick, New Jersey, 1996.

Conot, R.E., *Justice at Nuremberg*, London, 1983.

Cranston, M., *Human Rights To-Day*, London, 1955.

Divine, R.A., *Second Chance: The Triumph of Internationalism in America during World War II*, New York, 1971.

Dower, J.W., *Embracing Defeat: Japan in the Wake of World War II*, New York, 2000.

Dumbrell, J., *The Carter Presidency: A Re-evaluation*, Manchester, 1993.

Eichelberger, C.M., *UN: The First Twenty Years*, New York, 1965.

Feinberg, R.E., *The Intemperate Zone: The Third World Challenge to US Foreign Policy*, New York, 1983.

Forsythe, D.P. (ed.), *Human Rights and Development: International Views*, Basingstoke, 1989.
——, *Human Rights and US Foreign Policy: Congress Reconsidered*, Gainsville, Florida, 1988.
——, *Human Rights and World Politics*, Lincoln, Nebraska, 1983.
Forte, C., *Forte: The Autobiography of Charles Forte*, London, 1986.
Ginn, J.L., *Sugamo Prison, Tokyo: An Account of the Trial and Sentencing of Japanese War Criminals in 1948*, Jefferson, North Carolina, 1992.
Green, J.F., *The United Nations and Human Rights*, Washington DC, 1956.
Goldman, E.F., *Rendezvous with Destiny*, New York, 1952.
Goldstein, J., and Keohane, R.O. (eds), *Ideas and Foreign Policy: Beliefs, Institutions, and Political Change*, Ithica, New York, 1993.
Gourevitch, P., *We Wish to Inform You that Tomorrow We Will Be Killed with Our Families: Stories from Rwanda*, London, 2000.
Guest, I., *Behind the Disappearances: Argentina's Dirty War against Human Rights and the United Nations*, Philadelphia, Pennsylvania, 1990.
Gunther, J., *Inside USA*, London, 1947.
Hazzard, S., *Defeat of an Ideal: A Study of the Self-destruction of the United Nations*, London, 1973.
Heaps, D., *Human Rights and US Foreign Policy: The First Decade 1973–1983*, New York, 1984.
Heijden, B. van der, and Tahzib-Lie, B. (eds), *Reflections on the Universal Declaration of Human Rights: A Fiftieth Anniversary Anthology*, The Hague, 1998.
Hill, D.M. (ed.), *Human Rights and Foreign Policy: Principles and Practice*, Basingstoke, 1989.
Hobbins, A.J. (ed.), *On the Edge of Greatness: The Diaries of John Humphrey*, Vol. 1: 1948–9, Montreal 1994.
Hoopes, T., and Brinkley, D., *FDR and the Creation of the UN*, New Haven, Connecticut, 1997.
Hosoya, C., Ando, N., Onuma, Y., Minear, R. (eds), *The Tokyo War Crimes Tribunal: An International Symposium*, Tokyo, 1986.
Humphrey, J., *Human Rights and the United Nations: A Great Adventure*, New York, 1984.
Hunt, L., *The French Revolution and Human Rights: A Brief Documentary History*, Boston, Massachusetts, 1996.
Hyde, H.M., *Norman Birkett: The Life of Lord Birkett of Ulverston*, London, 1989.
Hyde, L.K., *The United States and the United Nations: Promoting the Public Welfare*, New York, 1960.
Ignatieff, M., *Virtual War: Kosovo and Beyond*, London, 2000.
Ismay, *The Memoirs of General the Lord Ismay*, London, 1960.
Kampelman, M.M., *Entering New Worlds: The Memoirs of a Private Man in Public Life*, New York, 1991.
Kaufman, N.H. (ed.), *The Dynamics of Human Rights in US Foreign Policy*, New Brunswick, New Jersey, 1981.
——, *Human Rights Treaties and the Senate: A History of Opposition*, Chapel Hill, North Carolina, 1990.
Keck, M.E., and Sikkink, K., *Activists beyond Borders: Advocacy Networks in International Politics*, Ithica, New York, 1998.
Kochavi, A.J., *Prelude to Nuremberg: Allied War Crimes Policy and the Question of Punishment*, Chapel Hill, North Carolina, 1998.
Kommers, D.P., and Loescher, G.D. (eds), *Human Rights and American Foreign Policy*, Notre Dame, Indiana, 1979.

Korey, W., *NGOs and the Universal Declaration of Human Rights: A Curious Grapevine*, Basingstoke, 1998.

Larsen, E., *A Flame in Barbed Wire: The Story of Amnesty International*, London, 1978.

Lash, J.P., *Eleanor: The Years Alone*, London, 1973.

Lauren, P.G., *The Evolution of International Human Rights: Visions Seen*, Philadelphia, Pennsylvania, 1998.

Lefever, E.W. (ed.), *Morality and Foreign Policy: A Symposium on President Carter's Stance*, Washington DC. 1977.

Leogrande, W.M., *Our Own Backyard: The United States in Central America, 1977–1992*, Chapel Hill, North Carolina, 1998.

Mayhew, C., and Smith, L. (eds), *A War of Words: A Cold War Witness*, London, 1998.

——, *Time to Explain*, London, 1987.

McCullough, D., *Truman*, New York, 1992.

Minear, R.H., *Victors' Justice: The Tokyo War Crimes Trial*, Princeton, New Jersey, 1971.

Morris, V., and Scharf, M.P., *An Insider's Guide to the International Criminal Tribunal for the Former Yugoslavia*, Vol. 1, Irvington-on-Hudson, New York, 1995.

Morsink, J., *The Universal Declaration of Human Rights: Origins, Drafting and Intent*, Philadelphia, Pennsylvania, 1999.

Mower, A.G., *Human Rights and American Foreign Policy: The Carter and Reagan Experiences*, New York, 1987.

——, *The United States, The United Nations, and Human Rights: The Eleanor Roosevelt and Jimmy Carter Eras*, Westport, Connecticut, 1979.

Muravchik, J., *The Uncertain Crusade: Jimmy Carter and the Dilemmas of Human Rights Policy*, Lanham, Maryland, 1986.

Neier, A., *War Crimes: Brutality, Genocide, Terror, and the Struggle for Justice*, New York, 1998.

Nolan, C., *Principled Diplomacy: Security and Rights in US Foreign Policy*, Westport, Connecticut, 1993.

Nolde, O.F., *Free and Equal: Human Rights in Ecumenical Perspective*, Geneva, 1968.

O'Neill, W.L., *A Democracy at War: America's Fight at Home and Abroad in World War II*, New York, 1993.

Paget, R., *Manstein: His Campaigns and His Trial*, London, 1951.

Pal, R.B., *International Military Tribunal for the Far East: Dissentient Judgment of Justice R.B. Pal*, Calcutta, 1953.

Piccigallo, P.R., *The Japanese on Trial: Allied War Crimes Operations in the East, 1945–1951*, Austin, Texas, 1979.

Power, J., *Amnesty International: The Human Rights Story*, Oxford, 1981.

——, *Like Water on Stone: The Story of Amnesty International*, London, 2001.

Pritchard, R.J., and Zaide, S.M. (eds), *The Tokyo War Crimes Trial, Index and Guide*, New York, 1981.

Proskauer, J.M., *A Segment of My Times*, New York, 1950.

Pruden, C., *Conditional Partners: Eisenhower, the United Nations, and the Search for a Permanent Peace*, Baton Rouge, Louisiana, 1998.

Robertson, G., *Crimes Against Humanity: The Struggle for Global Justice*, London, 1999.

Robins, D.B., *Experiment in Democracy: The Story of US Citizen Organizations in Forging the Charter of the United Nations*, New York, 1971.

Röling, B.V.A., and Cassese, A., *The Tokyo Trial and Beyond: Reflections of a Peacemonger*, Cambridge, 1993.

Rousso, H. (trans: Goldhammer, A.), *The Vichy Syndrome: History and Memory in France since 1944*, Cambridge, Massachusetts, 1991.

Russell of Liverpool, *The Scourge of the Swastika: A Short History of Nazi War Crimes*, London, 1958.

Sandifer, I.R., *Mrs Roosevelt as We Knew Her*, Silver Spring, Maryland, 1975.

Saunders, F.S., *The Cultural Cold War: The CIA and the World of Arts and Letters*, New York, 2000.

Scharf, M.P., *Balkan Justice: The Story Behind the First International War Crimes Trial Since Nuremberg*, Durham, North Carolina, 1997.

Schoultz, L., *Human Rights and the United States Policy toward Latin America*, Princeton, New Jersey, 1981.

Sebald, W.J. (with Brines, R.), *With MacArthur in Japan: A Personal History of the Occupation*, London, 1967.

Shea, N., *In the Lion's Den: Persecuted Christians and What the Western Church Can Do About It*, Nashville, Tennessee, 1997.

Smith, B.F., *Reaching Judgement at Nuremberg*, London, 1977.

——, *The Road to Nuremberg*, London, 1981.

Spencer, D., *The Carter Implosion: Jimmy Carter and the Amateur Style of Diplomacy*, New York, 1988.

Tananbaum, D., *The Bricker Amendment Controversy: A Test of Eisenhower's Political Leadership*, Ithica, New York, 1988.

Taylor, T., *The Anatomy of the Nuremberg Trials: A Personal Memoir*, New York, 1992.

——, *Nuremberg and Vietnam: An American Tragedy*, New York, 1971.

Tolley, H.B., *The International Commission of Jurists: Global Advocates for Human Rights*, Philadelphia, Pennsylvania, 1994.

Truman, M., *Harry S. Truman*, London, 1973.

Vogelgesang, S., *American Dream, Global Nightmare: The Dilemma of US Human Rights Policy*, New York, 1980.

Walker, S., *In Defence of American Liberties: A History of the ACLU*, New York, 1990.

Weingartner, J.J., *Crossroads of Death: The Story of the Malmédy Massacre and Trial*, Berkeley, California, 1979.

Wells, H.G., *The New World Order*, London, 1940.

West, R., *A Train of Powder*, London, 1984.

Wronka, J., *Human Rights and Social Policy in the 21st Century*, Lanham, Maryland, 1998.

Index